KEYS TO

THE WHITE HOUSE

and Other Stories of a Gig Warrior

Robert J. Boguslaw

MGySgt, US Marine Band, Ret.

Keys to the White House and Other Stories of a Gig Warrior
By Robert Boguslaw

Copyright © 2020 Robert Boguslaw

ISBN-13: 978-1-951492991
ISBN- eBook: 978-1-951492-11-3

Library of Congress case no._1-8603647601
Published by HigherLife Development Services, Inc.
PO Box 623307
Oviedo, Florida 32762
(407) 563-4806
www.ahigherlife.com

Recording copyright held by author
Printed in the United States of America
10 9 8 7 6 5 4 3 2 1
Second Edition

ABOUT THE AUTHOR

ROBERT BOGUSLAW is a pianist, composer, educator, and free-lance performer in the Baltimore-Washington, DC region. He leads the Rock Creek Trio in classical music performance. In the area of jazz, he heads The Way, a jazz ensemble performing his original compositions. From 1991 to 2013, he served as staff pianist and combo section commander with the "President's Own" Marine Band, a unit of the USMC. Boguslaw's artistry emerges through the performance of numerous musical genres, including classical, jazz, blues, folk, pop, musical theater, and world music. He has performed throughout the United States, Caribbean, in South America, and Europe. Currently, he resides in West Friendship, Maryland, with his wife, two of three daughters, and a granddaughter, Phoenix.

TABLE OF CONTENTS

FOREWORD

One important life event that motivated Bob to write this book was the loss of a dear friend and jazz aficionado, Dennis Askey. When Dennis passed away, we lost a great jazz historian along with his stories of encounters with jazz masters, stories worthy of sharing. Like Dennis, Bob offers first-hand accounts of historic events and encounters with political and cultural icons, particularly during his service in the "President's Own" US Marine Band at Marine Barracks, Washington, DC. There he served for twenty-two years during the administrations of Presidents George H. W. Bush, Bill Clinton, George W. Bush, and Barack Obama. Bob was pianist to heads of state, presidents, popes, and pundits. I sometimes imagine him as a Forrest Gump character, standing shoulder-to-shoulder with world leaders and celebrities at historic moments.

There are some who hold the value of his military service in low esteem. Some of the young recruits assigned to Marine Barracks Washington, DC resent these military musicians who enter the Marine Corps in a separate system of rank and promotion. They do not consider the musicians real marines. To them, being a marine is about defending our country. What does music performance have to do with national defense?

We once visited an attorney's office who asked about Bob's profession. "What line of work are you in?" When Bob told him that he was a pianist in the "President's Own," the attorney scoffed and remarked, "Our tax dollars at work." Some folks don't believe that US taxpayers should pay for a pianist or any kind of music. What does that have to do with the national defense?

The ceremonial aspect of our military is largely the function of military musical performing organizations. The Marine Band is always present at inaugurations, events of state, ceremonial parades, and military funerals. They were present with President Lincoln at Gettysburg. Their music has ignited the spirit with pride and joy, compassion and sorrow, respect and tribute throughout the events of American history.

While others commit brains and brawn to the mission, military music commits the mind and heart. At events of state, receptions of world leaders, and treaty and bill signings, music performs a diplomatic function. Music is present, whether in celebration or easing the spirit when tensions are high among the seats of power around world events. Military music provides the atmosphere for nations to convene.

No matter how you feel about the worth and value of these intangible, ceremonial and diplomatic services, Bob was fully committed, fully qualified, fully trained, armed and ready. He served with honor and relates his story with humility and a sense of humor. I believe that you, the reader, will find these stories of a gig warrior highly entertaining.

Mary Boguslaw

INTRODUCTION

My primary motivation to write *Keys to the White House* was my desire to pass these stories down to my children, grandchildren, and the generations to follow. My hope is they'll be able to someday read this book and say, "This is what Dad did," or "what Grandpa did." This is important to me because of what's probably a nearly universal human impulse to pass on a legacy to one's family. Secondly, in this book, I've documented what life was like for both a gigging musician and a member of the "President's Own" Marine Band in the late twentieth and early twenty-first centuries.

Ever since 1975, when I began studying at the University of Miami, I've heard musicians commiserating that live music is dying. I recently went to a sold-out Dave Matthews Band Concert, a world-class Baltimore Symphony performance of Mahler's 1st Symphony, and soloed with the Gettysburg College jazz band for an audience of approximately 500. There were large and enthusiastic audiences for each performance, and I suspect that if live music were really dying, it'd be dead by now.

But I do believe that changes in the way we purchase, access, and even perceive music these days are causing the decline of the "Gig Warrior" lifestyle. Listeners can now freely access any recorded music, getting whatever they've chosen to listen to recorded and played back with very high quality and fidelity. Hand-held devices have also made divided attention spans commonplace. These factors have made the corner bar or nightclub with a cover band or lounge act nearly obsolete. So, although I believe that in the twenty-second century there will still be live concerts attended by large and enthusiastic audiences, I also believe it will be difficult for future generations to comprehend the lifestyle of freelance musicians today. In the same way that we have to do research to understand the silent movie pianists and song pluggers of the early twentieth century, my hope is that this book will help with a historical understanding of the gig warrior lifestyle.

Before the reader dives into this memoir, there's one thing I feel I need to be very clear about. Playing piano for the "President's Own" was a truly wonderful career and I'm very fortunate, blessed, and grateful to have been able to spend a substantial part of my professional life doing so. I currently have, and have always had, a tremendous amount of respect for the institution and history of the Marine Band. In my twenty-two years of military service, I also developed a great respect for the Marine Corps and the men and women who've chosen to spend their lives serving our country.

Everything has been recounted as accurately as I remember, including all people, places, and events. The memoir has been divided into two parts, and generally speaking, the time frames of these anecdotes are:

Part I
1975-1985: Miami, Florida

1985-1991: Lexington, Kentucky

Part II
1991-2014: Washington DC/Baltimore

WHY MUSIC?

I've given a lot of thought over the years about why I chose to devote so much of my life to making music. I'm definitely not alone in having made that choice. Music schools, summer festivals, private studios, and even public schools regularly produce fine young musicians aspiring to spend a lifetime dedicated to making music. Most of these aspiring musicians are intelligent enough to pursue other lines of work that would yield significantly greater financial rewards. So,why music?

Quite a few strong motivational factors that influence young musicians tend to fade as they get older. These include competitiveness, the desire to prove oneself to peers and family, the desire to fit into a group, simply possessing an exceptional natural ability, and finally, the attempt to gain the attention of and impress those of the opposite (or same) sex. Over the years, I've become convinced that none of these motivating factors have long-term staying power. I've arrived at the conclusion that the primary motivation of the world's most accomplished and expressive musicians is this: Music is the most direct medium for the intense expression of the kaleidoscope of human experience. Period. Judging this depth of expression is, of course, subjective, but I'll give some musical examples that elicit in me palpable emotions and experiences:

- The tenor saxophone sound of John Coltrane on "A Love Supreme" which pierces my soul with sadness, joy, and creative ecstasy.

- The muted trumpet sound of Miles Davis on the *My Funny Valentine* album that takes me to an introspective and soul-searching place.

- The ecstatic trumpet of Louis Armstrong on songs like "West End Blues," which has the power to relate the entirety of the pain and joyful resilience of the African-American experience in every phrase.

- The beautiful tone and uniquely expressive compositional style of

Keith Jarrett on the *Belonging* album. Here, I experience gut-wrenching pathos and harmonically free creative joy.

- The slow movement of Beethoven's Seventh Symphony—the palpable grief that emanates from this funeral march.

- The final two movements of Beethoven's Fifth symphony make me feel I can touch the ecstatic joy that pours out in the triumphal closing movements of this masterpiece.

- Glenn Gould playing Bach's Goldberg Variations brings me awe at the brilliance of the construction of this work. His particular performance of it brings to mind a glimpse into what seems to be the creative process of the Divine.

- Maurizio Pollini playing Chopin Ballades, for me, contain the complete realm of emotions associated with human earthly love.

- Sting's "Fields of Gold" represents my deepest nostalgia for youth and young love.

- Sting's "Ghost" represents the deepest personal grief for the loss of a loved one. I can't hear it without feeling a deep sense of loss for my wonderful deceased father.

- Jethro Tull's Celtic folk-influenced songs elicit an intense connection of the human spirit to this earth that carries us on our voyage and nurtures us.

This list could go on for a long, long time. (How can I omit Brahms, Stravinsky, Debussy, Bud Powell, Stevie Wonder, and Paul Simon?) This is why we make music: to touch deep places in our souls and share that with our audiences, hoping they, too, might experience, in their own way, the kaleidoscope of human existence that we artists are always striving to glimpse. If this is truly one's approach toward making music, even an entire lifetime isn't enough. I hope that you enjoy these stories.

PART I

WHERE I
CAME FROM

THE WAR, PART 1

It's a typical spring afternoon in 1967. I place my books on the rack under my chair and take my usual seat in the dingy, grey, poorly-lit classroom. My fourth grade class ended earlier, but twice a week after school, I attend Hebrew school. I'm generally pretty disinterested in acquiring the necessary skills to navigate the Torah for my Bar Mitzvah, but I think that's mostly because studying Hebrew and Jewish history and philosophy is the last thing in the world I want to do after spending six and a half hours in secular school. Today, however, something unusual is going on. My professor, Mr. Borakov, is listening to a small transistor radio that's on his desk—not an effective aide for teaching the Hebrew alphabet. I notice Mr. B is sweating profusely. His face and bald spot are glistening, and he has large, dark stains on his shirt under his arms and on his back.

When the final busload of Jewish boys come in and take their seats, he quiets us and informs us that the State of Israel is under attack by Egypt, Syria, Jordan, Iraq, Saudi Arabia, and Lebanon, which is pretty much the entire Arab world. Even those of us who spend most of our time in class fantasizing about becoming hall of fame baseball players instead of studying Hebrew understand how grim things look for the Jewish state. It would be like having the entire United States attack New Jersey.

We spend our entire hour and a half long class listening to battlefield reports coming in live from Tel Aviv. When we hear the Israeli Army has taken the Golan Heights from Syria, we follow Mr. Borakov's cue: we all cheer.

When we hear that the Egyptian Army has been repelled back across the Negev desert by Israeli tanks, we cheer again. When we hear the French have sent in fighter jets to help the Jews, we cheer for the French. Today, in Hebrew school, we glue ourselves to the radio to hear whether or not the State of Israel will survive. By the time class ends, the odds look pretty good.

As Jews raised by a previous generation that witnessed and managed to survive the Holocaust, we've grown up knowing that you certainly can't take your freedom and security for granted. I was eight years old when I first saw films of skeletal, emaciated corpses being bulldozed into mass graves at Dachau. The faculty showed us the films in Hebrew school and right then and there, I vowed that I would never become complacent.

THE TREATY, PART 2

Standing in uniform outside the open doors of the State Dining Room, thinking back to that spring afternoon spent in Hebrew School cheering Israel and its allies on to victory in the Six-Day War, I find myself amazed by what I'm about to witness. Yitzhak Rabin and King Hussein of Jordan are standing on a podium with President Clinton. The president lays the document out in front of both men and hands pens to them. They both sign and then shake hands as a long series of exploding flash bulbs punctuates the ceremony.

King Hussein doesn't look terribly happy. Prime Minister Rabin looks even worse, as if he's been eating lemons all day. These leaders' signatures, however, just declared hostilities between their two nations to be over. Jordan has finally recognized Israel's right to exist. It's 1994, and it took twenty-seven years to get to this point.

After the Six-Day War back in the late 60s, Rabin probably would've been voted "least likely Israeli general to ever sign a peace treaty with Jordan." I guess as he aged, he decided he didn't want to condemn his grandchildren and future generations to fighting the same war over and over again. And I lived to see it happen. Up close. Congratulations to Yitzhak!

GO-KARTS

Doug, Glen, Jay, and I are all piled into one car on our way to our rehearsal warehouse. We pay twenty-five dollars a month so we can have a guaranteed private space to work up songs for our funk/fusion/rock band. This month we're going by the name Pegasus. These guys are all really fine musicians. I'm grateful to belong to a group like this, as it's a welcome relief from the intensity and seriousness of the Beethoven, Brahms, and Bartok that I study all day at the University of Miami. The classical stuff is great, but it's nice to do something mostly for the fun of it.

The problem is, Jay tends to take a lot of the fun out of being in the band by frequently instigating arguments with Doug. I'm still pretty young, but I've been doing this for long enough now to know that almost all rock bands have personality clashes like this. My theory is that Jay, who plays drums, doesn't like Doug "hot dogging" for the crowds with showy gestures, faces, and quasi-dance moves with his guitar. Sure, Doug has an ego. But so do all of us, especially Jay. As far as I'm concerned, Doug can do anything he wants to on stage. He's both a good guy and a musical genius. His guitar playing and natural ability are off the charts. He can mimic the styles of John McLaughlin, Dickie Betts, and Jeff Beck. He idolizes Beck, who's a pretty good choice, if you're looking for a guitar hero.

Doug's my roommate this year, and I've noticed that whenever he's in the apartment, he has his Gibson Les Paul guitar strapped around his neck. He does his homework while wearing it. He cooks dinner while wearing it. The guitar even accompanies him on trips to the bathroom. Yes, he practices while pooping. He's also one of the funniest people I've ever met. When he's around, practical jokes are constantly happening. One of his favorites is to come into the room we share at night when I'm either sleeping or trying to sleep and stomp around on my mattress, which is on the floor as I'm not financially sound enough to afford a bed frame, apologizing vigorously, "It's so dark in here," and "I just couldn't see you." With almost anyone else, this would get old really fast, but Doug somehow always keeps me laughing.

Tonight, the tension between Jay and Doug is spreading. Glen and I join in on these exceptionally silly arguments about "professional demeanor" and "stage presence." All for a band that plays about a half-dozen gigs per semester, mostly for beach parties on Key Biscayne or at the Rathskeller, the University of Miami campus bar. The heated discussions usually start with something like this:

Jay: Doug, it's just unprofessional to be making eye contact with every girl in the audience!

Doug: Come on, Jay. Give me a break!

Bog (my nickname): Jay, why do you think Doug practices all the time if it's not to impress the chicks? (I'm half joking).

Glen: Guys, stage presence is something we really do need to take seriously.

Bog: Does stage presence mean telling somebody who they can or can't look at while they're playing?

Jay: Come on! I'm just trying to get us to a place where we'll have the best possible stage show!

This exceptionally silly argument degenerates into everyone talking at once. We're so busy arguing about nothing that none of us notice that Doug has pulled his '67 Pontiac Firebird off the Palmetto Expressway two exits early. And now we're pulling into a go-kart track parking lot.

Doug parks and turns to us and says, "OK, enough! We're racing go-karts. We can argue some more afterward if you want to."

"Doug, you've got to be kidding me," says Jay.

"No! This is important," Doug says. "We need to do this."

Four grumpy jazz/rock/fusion musicians put on their safety helmets and climb into their little motorized wagons. We zoom around the track five times at about twenty miles an hour. I'm the slowest and easily the poorest driver, but I realize about halfway through the third lap that I'm really having fun.

After coming in last and hearing about it from the rest of the band, we all pile back into Doug's car, talking about nothing but our juvenile go-kart race until we arrive at the warehouse and start rehearsal. It's an excellent rehearsal as we iron out the kinks in some Tom Scott, Jeff Beck, and Chick Corea tunes. We also start learning our first Steely Dan song. Overall, it's a pretty productive night. On the way back to Coral Gables, everything is peaceful and everyone seems content. Mercifully, the conversation doesn't go anywhere near "stage presence." Yeah, Doug's definitely a genius.

BOB

We just dropped Bob off at Miami International Airport and now we're back on the Palmetto Expressway heading for home in Mary's beat-up '67 Chevy Caprice that she affectionately calls "Old Gray." No functional AC and my back feels like it's covered with steaming adhesive, causing it to stick tightly to the vinyl upholstery. This is Miami in August.

Two days ago, Bob and I were recording three original songs at Criteria, reputed to be Miami's best recording studio and maybe one of the best in the entire country. Eric Clapton just wrapped up his new album at Criteria the day before our session. Our recording session was the fulfillment of a dream for Bob and me and probably the entire band. The songs we recorded represent an entire summer of rehearsing, composing, and arranging with our band, PRNDL (pronounced "per nin'dle"). We were all crazy nervous going into the studio (mostly because of the expense), but somehow we pulled it off, completing the session close to three in the morning.

Then yesterday, Bob got a phone call from his mother, telling him that his father had died. And today he's leaving for Luquillo Beach in Puerto Rico to attend his dad's funeral. Talk about an emotional roller coaster.

Bob and I met and became friends for life at the 1968 Complex dorm at The University of Miami. Away from home for the first time without adult responsibilities but with adult freedoms, we both began doing lots of partying. But even with the partying, I was driven to work hard at my music. I felt I had something to prove to my plentiful doubters and at UM, I also discovered I truly love music. Not just because I could impress potential high school dates or get compliments from friends and family, but I realized that music has the power to touch the spirit in a way that nothing else can. So in general, I wouldn't start partying until I had gotten in my four hours of practice and completed my theory assignments. But when the work was done, Bob was always my favorite party buddy. He was possibly the funniest person I'd ever met, and he was really smart—whether sober or not. He was also a great persuasive speaker who could seemingly talk anyone into believing anything. Quite the barstool philosopher. But we didn't just smoke and drink together. Bob also played the twelve-string guitar, and we almost never hung out without me breaking out my classic Gibson mandolin to jam.

Sometimes we played Grateful Dead, Allman Brothers, or Beatles songs, but most of the time, we just jammed. Bob was a self-taught musician. He once confessed to me that he thought counting off at the beginning of a song was the musical equivalent of "Ready, set, go!", rather than an indication of tempo. But none of that mattered because Bob had remarkable musical instincts. The chord progressions he would come up with were completely unique, and he put a variety of infectious rhythmic grooves to them that you'd never expect to hear coming from an acoustic instrument. I'd improvise melodies, trying to follow his surprising chord changes. Some of our improvisations would stay with us and eventually, we ended up with a number of completed songs. That's when we decided that it was time to put together a band.

At the end of our freshman year, Bob decided that he'd had enough of college and that he was not going to return to UM. I wasn't sure I would return either. My piano teacher had been less than inspiring and I missed the changing of the seasons. There was also far too much disco on campus in 1976 for my taste. I did know that I'd be spending my summer at home in South Jersey with my parents and my brother Dave. Dave had recently graduated from college and was teaching guitar in a local music store and doing a few society gigs and shows. Somehow, I managed to convince my parents that it was a good idea to have Bob come up from Puerto Rico and spend the summer with us. The two of us and Dave wanted to put together a hybrid bluegrass, folk, country, blues, world music trio, consisting of two guitars and a mandolin. Mom and Dad (reluctantly) gave us the OK, and in mid-June, I picked Bob up at the airport with his twelve-string guitar and backpack. Thus began our band, The Final Frontier.

Musically, Bob and I picked up right where we had left off in Miami, but once my brother joined us, we had a competent professional to play the improvised solos. Dave naturally fit right in, coming up with interesting melodies or harmony lines to join with the melodies I'd composed. The group's main drawback was that Bob and I didn't play our instruments terribly well.

Although I have a certain level of technical command of the piano, I'd never received any formal training on the mandolin; I was completely self-taught. So even though I used my ear to come up with some really creative lines, I couldn't make anything I played sound effortless. Dave's guitar proficiency was a welcomed addition. That summer, we played together and wrote music daily, coming up with songs like "Red Cloud," "King of the Equator," "Say the Word," and "Bogie on the Rag." We worked on drumming up gigs with a little bit of success, but none of them paid well. And the work was certainly not frequent enough to pay our bills.

We played a few bars. At one particularly dark and mildewed South Jersey lounge, the bartender asked us to maybe try and increase the audience interest (all seven of them) by "singing something dirty, maybe with the word 'fuck' in it!" Bob had written a particularly obscene number that Dave and I didn't know, and he promptly performed it solo with the suggested expletive and more.

There was also a bar in Philadelphia's Penn's Landing where the management neglected to inform us that we'd be joined by an exotic dancer. The young lady told us that she was supporting herself through college by belly-dancing at this club. She wore only a G-string and nipple pasties, but at the time, I wished that she would have thrown on a bathrobe or maybe even a quilt over the entire package. Not terribly attractive and was carrying a good deal of extra weight. And judging by the audience's reaction to her, I guessed they shared my opinion. At the very least, it was pretty incongruous and a bit surreal to be playing Doc Watson's bluegrass classic "Way Downtown" with semi-naked female gyrations going on so close to us on the stage. The whole scene definitely shattered my overly-romanticized preconception of what a strip club was like.

The best gigs Final Frontier did during the summer were for the Philadelphia Folk Life Festival sponsored by the Bicentennial Commission. We performed two little daytime concerts on small stages set up near Philadelphia's Art Museum in Fairmount Park. We didn't have big crowds for either show, but we were well-rehearsed by then, and the small audience did show appreciation. When we arrived a half hour early for the first show, we caught the first group of the day concluding their set with a bluegrass version of the Beatles' "I've Just Seen a Face."

"Where'd you guys get the idea to do that Beatles song bluegrass?" Bob asked one of their band members.

"Oh, we heard some group doing it that way on WXPN."

That "some group" was us, Final Frontier, doing a promotional radio appearance. I guess I should have been flattered they stole our arrangement, but I couldn't be because their version sounded better than ours.

During the second of the two bicentennial shows, Bob broke a string on his guitar. Our fifteen-minute break turned into forty-five, while Dave and Bob drove frantically around Philly trying to find a music store to buy a replacement string. There's no good excuse for not being prepared for something like that, so all I can say is, "We were young, and we needed the money." Literally. Even the minimal cost of replacing strings was a big deal to us.

While Dave and Bob were getting lost in South Philly's streets, I went on stage solo and played and sang "Billy the Kid" by Ry Cooder and "Paradise" by John Prine. I hoped they'd return, strings in hand, by the time I finished. No such luck. The tunes went pretty well, but my entrance and exit from the stage under the circumstance was painfully awkward.

Two months came and went, and all the composing, arranging, and rehearsing was for naught. Even the promotional photo session (all three of us wearing matching overalls) that my high school friend, Steve, did for us couldn't delay the inevitable demise of Final Frontier. Understandably, Bob just didn't want to live off the kindness of his friends' parents anymore, so in mid-August, I drove him to the airport once again. I returned home, not knowing whether I'd ever see him again or if any of the music we'd written would be played again.

A few days later, at the persistent urging of my jazz fusion virtuoso guitar playing friend and UM classmate, Doug, I decided to return to college. Back to Florida. It was very much a last-minute decision and I can only imagine what twists and turns life would have thrown me if I hadn't.

But the summer of '77 was different. I decided to spend it in Miami to practice and take lessons. I was surprised my parents didn't insist that I get a job, but fortunately, they didn't. I think they were convinced I was working hard on the piano. I was. But I was also partying a lot and living in a "band house." Bob returned to Miami and moved in with me, Wayne (a good friend and woodwind player from my high school days in New Jersey), and Richie.

Bob, Wayne, and I wrote lots of music together throughout the summer, and when everything was clicking, we ended up literally dancing through the house playing our new material, sometimes to the chagrin of our roommate, Richie, a great jazz bassist, who worked a gig in Fort Lauderdale most nights until three in the morning. When we were done, we'd collapse on our Salvation Army couches, high-fiving and laughing.

But when he was down, it seemed to me that Wayne could sink into depression and I was prone to follow him. Whenever that happened, I generally got on my bike, rode to the music school, and closed myself in a practice room with Ravel and Beethoven. Wayne's negative moods could be infectious. But his musical contributions were substantial and they helped our sound evolve into something really unique. Then I managed to convince Jay, Glen, and Sheldon to join our band. Now we had drums, bass, and a lead guitarist. For the first time, we had a complete band.

With the added input and some compositional ideas from our new bandmates, the character of the songs evolved once again. Sheldon was a virtuoso rock guitarist who had also studied jazz. Wayne and I came from a classical background, but we both leaned toward progressive rock and jazz fusion. Glen and Jay also loved the progressive rock idiom but leaned a bit more toward the hard rock tradition. And Bob just loved great songs, whether by the Beatles, the Grateful Dead, or The Band.

All these influences eventually came together in three tunes: "Gargoyles," "Total Blue," and "Latin Bebop." A lot of pot was smoked, lots of beer was drunk, and we laughed until we cried nearly every night. But we also rehearsed a lot. I played both keyboards (Fender Rhodes and a cheesy synthesizer) and mandolin and developed steel string callouses and a bit of chronic soreness in my right wrist. This was probably caused by a combination of poor mandolin technique and pounding the keys to compete with our group's outrageous overall volume level. We rehearsed in a very small room that was really a converted tool shed. By August, we decided we had enough music to go into a studio and record.

Our "band manager" (a strictly honorary title since we never performed live), Darryl, was interning at Criteria and suggested we record there. Criteria was one of the world's greatest studios. We agreed, failing to consider the kind of pressure that an hourly rate of 130 dollars would put on us. We could only afford three hours and that was pushing it. We were just plain ignorant of the fact that setting levels and mixing probably represented two hours of studio time in and of themselves. But somehow, we pulled it off.

"Gargoyles" rocked out. "Total Blue" floated in space, then drove with a relentless forward momentum. "Latin Bebop" just brimmed with reckless fun. Yes, we pulled it off. A summer band house, an original group concept, and creating something exciting and unique and sharing it with my good friends were all elements of my youthful dream coming to life at the age of twenty. Right at the three-hour mark, we finished laying down our last track.

Our recording engineer seemed a bit detached throughout our late night session. A few times, I thought I even detected a bit of amusement on his face when a few of us (myself included) demonstrated a lack of even a rudimentary understanding of studio recording protocols. But at the end of the session, he came through for us.

"I like you guys and I like your music," he said. "Your time's up, but I'll give you a few extra minutes, so we can do a quick rough mix."

We thanked him, then took our places sitting quietly behind him while he equalized our individual instruments and blended them together. The recording booth had a wall of the best speakers money could buy pointed directly at us. I had never heard anything that sounded that rich and full. I also hadn't imagined that our songs could sound so good. I don't think I'll ever feel as satisfied as I did sitting in that booth at three-thirty in the morning in August of '77 listening to our musical dream child.

Bob felt the same way. As a matter of fact, we were all pumped enough that we stopped at Denny's for a four-in-the-morning breakfast. We were exhausted but still buzzed with the adrenalin rush created by the recording session. When we got home, I lay awake in bed for a good while just staring into the darkness and wondering what life would have in store for me next. I finally fell asleep.

It seemed like I woke up immediately with Bob standing in the doorway of my bedroom. "Bogie, my mom just called. I need to go home today... My dad just died." You've got to be kidding me! What a rollercoaster! What a real-life dream come true followed by a devastating nightmare. Snatched from the clutches of dreams back to life's reality.

As Mary and I drive home after saying a heartfelt but sad goodbye to Bob at the airport, I realize I find great comfort in being with her. The other really special thing that happened to me this summer is that I fell in love with this wonderful, unique, and unpredictable woman, and as far as I can tell, she seems to have fallen in love with me, too. It's been quite a summer.

CODA

Bob eventually returned from Puerto Rico and we tried putting the band back together. We still made some very creative music, but personality conflicts and finances eventually led to our final break up. As to our recording, Wayne and I took the initiative and pounded the New York pavements, leaving our unsolicited demo with every recording company we could find in the phone book. It was an amazingly naïve approach, but what is even more amazing is we received a letter of interest from Warner Bros. We didn't even get past the receptionist's desk when we visited their New York offices. An entirely unsolicited instrumental demo, and Warner Bros.' A&R (artists and repertoire) division was asking to see us play a live show. Unfortunately, the band was going through changes as our immaturity led to interpersonal conflicts. The group splintered into factions. Darryl, our "manager," decided it was best to be up front, so he promptly informed Warner Bros. that we were undergoing personnel changes. Somehow, that caused them to quickly lose interest in us, which was not surprising.

Wayne graduated from UM, worked some cruise ships, toured for a short time with Blood, Sweat, and Tears, and eventually settled in Long Island to teach music. I played a top 40s rock gig with Jay, Glen, and Sheldon for a short time at a depressing "drunk college kid" bar called Rum Runners, my first "steady." But secretly, I swore to myself that I would never again put all my eggs in one basket. I decided to get my own act together and not rely on any one particular band as a career path.

Bob moved to Long Island, got married to his lovely high school sweetheart, Jean, and played with a few new wave bands. He eventually ended up managing a successful congressional campaign for an old friend, putting his powers of persuasion to good use. Somehow, that morphed into a good job in DC at the Environmental Protection Agency (EPA). Then, as unlikely as it seems to those of us who knew him back in the 70s, he also found Jesus and grew increasingly involved in his church. Bob eventually became a minister. He left his job with the federal government and put his persuasive speaking gift to the best possible use: weekly sermons and promoting programs to fight hunger. Since we live relatively close, Bob and I still get together once in a while and have multiple laughs about old times. There's still a definite synergy when we play a bit of music together. Nowadays, we generally don't talk religion or politics, but our spirits still connect in the same deeply rooted common ground we've had since the 1970s.

The Final Frontier, 1977
Left to right: Bob Hahn, Bob Boguslaw, and David Boguslaw

VOODOO

For the last two weeks of my gig on the Costa Cruise Lines' Renaissance, the ship was chartered by a French Belgian Rotary Club. They were quite a grim and joyless group of Caribbean tourists. While the knife-throwing husband hurled flaming tomahawks at his wife who was tied to something that looked like a giant spinning roulette wheel, the Rotarians looked like they'd just finished balancing a bank account.

While docked in Grenada, a troupe of scantily clad quasi-communist dancers, brought on board to provide some local color, delivered a "power to the people" anthem to close their performance, climaxing with the classic Che Guevara raised fist. The Rotarians again reacted as if they'd been watching paint dry. The Belgian men always wore their sport jackets and the women their shoulder-covering knee-length dresses everywhere they went, even to a steamy open-air market in Port Antonio, Jamaica.

There's been one exceptionally cool aspect to this fourteen-day charter. We dropped anchor in twelve ports in a two-week span. I went to a lot of places I'd never been to before and probably will never visit again. Places like Guadeloupe, Martinique, Union Island, and now Haiti.

As we pull up to the dock in Cape Haitian, I feel a combination of fascination and dread. I'm not an expert on history and sociology, but I do know that we're visiting the poorest country in the western hemisphere. After three months in the West Indies, I'm accustomed to peddlers and beggars, but from what I've heard, Haiti is the worst. It seems that everyone in the Caribbean thinks that all Americans are millionaires. They don't know my income on this cruise ship puts me squarely on the poverty line at home. I suppose, though, that when the Haitians compare themselves to my standard of living, I might as well be a millionaire. After all, I do have running water, electricity, and enough to eat.

The island is extremely mountainous with thick forests nearly everywhere. It's beautiful but mostly impossible to farm. As we pull up toward the dock, our ship is approached by ten to fifteen rickety-looking rowboats. Their occupants are dressed in ragged looking khaki shirts and shorts and their cargo is all local wood carvings. They could have waited for us (and our Rotarians) to disembark before trying to sell to us, but I guess they figure their boats give them a first crack at the tourist dollars.

"Hey Americans," they yell. "You want to buy a very, very nice statue? Very nice! Very cheap!" They hold up several two- or three-foot tall carved mahogany statues that, from our vantage point on the ship, look to be human figures, probably peasants.

I have no intention of buying anything in Haiti except possibly some coconut milk. I just spent a half week's salary to buy black coral in Jamaica and a gold chain in St. Thomas as a nice, romantic gift for Mary. But my roommate, Louie (guitar and trumpet), takes a liking to one of the figures. After a little bartering, the rowboat captain flings a rope up over the side of the ship and somehow attaches the statue to a pulley and sends it up to Louie. There's also a small cigarette case for Louie to deposit five dollars into and send back down. These Haitian entrepreneurs have done this before. As Louie looks at his beautifully crafted new acquisition, one of the Jamaican waiters on the ship, Herb, who's become a friend of ours comes up behind him:

Herb: "Oh, mon! You shouldn't have bought that! You don't know that it's cursed?"

Louie: "What do you mean, cursed? How would I know that?"

Herb: "In Jamaica, we believe it's a sin to carve wood or stone into the human form. These Haitians worship Vodun, and that's why their island is cursed and Jamaica's blessed. And look there! At the bottom! Look at his feet!"

Sure enough, at the bottom of the statue where you'd expect the carved peddler's feet to be but aren't, there's a small crucifix with a snake wrapped around it. Louie's eyes widen, and he immediately yells down to the rowboat captain that he wants his money back. It's quickly apparent that's not going to happen, so Louie takes his new wooden friend to our cabin, carrying it as if the snake's alive and poised to bite him.

Our drummer/band-leader, Rick, and I disembark and find that Haiti is not much different from other Caribbean islands. A lot of panhandling, nice people, and a large assortment of both sweet and objectionable organic smells. But I do notice there are no dogs anywhere to be seen and absolutely no overweight people. In that way, it's unlike any of the other islands we've visited. When I return to my cabin, drenched in sweat as always, I find Louie sitting on the top bunk, staring at his new statue. People in the Caribbean don't laugh about Voodoo and Louie is a Catholic of Puerto Rican descent. He's convinced the statue's staring at him. I just laugh about it and tell him to forget it. It's time for dinner and then our cocktail set.

Later that night, in the middle of my deepest REM sleep, I'm awakened by some serious screams.

"Aaaaaaaahh...Aaaaaahh...Aaaaahhh!"

It's Louie, and he swears the statue's eyes had lit up and it was looking at him. He's sure the Voodoo curse is starting its work on him. I saw nothing, but I tell Louie I think it's time for a burial at sea. Louie doesn't want to lose his five dollars. But when I offer to give him the money so I can get a good night's sleep, he declines the dollars but agrees to toss the cursed statue over the side. We both throw some clothes on and climb a few flights of stairs to the top deck. We go outside; Louie hesitates for a second, then throws the carving into the sea. We both watch it bob in the waves for a minute, then disappear in the ship's wake.

Back at our cabin, we spend a couple minutes talking about the supernatural, and then we turn in. As I'm falling asleep, I wonder for just a moment if the next time something bad happens to me, it might be because a Voodoo curse can't be reversed by drowning.

RICK, PART 1

Rick and I met on my first full-time playing gig after graduating from Miami. I finished school in May and still hadn't found any work outside of moving furniture a few times for Manpower. In mid-June, the slow season for gigs in Miami, I was offered a three-month run on the Costa cruise ship Renaissance. Three and a half months of steady employment in a show band seemed like a great idea. Plus I'd be working on a floating hotel. No dealing with our old junker of a car. No grocery shopping or preparing food. Visiting Venezuela, Aruba, Santo Domingo, San Juan and St. Thomas on a weekly basis, and the commute would be a simple three-deck stair climb from my cabin to the main show room. I could put down a book I was reading at 5:55 and be playing a Jobim bossa nova at 6:00 for the cocktail hour. These negligible responsibilities made the gig seem almost like a second childhood.

Rick and I had lots of adventures on that ship. We nearly crossed paths with Hurricane David (150-mile-an-hour winds and forty-foot waves) while trying to make it to port in Santo Domingo. As it happened, the storm unexpectedly turned north and hit Santo Domingo head on, completely destroying the port. Luckily, our captain had the good sense to turn around and head south, waiting out the hurricane for three days in Curaçao. That night, I remember playing Chick Corea's "Spain" as a show opener before the ship turned around. The swells were already up to twenty feet and the winds were at forty miles an hour. I was always amazed the dancers we played for could keep their balance on a rocking ship, but that night a couple of them hit the floor. So thinking that "Spain" might be the last song we ever played, Rick and I totally smoked it.

While working on the Renaissance, we often rented cars to take a trip ashore. One such trip was to the "German Village," a few hours up into the mountains from Caracas. On our drive, we stopped at the side of the road to rent horses from a group of ten- to twelve-year-old Venezuelan boys. They had us take a ride up a two-mile muddy, hilly, and rock-filled path. The Venezolanos thought it would be entertaining to follow us on their own horses, regularly whipping our horses' hindquarters to make sure they never slowed down. I could see Louie, Rick, and John ahead of me, thrown from side to side at a frightening speed. When I looked behind me, I saw the boy who had been given the "whip Boguslaw's horse" job smiling and laughing. I probably looked even more precarious than the three gringos in front of me. Fortunately, we made it back to the car without fracturing any spines, skulls, or buttocks. John and Louie said a few unpleasant sounding things in broken Spanish to our "tour guides," but they just laughed.

One evening, our entire band (called "El Cohunto Renaissance") was dragged into a rabid conga line in the disco by a large group of drunken Venezuelan passengers who were screaming the lyrics to "YMCA." I can still remember my Heineken splashing onto the back of the girl in front of me. No one cared because they were all having such a great time screaming Village People lyrics (which they didn't understand) at the tops of their lungs. Dadaism on our floating hotel. Yeah, Rick and I had some fun on that ship.

I also recall Rick hunting for weed in Aruba. The dealer told us only one person could accompany him, so he and Rick set off and left the rest of us on a street corner. We waited for him over an hour and eventually had to leave to get back to the ship or we were in danger of being left behind. Once on board, I quickly threw my tuxedo on and ran up to the bandstand. Still no sign of Rick as I felt the ship moving away from the dock. I sat down at the piano, convinced that Rick was bleeding out in some alley with an Aruban knife in his neck. But right when we got to the bridge of our first tune, I heard some cymbal rolls and looked back in time to see and hear Rick come in with the typical bossa nova pattern he favored. Turned out the dealer had taken Rick's money and left him standing on a different street corner. Rick had waited until the last possible minute and then ran full speed back to the ship, arriving just before they pulled up the gangway. Live and learn, one would hope.

Rick and I didn't really know each other when we set sail. We'd rehearsed only once, but I had the feeling we shared lots of common ground. Both of us were neurotic Jewish guys from the northeast who were liberal and open-minded. We'd both read Herman Hesse and Jerzy Kosiński. We both thought it was very cool to get paid to travel. We both had the same sarcastic sense of humor. But what we had most in common was music. We both loved the innovative jazz/rock fusion of the seventies: Weather Report, Return to Forever, Frank Zappa, Mahavishnu Orchestra, and Miles Davis. We also shared a love for the creative acoustic jazz artists of the period such as Keith Jarrett, Jack DeJohnette, McCoy Tyner, and Charlie Haden. And even though Rick hadn't studied classical music, he was open to all styles and was particularly into twentieth century composers. I'd practice a Prokofiev concerto at night after the shows were done, and Rick would improvise exceptionally musical drum parts to accompany me, something I wouldn't have thought possible. This was in addition to the almost nightly jam sessions we'd do after work. It's probably safe to say I became a competent jazz pianist, in large part, because of those sessions with Rick.

In the summer of '80, I once again found myself unemployed. And once again I got a call for some cruise ship work. Two weeks on the Mardi Gras and six weeks on the Carnival. The Mardi Gras was uneventful with the typical weekly route of Nassau, San Juan, St. Thomas, and Miami. But on the Carnival, when I walked into the main show room for a meeting of the new musicians with our gay, operatic cruise director, I looked behind the drum set to find none other than Rick sitting there, practicing his favorite hobby, juggling. A tennis ball eluded him and rolled across the stage toward my feet.

Rick looked up and yelled, "Bogie!"

I was amazed. It turned out that Rick was on the road with a Top 40 band somewhere in the Midwest when he decided he'd had enough. He called one of the cruise ship booking agents and decided to take the gig on the Carnival when he heard he'd be working with me. It turned out that we did even more jam sessions on this gig than we had on the Renaissance. There were three bands full of young jazz hopefuls on this ship, mostly from the Berklee College of Music in Boston, so there was never a shortage of musicians who wanted to throw back some beers and play some bebop after hours.

But my favorite memory of the Carnival had to be of myself, Rick, and two other tuxedo-clad musicians running an extension cord out of my cabin onto the deck, plugging a small TV into it, setting it on a table, turning it on, and settling back in deck chairs to see what was on at five-thirty in the morning as we approached the port of Miami. We felt justified because, after all, we were still too far out to sea to get reception in our cabins. The jam session/party had concluded about an hour earlier. I can only imagine what the Italian officer was thinking as he walked by us while making his morning rounds. Here we were: four musicians still dressed in last night's formal wear, trying hard not to fall off of our deck chairs because of uncontrollable laughter. After all, on the TV screen Moe was slapping Larry, and Curly was responding with "Soitenly!"

We did get to work one more ship gig together briefly, but it was so miserable that I quit after a month. It was a ferry from Maine to Nova Scotia, and you couldn't get off the ship except for forty-five minutes every morning and forty-five more each evening. Talk about going stir crazy. It's possible I would have killed myself with bourbon if I hadn't quit. But it was on that ship that we swore we'd record together someday.

Shortly after I left that gig, Rick was fired for sneaking onto the bridge in the middle of the night and "steering" the ship, even though it was on autopilot. When one of the officers caught him, he wasn't amused, and they put Rick ashore in Portland, Maine, a short drive back to his new home in Boston. Rick has never been a person to be constrained by rules and conventions.

Bob is second from the right, Rick Klane is at far right
"El Cohunto Renaissance" Cruise Ship Band, 1979

NEW YEAR'S EVE

It's two in the morning on January 1, 1980, and we're paying our check at the cash register, trying to get the hell out of here as quickly as possible. As Mary and I finished up our coffee and eggs at this Hallandale, Florida diner, feeling a genuine sense of relief that the night was almost over, the server at the counter made a big issue of throwing out a homeless guy who apparently had been nursing a cup of coffee for too long. The restaurant is nearly empty, and it's cold outside. That's right, cold in South Florida. A few nights a year, it gets into the thirties in Miami, and tonight's one of those nights. Apparently, it's more important to diner management for "homeless guy" to hit the road and do his best to keep himself warm than to take the risk of alienating the five customers currently enjoying their pancakes, eggs, and burgers. I know full well how cold it is tonight because I just finished what proved to be an exceptionally traumatic outdoor New Year's Eve gig.

Back in September I returned to Miami, having finished three-and-a-half months on my first cruise ship gig. I've played a few jobs since then, but mostly I've stayed home watching the small amount of money I managed to save gradually run out. I'm shy enough that just the thought of making phone calls to solicit work makes me nervous. So I sat, practiced, and waited for the phone to ring.

I got a call on December 20 for a New Year's gig. The guitar player made the job sound like a dream come true. We would board a cruise ship at nine that evening, sail up the intercoastal waterway to Hallandale, take a right turn out to Key Biscayne, and then back to Miami by one in the morning. We'd be playing jazz, and we'd each make three hundred dollars, by far my best paying gig ever. I'd be able to pay my portion of the December bills and still have a little bit left for recreational activities. And to top it off, Eric Traub was on the job. I'd seen Eric play at the university and with Ira Sullivan a number of times. He's a brilliant, 100 % committed jazz sax player whom I've aspired to play with since first hearing him. Eric has played with Maynard Ferguson, Michel Legrand, and one of the Army jazz bands in the DC area. He's a world class musician and was a great addition to what already sounded like a great gig.

A couple of nice but seemingly clueless young women came and listened to us play a few standards and George Benson's version of "This Masquerade" as our audition. They thought we'd be fine and committed to us, telling us that a '40s swing theme would be fine for this particular party. It sounded like such a good time that I convinced Mary she should go with us as a guest. Unfortunately, the job quickly became a nightmare.

The first clue my expectations might have been a bit too high was when we arrived at the dock and got our first look at our "cruise ship." It was a barge—a not terribly well-painted one with iron benches, open sides, and no heat. The whole thing stunk of diesel.

It was probably about fifty degrees outside when we boarded, and it continued to get colder as the evening progressed. We set up and played a couple tunes as the passengers boarded. Then we met our boss for the evening. After our second tune, the evening's surly young event planner walked up to Neal, our band leader.

"You guys are playing jazz!" he said. "Jazz sucks. Jazz is boring! You guys were hired to play disco and Latin music, and if you want to get paid you better start right now!!!"

The two girls who thought the '40s swing theme was a good idea were nowhere to be found. I felt a little sorry for Neal, but the reality was he became pretty useless for the rest of the gig, mostly because of his concern about the boss's "not getting paid" threat.

Half an hour in, the job was a disaster. Eric and I knew a bit of Latin music (in my case it was due to playing for Venezuelan passengers on my recent cruise ship gig). But the only disco ideas we could come up with were standards such as "Our Day Will Come" and "What a Difference a Day Makes" played with the dreaded disco drum beat and eighth-note bass octaves. We dragged the songs out for as long as we could, but it wasn't long enough. I guess the misery of trying to play with cold fingers, repeating run-on versions of songs I didn't want to play in the first place, and the lack of any musical guidance from our leader must have shown on my face. An exceedingly drunk, tall, and irate young Canadian passenger took exception to my negative attitude. He came around my Fender Rhodes electric piano, stood next to me (while we were in the middle of playing "Guantanam-era"), and proceeded to bang on the top octave of my keyboard with his fist, yelling, "WHAT THE FUCK IS THE MATTER WITH YOU? THIS IS NEW YEAR'S EVE!!! YOU'RE SUPPOSED TO BE HAVING A GOOD TIME!!!"

I stopped playing, stood up, and pulled my fist back. "Drunk Canadian guy" started to come at me, but somehow Eric got between us. After a few quick words, our disgruntled guest turned and waved us off in disgust. It seemed like a good time for a break. The barge had stopped moving, and I saw that we were tied up at a bridge in Hallandale. We had travelled all of three miles, and the party planners were out of alcohol. A couple of catering grunts went to comb the streets of Hallandale to try and find an open liquor store. Maybe it was the empty, useless barge bars that had more to do with the Canadian guy's disgruntlement than my unhappy facial expressions. I'll never know. But I do know that it was New Year's Eve, and we were playing for a party that ran out of alcoholic beverages at eleven-thirty.

When we disembarked with our gear at the end of the evening, I didn't think I could ever feel so glad a gig was over. There was also a sense of gen-uine relief when we got paid. At least I could afford to take Mary out for a late night Miami breakfast. She was such a good sport throughout the entire travesty. Then we watched a homeless guy get thrown out into the cold. So now I'm thinking that it's just not a good karma day, and it's best to just get home as quickly as possible and turn in with the hope that January 1, 1980 will bring better things.

CODA

Fortunately, a few years later, I spent four months playing a steady five night a week gig with Eric at a Coconut Grove restaurant. I was the leader, so this time I was the one who had to worry about getting paid by a slimy club owner. But we got to play lots of straight ahead jazz. At the time, Eric was probably the most committed and intense jazz horn player I'd ever worked with. I learned a lot from him. I picked him up and dropped him off nightly. Somehow, he didn't have a car or much money after three years on the road with Maynard Ferguson. He frequently invited me into his apartment to give a listen to some Coltrane, Sonny Rollins, or Dexter Gordon. He talked a lot about moving to New Orleans, and when the gig in the Grove ended, he left Miami for good, moving to the Crescent City, where his favorite music originated. The last I heard of him, Eric was doing well there, playing and recording some with Dr. John and Kermit Ruffins.

I never saw the other band members from that traumatic New Year's Eve gig again. But I guess we shared something special that evening that we'll all remember: a "worst gig ever" story. Every musician has a "worst gig ever" story. Mary was on one where the bass player was dragged off the bandstand by his collar, and the guest tried to beat him up. Just for not knowing a song. I was on a gig in Liberty City, Miami, where at the end of the night, the DJ who was taking over following our last set announced, "I'd like to thank Ms. Jackie and her band for playing. Too bad it wasn't any better." Ms. Jackie was possibly the most unprepared singer I'd ever worked for. I also played for numerous talent shows on cruise ships where the acts were lined up by the scores, all of them passengers who were completely incapable of expressing in musical terms what they wanted from our show band as we backed them up. At first it was laughable, but as a seemingly endless parade of bad musicians and music progressed, it became really depressing. And then of course there was Sonny. Every time I worked with him, he would hurl at least a few profane insults at me. So why has this particular New Year's job stood out in my memory as top of the "nightmare gig" list for thirty-four years now? I think it's because of expectations. I went into that gig thinking Jazz...cruise ship...working with a musical genius. I walked off that barge chilled to the bone, feeling like I hadn't played a meaningful note during an entire four hour job, and filled with gradually ebbing anger at a belligerent passenger and a supremely obnoxious boss. This was my worst gig ever because the expectation vs. reality gap was easily the greatest.

SUMMER, 1980

SONNY

WARNING: *X-rated dialogue is recounted here in the interest of historical accuracy, with absolutely no regard for good taste.*

"I'd like to throw that fuckin' Fender Rhodes in the swimming pool; it sounds so bad!" That's my band leader talking to me. He's a Brooklyn transplant living in Miami who goes by the name of "Sonny," though his real name is Angelo. He's right; my electric piano sounds less than wonderful, but his uncompromising way of expressing himself has me feeling dispirited, worn down, and deflated. I never wanted to play weddings such as the one we just finished: 50 percent syrupy pop ballads, 25 percent disco, and 25 percent Sinatra and Bennett standards. I don't have the money to take my keyboard to a repair shop, and I've been working on fixing it myself with mixed results. It's going to need regular maintenance as long as I keep loading its 124 pounds in and out of the sunken trunk of my car on a regular basis by myself. Even though I've been doing this type of work for almost a year, I'm still not used to the way no one on the gig helps anyone else with their gear.

I guess it's because when you play union jobs everyone gets paid a few bucks extra for "cartage." Ergo, it's every man for himself. Without a bass player or guitar player on this gig, I'm a one-man rhythm section playing with only a singer and a drummer, Sonny, who plays too loud, rushes and jumps down my throat every time I don't know a song or have difficulty transposing one (changing keys).

This wedding was at a beautiful Spanish Colonial home in the Brickell area of Miami, just north of Coconut Grove. I think the guests liked us reasonably well, though it's possible they heard Sonny swearing at me on the bandstand when I struggled with transposing Donna Summers's "Heaven Knows" and couldn't play the Bee Gee's "Night Fever" at all. Some of Sonny's other choice tirades come to mind as I'm packing up:

"I'd like to blow up that fuckin' University of Miami. They don't teach you kids shit!"

"If you don't know the tunes, what the fuck good are you to anyone?"

"Today I started havin' chest pains. That's all I need! Another fuckin' heart attack!"

"Holy shit! You're wearing fucking blue socks with a tuxedo! Do I gotta do fuckin' everything for you??!!"

Admittedly, the University of Miami never taught me about color coordinating my socks with my tuxedo. I visualize a time in the not-too-distant future when I don't have to play this kind of music or accept jobs from people who constantly berate me. This raises the questions: Why am I working for this guy? And why is he hiring me? The answer to the second question is simple. In Sonny's own words: "None of the veteran society music guys'll work for me 'cause they know what a son of a bitch I am, so I've gotta hire you kids from the fucking University of Miami." I don't argue when he confesses that to me, but then why do I work for him? That answer's simple, too. Money—and for no other reason. Sonny and I have an arrangement. He'll get me nearly nightly work playing shows in Broward and Palm Beach County retirement communities as long as I make myself available on the weekends to play weddings with him. Most of the time, the shows are solo piano, and even when they use bass and drums and Sonny plays with me, he refrains from his usual abuse, knowing he's got to follow me or there'll be a musical train wreck.

The math is simple. If I play night clubs, bars, or hotels in Miami, my income is two to three hundred dollars weekly. Doing Sonny's shows and weddings, it's anywhere between five and seven hundred. So even though my ear is always to the ground for better gigs, it's nice to know that there's no problem with paying my rent and utilities when I work for Sonny, or paying for my piano lessons with my brilliant new teacher, Fred Coulter. As I'm lowering my keyboard into my trunk, one last "Sonny-ism" comes to mind before I start thinking about the Chopin ballade I'll be playing at my lesson tomorrow:

Bob B: "So you stayed married for seventeen years, even though you say you and your wife knew you hated each other's guts after just one year? Why'd you stay married so long knowing that?"

Sonny: "I wasn't gonna give that bitch the satisfaction of collecting alimony from me!"

As miserable as Sonny can sometimes make my life, he's made his own life exponentially worse.

CODA

My phone rings on Sunday morning and I answer.

Me: "Hello."

Sonny: "It's Sonny. Listen, kid, I know what an asshole I can be on these jobs sometimes."

(Sometimes?)

"I want to say two things. One is that I just really care about these gigs coming off good and that's why I get so worked up. The other is I think you've got great potential, so just keep learning the tunes, and you're gonna have a great career doing this."

Me: I pause for a moment, feeling a very slight amount of empathy for Sonny. "Don't worry, Sonny. I'll make next week's gigs. I'm not gonna quit." (Yet.)

LESLIE BURRS

Leslie is an African-American jazz flutist. He's relatively young but has already toured with the Duke Ellington Orchestra and appeared with Grover Washington. He's a brilliant player. Leslie definitely exudes an air of self-confidence, at times bordering on arrogance. Certainly, working with him on a daily basis for the last two weeks has been one of the highlights of my career. I've been hired to accompany Leslie for a two-week run playing for schools and homes for the disabled. There will also be one public concert at the end of the run. It's sponsored by the Music Performance Trust Fund. I'm just glad to spend two weeks playing jazz professionally. The programs consist of Leslie and me playing tunes, mostly jazz standards, interspersed with some extended discussion and Q and A.

Yesterday, when Leslie asked for questions, one mentally disabled patient in the audience asked him if he was God. Apparently, Leslie needed to be ready for anything on this gig. We both were taken aback, but he fielded the question well with some discussion of subjectivity (asking the patient if he thought Leslie was God) and the role of the performing artist in society. He's pretty good at this.

Today we're playing for a classroom of gifted teenagers who are studying at a magnet school for the arts. We start with Jobim's "Corcovado" with a lot of interaction between the flute and piano and some harmonically adventurous chords and scales. Yesterday, Leslie said that I had set the stage for this approach in our first rehearsal. I told him I thought it had been him; I had just followed his lead. Either way, our performances have become highly conversational. As always, at the end of our first tune, Leslie asks the students, "What did you think of that?" One student calls out, "That was great!"

Leslie gives the student a sardonic little smile and says, "Well, of course that was great."

The students all look shocked at his overt display of ego. I probably look a bit shocked, too. Their opinion of us seems to be going quickly from something bordering on awe to disdain and I don't blame them. Leslie looks around the room with a smug smile and says, "I can tell what you're all thinking: Who does this guy think he is? What kind of self-centered, conceited musician did they send to play for us? Can we learn anything from someone with that kind of attitude?" I have to confess that's exactly what I'm thinking, but I know him, so I'm not quite as surprised as the kids are.

Leslie continues, "Think for a minute. What if I didn't believe what we're doing here is great? Then I'd be up here wondering and worrying about how we're doing and what you in the audience might be thinking about us. Do you think we could give a committed and convincing performance if we felt that way?" He pauses for effect, then says, "If you want any chance of being successful as a performing artist, it's essential for you to be convinced that what you're doing has value to your audience, that you have something to offer. And that it's not just OK but that it's great!"

As we get ready for our next song, Charlie Parker's "Au Privave," I can see a look of understanding come over the faces of the students. I think about my dreams of playing concerti while sitting in front of the Chicago Symphony or the Philadelphia Orchestra, and I realize I, too, just learned a really important lesson from Leslie.

NEW YEAR'S EVE

New Year's Eve is to gig warriors what Black Friday is to retailers. Sometimes demand can even outstrip supply. Most musicians actually get paid more than a livable wage on this one night of the year. And why not? We're all rolling the dice by being on the road at two or three in the morning, threatened by lots of sloppy-drunk vehicle operators and overly zealous police officers manning sobriety checkpoints. The money makes it worth it though, which is usually three or four times more than what a regular gig pays. And sometimes, if we're lucky, we even get to meet and play for some very interesting people.

We're packing up our gear. About an hour ago, we counted backward from ten to one, then shouted, "Happy New Year!" Immediately, we dove into "Auld Lang Syne," followed by "When the Saints Go Marching In" as a large group of septa- and octogenarians blew on noisemakers, burst balloons lying underfoot, and generally raised as much hell as you'd find in an unsupervised middle school cafeteria.

I've been playing gigs for a few years now, but I'm still amazed at the capacity of adults (especially ones with more life experience) to revert to the diversions of childhood when given the right environment and stimuli. I think about how I still get a big rush out of reliving my high school days by playing and singing Grateful Dead, Bob Dylan, and The Band songs with my old friends. I don't, however, long to relive the days of the "Itsy, Bitsy Spider."

Mary is folding cords for the PA system. She sang well and looks exceptionally lovely in a silver sparkling gown. This was our first New Year's gig together and it was a lot of fun. The drummer is my good friend, Louis, and we also had a fine bass player with us nick-named Bebob. At this point in my life, any job for a retirement community where we don't get bitched at a lot, I consider a major success. I have a few personal theories about what contributes to the irritability of our aging clients:

We're a very young band. They're a very old group of partiers. Our youth reminds them of how old they all are.

Because we're a young band, they think we won't know a lot of their WWII era favorites. To a large degree, they're correct.

Most of them are in some sort of pain most of the time.

But tonight things went well. The dance floor was full, leading up to midnight. The group got a good swing feel going; we had quick, smooth transitions from one song to the next and, most importantly, no one made a request we couldn't play. Hallelujah! There were no whining or dismissive hand gestures from the crowd.

We just got paid, and Mary and I get into our 1975 Pontiac Grand Prix. She asks me to stop somewhere so she can get a cup of coffee. I give her a clearly concerned look and ask, "You're going to be able to stay awake until we can get to Bob's party, aren't you?"

"Of course," she answers. We stop for some coffee, but she's completely unconscious by the time we make the twenty-minute trip to the chamber music party in Coral Gables.

Chamber music reading parties are fun, but ordinarily, I would just skip this one and go home, with Mary sleeping in the passenger seat. Even with string players from the Chicago Symphony Orchestra and the Concertgebouw expected to be there. I ask Mary if she wants to get up and go in. She mutters something unintelligible, but I've been with her long enough to know that she's out for the night. I think about the string quartet I composed and brought with me. Our friend, Bob, promised to help me get a reading of it. Not just any reading, but a reading by some truly top-notch professional string players. It took me over a year to compose and copy this three-movement, fifteen-minute piece. It's my first large-scale composition, written for the most part while working on cruise ships. I vacillate and then ask Mary if she minds if I go in for a bit while she rests in the car. She mutters something which I loosely interpret as, "No problem." I feel guilty about it, but I crack the window, lock her in the car sleeping, and go into the party with my string quartet tucked under my arm.

When I come through the front door, I find that my friend, Bohdan, is playing the Brahms E-minor cello sonata with the Chicago symphony cellist. It's as good as I expected it would be. A number of people are drinking wine and beer, and another group is rolling and smoking joints in the corner of the room. The sound of a string quartet is drifting in from a back bedroom. I'm pretending to be patient, but I'm actually worrying about leaving Mary in the car and wondering when I'll be able to get my piece read. Bohdan invites me to play the final movement of the Brahms (the most difficult part), so I move to the piano bench. The cellist goes with a faster tempo than I've ever played this sonata, and I'm distracted by my concern for Mary. I play like a dog.

I'm thinking maybe this wasn't such a good idea, that I should just leave and take my slumbering girlfriend home. Before I can say my farewells, though, Bob finds me and tells me he has a quartet that will give my piece a reading. I follow him to the back bedroom and listen as the group plays Mendelssohn, Schubert, and Mozart. They sound quite beautiful. It's now nearly three-thirty in the morning, and I'm having trouble staying awake, too.

As I'm drifting off, I hear Bob say, "Let's try Boguslaw's piece." Everyone looks pretty tired as I place the parts on their stands.

The first violinist is from the Concertgebouw Orchestra in Amsterdam. I give him a tempo and then count the group in. They get about three measures in and it falls apart. They try again, and this time, they make it to measure five before they have to stop again. The parts are very independent, and these are some tired string players. I explain that their entrances are staggered to give a pyramid effect. They give it another shot with the same result. Without looking at me, the first violinist says, "I'm not into doing this right now" and gets up and quickly leaves.

The other players begin to pack up, and Bob apologizes to me, saying we'll give it another try sometime soon. I'm devastated and fighting back tears as I leave. As far as I know, the years' worth of work it took for me to compose this quartet was a total waste of time and energy. In addition, I've proven to myself that I'm more than a little self-absorbed, having left my trusting girlfriend sleeping in the car for over two hours. Happy New Year! I think that it's likely that God is sending me a message having to do with my priorities.

STRING QUARTET NO. 1

Damn! I'm a terrible conductor! Actually, even calling me a conductor is a stretch. I'm sweating because I'm trying to direct tempo (the speed) and meter (the beat) changes for the last movement of my string quartet. I have a hard enough time just putting four consecutive beats where they belong.

Conducting is the only music class I didn't get an A in while at UM—and with good reason. But now, some really good friends have worked my piece up to performance level. It's unusual to have a conductor for a string quartet, but I've composed a difficult piece that makes it necessary for someone to beat time in an array of patterns. The musicians, who unanimously voted for me to conduct, all claim I'm doing more good than harm, but I'm doubtful.

The slow canon in the last movement gives way to a brisk and rhythmic 6/8 return of the first theme to close. I don't quite end with the group, but we get a nice round of applause with a curtain call and a brief standing ovation. The concert is all new music and it's being performed at one of Miami's art museums. In my mind, the piece is pretty successful. Not a masterpiece, but a good try for a first major work. Sounds kind of like a poor man's Bartôk. I'm actually ecstatic, thinking back on my humbling experience the previous New Year's Eve and how, at the time, I despaired of ever seeing my quartet come to life.

Fortunately, Bob took the initiative following the party and recruited three other string-playing friends of ours with the idea of giving me a credible reading. After the first reading, the group seemed to like it and agreed to keep meeting to work the piece up to performance level, at least as long as I kept providing beer for the rehearsals. Even classical musicians have simple needs. Anyway, they deserved a lot more than a few beers. At the end of each rehearsal, I found myself wanting to pay them all something, but that wasn't going to happen with what I'm making working four nights a week at the Grove Club.

Eventually, following suggestions by the group that we find somewhere to perform the quartet, I hooked up with an old friend from the University of Miami who told me they were looking for a few more pieces for today's new music concert. So here I am, taking bows, hoping the applause is more about the composing and the strings' performance than my conducting. Backstage, I invite Bob, Heidi, Al, and Alfredo to join me and Mary for a few beers. Once again, I'm buying—gladly.

GIL'S KEY PUB

I'm in the fifth hour of my daily practice session. I've already worked on scales, Hanon, Chopin Etudes, a Haydn Sonata, and Brahms's magnificent Handel variations. Now I'm working out of a book of Bill Evans's jazz piano transcriptions. I'm starting to feel tired, and I'm paying more attention to the sweat that's pooling in my navel than I should. The piano is in the Florida room of our rental home and there's no A/C in here. I keep a fan directly on myself and there are lots of jalousie windows, but the intense mid-June Miami heat and humidity are inescapable.

Right now, what's troubling me even more than heat exhaustion is an overwhelming feeling of futility. I'm beginning to seriously consider the possibility of abandoning my music career and going back to school to study law, which I think my parents would have preferred, or literature, my second choice. I've spent all my waking hours today working on great works of musical art, but I'm feeling dark right now. I'm in my third month of working with a country band at Gil's Key Pub in North Miami, so Chopin, Brahms, and Haydn seem completely irrelevant to anything I play to earn my living.

The music we play at Gil's isn't my favorite, but I do like it better than I thought I would when I accepted the gig. One-third country rock (Eric Clapton, Eagles, Kansas), one-third old time country (Merle Haggard, Hank Williams, etc.), and one-third bluegrass (Orange Blossom Special, Shady Grove, Rocky Top). The fiddle player kicks butt. The drummer, Louis Rainbow, is one of my closest Miami friends. He does a great job, and the guitar and bass players are a bit better than average at playing the style.

One big problem is that I'm working for forty dollars a night to play from ten until four in the morning. Hourly, I could make nearly as much working at McDonald's—so much for skilled labor. Louis and I usually drive together and get home at around five, then we make some breakfast. I'm generally asleep by six.

Another problem with Gil's is there's frequent vomiting in the men's room and the ventilation isn't the greatest. But the worst thing is that there are lots of fights. Bikers like to hang out at Gil's and their fights tend to be pretty serious. I've seen a beer bottle broken on a head, and a woman clawing at her boyfriend's face while screaming at him that he had been "out fuckin' that other whoredog." Pretty ugly. That went down at around three one morning when the bar was almost completely deserted. And let's not forget that the place just plain stinks. Kind of like an organic landfill with an overflowing septic field rising up underneath it. (Maybe I'm exaggerating, but it's pretty foul.)

Last night, Bob, our bass player who's six foot eleven (and that's without his cowboy boots and ten gallon hat on), caught a punch in the gut as he exited the men's room. Some borderline incoherent drunk at the bar had thrown the punch and, not surprisingly, missed his target and ended up stumbling toward the restroom where it landed with almost no force on Bob's solar plexus. The drunken fighter muttered something that might have been an apology, and Bob just shook his head and headed to the bar for a Heineken, completely unsurprised and unfazed.

Once, while between sets, I played pool with a biker, a small muscular black haired guy wearing a denim jacket with the arms cut out. In the middle of his humiliation of me with a pool cue (I'm a notoriously bad pool player), he asked me what I thought of George Jones.

"Who's George Jones?" I asked.

He gave me a skeptical half smile and didn't answer. Our game ended, and as he took my dollar (I know better than to wager big on pool), he looked at me and said, "Tell me something, buddy. You can't really be into country music and not know who George Jones is."

"You got me!" I said. "I'm not. I'm just makin' the gig." I'm into classical music, jazz, and progressive rock, all styles that nobody wants to pay me to play.

As the sweat pours off of me, I get up from my Steinway upright (a very nice gift to me from my step-grandmother) to take my second cold shower of today's practice session. I keep telling myself that maybe if I continue studying with Fred and Mike (my blind genius of a jazz piano teacher) and working my butt off, someday soon I'll be making a living playing what I want to play. But right now, my patience is really being tested.

VEGA

As usual, after my most recent cruise ship gig ended, I was unemployed. After spending a week looking for work and considering a change in my career path, I got a call for a gig unlike any I'd ever had. I was to audition and, if considered qualified, I would begin daytime rehearsals with a Latin/Disco show band doing exclusively original music while being paid 150 dollars a week. I was told this band was going to hit it big, "nothing but large concert venues and TV appearances." Even at the age of twenty-three, I'd heard that line before. Believe it when you see it. But this time, it was backed up with cash.

The band was called "Vega," and it was a regular United Nations of disco. Of the nine members, four were Latino (Columbian, Cuban, and Puerto Rican), one was African American, one Iranian, one Canadian, and a Jewish guy from Jersey (me). The drummer had just quit and they were auditioning, so I thought why not Rick? Rick agreed to audition and was the only drummer who nailed the new beat that our leader, Willie, had come up with. It was an Afro- Latin 6/8 beat superimposed on top of an early '80s disco groove. Actually, Stevie Wonder had used this groove on his hit, "Another Star," five years earlier.

Although Willie was a fine musician and a very nice guy, I was pretty certain we weren't destined for stardom from the beginning. But then again, I never would have guessed the Bee Gees were destined for musical glory either. Shows how much I know! At any rate, Rick and I were definitely having some fun. Willie liked to call me "professor," I suppose because he found out I played classical music and, as always, I took my job seriously when it came to putting together our shows. But there was lots of partying that went on in Vega. Lots. Star Island, Miami, 1981. Bankrolled to rehearse in the home of Willie's older brother and sister-in-law, both millionaires. Use your imagination.

We eventually morphed into a Salsa band, alternating sets with a DJ from eleven at night to five in the morning at a Latin club named El Ultima. The club DJ implied he was smarter than us because he "used to play the drums, but then I realized that DJs don't have to carry around hundreds of pounds of instruments or spend hours rehearsing." I figured the music profession was far better off with him becoming a DJ.

The club was a hotbed of drug activity, and two Hialeah police officers spent their entire Friday and Saturday evenings either inside the club or in the parking lot. Once, I found a large vial of white powder in the men's room and thinking it must be cocaine, I considered putting it in my coat and taking it with me. It was probably worth three months' of rent, about fifteen hundred. I thought better of it. I had never sold drugs, and I certainly didn't want the vial's owner to come looking for me with a gun. There had been a number of shootings at El Ultima prior to Vega's gig there. Some of the band members even carried guns, an aspect of this lifestyle I really wanted to stay away from.

At times during the DJ sets, we'd grab a table and watch the dancers, all of whom were good. Some were world-class. But mostly, Rick and I hung out backstage. I'd drink bourbon and ginger ale, smoke cigarettes, and play chess with Rick or Joe, the bass player. Besides, the DJ's music was monstrously loud, ear-drum shattering loud. Vega was probably the loudest band I'd ever played with, but the DJ won. How loud was it? Well, if you could take seven or eight of the world's most tastelessly loud garage band rock guitarists and have them all play The Who's "Won't Get Fooled Again" with their amps turned up to eleven, the DJ would still have won.

Willie taught me how to play salsa on that gig and I'll always be grateful to him for that. I never became an expert, but I learned enough to be able to incorporate it into some of my jazz playing and composing. Willie was one of those composer/arranger musicians who could play every instrument in the band. He wasn't an expert on any of them but was better than adequate on all. Very impressive. When he first taught me a few montunos (salsa piano patterns) and I finally got the right feel for it, I felt like I never wanted to play any other kind of music again. But about halfway through our gig at El Ultima, I began to change my mind. As infectious and addictive as the salsa rhythms were, I was nearly always playing on one chord. For a young keyboardist who loved harmony, the gig started to feel a bit stifling. I needed more chords to play. More chords, please!

About this time, we were given notice by the club that our contract wouldn't be renewed. Willie fell into a serious state of depression because of the financial investment his family had made in him, and all of us started looking for other work. Rick decided to jump the sinking ship. He'd been talking about moving back to Boston from Hollywood, Florida. He had a girlfriend there and he thought Boston offered more jazz opportunities. Neither of us wanted to be career cruise ship or disco/Latin show band musicians. After packing up his gear following his last gig with Vega, Rick and I said goodbye, and as he hit the road, I wondered if we'd ever get to make the recording we'd sworn to do or if our musical relationship had peaked with Vega and the cruise ships.

REGGAE TOUR IN THE BAHAMAS!

I don't want to see the bottom of the barrel if this tour isn't it. The most positive thing I can say about it is that it's only four days long and tomorrow we return to Miami. James is the band's drummer and my current roommate. We were promised 250 dollars to play concerts in Freeport and Nassau with Eddie Lovette, who's had three number one hits in the Bahamas in the last two years. When I got the call, I'd been in-between gigs for two months, so it sounded like a great idea at the time.

We rehearsed just once with the rhythm section and once with the full group. Eddie had a nice voice for this music, but there was really nothing creative or original about his records. All his hits were American pop tunes done with a reggae groove, songs like "Under the Boardwalk" and "You Are My Shining Star." The group was completed by Popcorn, an exceptionally funky R&B electric bass player. He was the one who hired James and me. He's the one I hold responsible for being stuck in this dingy Nassau motel miles from the beaches, with inadequate air conditioning, spending the last two days of our "tour" eating nothing but carrots, celery, cheese, and peanut butter. That's all James and I could afford with the four dollars we had left when we arrived in Nassau. Popcorn got his own room, but I don't think he's eating much better than we are.

The problems started after our first show in Freeport. We were told we'd be paid in cash following each performance. Dickie, the "promoter," came to Popcorn and told him there were lapses in promotion for the show by a local radio station, so he hadn't taken in enough money to pay us. James and I had spent most of the little bit of money we arrived with in Freeport on dinner and a few Heinekens, having been promised we'd be paid that evening.

This is where I would have loved to give an ultimatum: "If there's no money, I'm on the first plane back to Miami tomorrow morning!" But I couldn't. Bills were due, and I was without a credit card to book a last minute flight. At this point, I haven't been in the professional music business long enough to establish positive patterns of income. At the rate I'm going, it'll be a long wait before I get my first Visa card.

Then Dickie took our passports, telling us he needed to present them to some sort of immigration office. Right. I'm pretty convinced that Dickie is some sort of gangster. He's a very large man who speaks loudly at all times in a thick Bahamian-calypso accent and wears multiple gold chains around his neck. His colleagues look and sound a lot like him. He first met us at the airport and drove us to the gig in a large, black Mercedes limousine. At every street corner in Freeport where the limo stopped, it seemed like someone was yelling something angry and incomprehensible at him. I'm not intimidated by Dickie because of his race. I'm intimidated because I'm convinced he's a criminal. He kept our money after the first show when it seemed to me to have been pretty well attended. The audience was receptive, though definitely not frenzied. With this show, frenzy would have surprised me.

Following our third consecutive meal that features a main course of peanut butter dipped carrots, Dickie picks us up in his limo and drives the group to a boxing ring that seems to have been randomly dropped into the middle of a field of sawgrass. There aren't a whole lot of cars in the parking lot, and as we prepare to go on, Dickie comes into our locker-room (which smells of some unknown farm animal) and informs us that once again, he's not going to be able to pay us tonight.

"You can play or not, whatever you want. I'll just have to catch you up with the money next time I'm in Miami." We all look at each other, then at Dickie and his friends, and agree to play, knowing that if we don't, there's no way we'll ever see a penny for any of this. If we do agree to play, the odds are one in ten at best. The show goes well for an audience of about fifty.

As we're being driven back to the Royal Bates Motel, I think about the two last slices of Swiss cheese I've saved out to celebrate my Bahamian tour before turning in and how glad I'll be to get on that plane tomorrow. I'm sure I'll laugh about this someday, but right now, it's not so funny.

CODA

Not surprisingly, Dickie never showed up with our money. I heard through Popcorn that he had landed in a Bahamian jail. I kept working occasionally with Popcorn, though our relationship became strained as I held him responsible for hiring me. The lessons I learned on this tour about protecting myself in the future were obvious. Mary paid the bills that month without complaining and got a good laugh when I described our gourmet motel meals.

CRUISE SHIP HOSTAGE DRAMA

I've been taken advantage of enough! I've been lied to and screwed out of my pay enough! I've had it! That's why I'm carrying my 120-pound keyboard down the gangplank and off of this cruise ship. My amp is already sitting next to a bench on the dock. Mary and Popcorn's new wife, Sharee, are sitting on the bench keeping an eye on it. It's even more of a pain carrying this equipment off the ship than usual. I'm making my way through a large crowd of Hawaiian-shirted, optimistic looking, sunburn-candidate tourists from Nebraska who are coming up the plank while I'm going down. We're docked at the Port of Miami and preparing to embark on a four-day cruise to the Bahamas. But Popcorn and I won't be on board.

The band's going to be without its keyboard and bass players. It's going to be just trumpet and drums tonight and for the next three nights in the lounge. I don't feel good about this because Mike (trumpet) and Moss (drums) are good friends of mine, but I'm determined not to be taken advantage of this time. Mike is an old friend from other ship adventures. He plays trumpet like Miles Davis from his nineteen-fifties' "cool" period, drinks a lot, and loves to laugh. This is the last cruise before our band goes on to better things, or at least to dry land in Miami...or so we thought.

How did it come to this? When I accepted this gig and was welcomed on board six weeks ago, I told Mike that I'd love to bring Mary on board for a cruise. Popcorn had just married Sharee and was honeymoon-less, so I was sure he'd like to bring his new bride, too. Mike, being the nice guy he is, came up with a plan.

He told us, "If you've been employed for six months, you get to bring a guest on for a cruise and pay nothing but port tax. I'm not bringing anyone on, so Mary can be my guest. Popcorn's going to hit six months, so he can just bring his wife along himself."

Mike cleared it with the purser's office and gave us the go-ahead to bring our ladies on board. Just as Popcorn and I were about to bring Mary and Sharee on board, Mike came and told us that the purser changed his tune. Yes, we could bring the ladies on board for the cruise, but only if we paid full price. No explanation was given for the change. A flood of memories arose, bringing to mind how many times I've been taken advantage of during my three years freelancing in the Miami area.

For one, the country singer, Ronnie, hired me to work a duo gig with him and his Ray Price-looking hairdo in Key Largo. He promised to pay three hundred, had me drive him down there ten times in two weeks, then only paid me seventy-five dollars. After numerous phone calls, I managed to track him down months later and walked into his open and empty apartment, leaving an unpleasant handwritten note on his kitchen table. At the time, I considered holding on to his Nikon camera for ransom but decided it wasn't worth going to jail over. He eventually changed addresses and phone numbers. I still regret passing on the camera.

The R&B singer, Al, who called himself a jazz singer, owed me a couple hundred from a club we played in Kendall. He still managed later to smooth talk me into writing charts for a seven piece band, a forty-five minute swing era show, paying me only half of what he'd promised. That was another five hundred I never saw.

And Dickie, the high-end reggae promoter...Well, you've already read what happened there. I told Mike that if Mary and Sharee couldn't come with us, the Caribe could do this particular cruise without me. Popcorn agreed. I immediately walked up a few decks and packed up my gear.

I excuse myself as I walk past the last few tourists, set down my Fender Rhodes by Mary's bench, and sit down next to her to catch my breath before the final long hike back to the car. But now I see Mike walking briskly down the gangplank toward us. That's unusual because Mike is a really laid-back guy. He comes over and asks me and Popcorn to wait a few minutes before we split, telling us he's going to talk with the chief purser to attempt to straighten out this mess. I state the obvious by telling him the ship sails in a half hour, but we'll wait until he gives it one last try.

Ten minutes later, I'm hauling my keyboard back up the gang plank. Mary good-naturedly registers with an impatient looking officer in a spotless white uniform. I think my main motivation in boycotting the cruise was probably my intense wish not to disappoint her, but the outcome makes me feel a little bit better knowing that for once, I was the hammer instead of the nail. We're on our way to Nassau.

CODA

We had a great little working vacation. Mary and I spent a marvelous romantic day on Paradise Island beach, right across a short causeway from Nassau. We also went on a short snorkeling trip to see some remarkably beautiful coral reefs.

Somehow, the DJ on the ship managed to "moon" the entire band without the passengers noticing. They were too occupied, being whipped up into a disco frenzy with Moss singing "Get Down on It." Mike got out of the music business after this last cruise and became a very successful businessman. Moss got off the ship and worked successfully for many years as a freelance jazz drummer and a brilliant photographer. I don't know what became of Popcorn, but I wish him well. That was the last of five ships I worked on, but I never let myself be taken advantage of again. It's a lesson I'd finally learned.

RADIO STARS IN BOGOTA

I'm having a hard time sleeping in Bogota because I can't breathe. The elevation is nearly nine thousand feet above sea level. The thin air and too many cigarettes are a bad combination. I'm here with the Freeman Sisters Band, playing Top 40 covers. We do "Flashdance," "Holiday," "Fame," and probably five songs from Michael Jackson's *Thriller* album. Quincy Jones would be pleased with me because I took more trouble than usual learning the keyboard parts from the Michael Jackson record. Top 40 bands and I generally don't mix terribly well because I can't get motivated when I have to play the same parts the same way, night in and night out. Just one of my tragic flaws as a musician.

However, this band needed a keyboard player to make a two-week trip to Bogota and Medellin on short notice, and I was available and learned the tunes quickly. The band members are all nice people, though one of the sisters is something of a diva. She doesn't know how to adjust a PA system, and she complains a lot when her monitor speakers don't sound pleasing to her. The other singer is married to Rick, the guitar player, who's a good musician and a tremendously nice and patient guy.

But mostly, I hang out with the drummer, Nick, and bassist, Sergio. Sergio is from Naples and recently moved to Miami after marrying a nice Jewish girl, Fran, who joined him on the trip to Colombia. Sergio claims to speak English, and although he gets by, his English is more than a bit limited. Nick's a skinny Italian guy from Long Island with a head full of permed curls and is a top-notch rock and jazz drummer. He's also probably as funny as Steve Martin. We're basically the Three Stooges on this trip.

We laugh at everything. A lot. We laugh at restaurant signs that read: "Kentucky Pollo Frito," "Papas Fritas Ristorante" and "Whopper King." We laugh all night long, telling jokes while drinking "Agua Diente," a Colombian version of nasty vodka. We laugh the next day when Fran tells us Sergio's limited English prevented him from "getting" probably even one punch line. We laugh when our driver stops the car in the mountains, so we can pick coca leaves and rub them on our gums. This leaf doesn't give the full effect of cocaine, but it numbs our mouths to the point where we're all talking as if a large wad of dry cotton has been placed under our tongues. We laugh, following a guest appearance on El Show de Jimmie (The Jimmie Show) because I had to interrupt the taping twice to run and use a seatless toilet due to something I either ingested or imbibed the day before. We laugh, but look the other way when our driver and tour guide, Jaime, speeds in the wrong direction down a one-way street yelling, cursing, and laughing, seemingly all at once. I'm amazed that someone as crazy as Jaime has a job. We laugh when we can't make a maître d' understand that we want to know if they're serving dinner, and after asking Sergio to help (thinking the host might understand Italian), he puts his hand, palm up and fingers together under the maître d's chin and says in his most practiced English: "Wee waaant to half deeener." The maître d's puzzled expression gets us laughing so hard that we feel compelled to leave, consequently ending up dining at the "Papas Fritas Ristorante."

But we don't laugh when we take a tram up a mountainside that overlooks the city and some neighboring valleys. The rain just stopped, and we're lucky enough to see a double rainbow below us! The two bows intersect at their apexes, stretching in four directions across the valley that's home to Bogota's millions of residents.

From up here, we can really see the extent of the slums that climb the mountain sides, radiating out from the center of the city. Millions of people live here with no running water, no electricity, and no sewer systems. I've been told that most people who live in the slums have come from rural areas, having been squeezed out by large farming interests and the violence of a brutal drug war. They're looking for a better life.

We can also see the downtown area with quite a few modern skyscrapers, crowded and well-maintained roads, and lots of nice apartments and condos protected by armed security guards and accordion wire. The rainbows seem even more striking, hovering over this vibrant yet troubled city.

We also don't laugh when we're taken to see the Catedral De Sal (The Salt Cathedral). It's actually a cathedral carved out of salt. Hundreds of years ago, the Spanish used slaves to tunnel into a mountainside to mine for salt. About a half mile in, they came to a huge open cavern, filled with huge salt columns and a variety of salt rocks and boulders that their artisans carved into altars, the twelve Stations of the Cross, votive candle holders, and other adornments of Catholicism. These days, the cavern is lit by electricity, but I'm imagining what it must have been like in here three hundred years ago as Mass was celebrated strictly by candlelight. To me, this place is one of the wonders of the world and I take a few minutes to pray.

On the way back to the city, our driver crosses herself and mouths a prayer just because we're being followed for a brief time by a police car. She's doing nothing illegal, so her reaction amazes me. I usually feel safer when I see a police car, but not here. This entire country really does make me appreciate the US of A.

I should feel some guilt for being on this trip under false pretenses, but I don't. For me, it's a free trip to a place I never would have gotten to visit otherwise. It happens that the Freeman Sisters Band was sold to club owners in Bogota and Medellin under the pretense that they were once background vocalists for KC and the Sunshine Band. In truth, at one time, they alternated sets with KC at the famous Castaways Hotel on Miami Beach, but they never sang with him. He never sang with them. Nobody in Colombia knows this though, so we're now on our way to a local radio station to do an interview intended to drum up business for our weeks' worth of club gigs in Medellin. I assume the Sisters will anticipate questions about their relationship to the big American disco star, KC. Maybe that's not a safe assumption though...

As we enter the radio station, I notice the age of the equipment. In the US, all these microphones and mixing boards would have been discarded long ago, or the station would have been put out of business ten years ago by the high-fidelity competition. Surprisingly, the DJ is a Scotsman. He tells us he's been living in Medellin for the last eighteen years, having married a local. I figure they're having him do the interview, so we'll have a truly bilingual translator.

First, he talks to the Freeman Sisters, and they respond to the typical questions about where and when we'll be appearing in Medellin and how we like the country and its people? He then has the nerve to ask them which songs the two of them recorded with KC's Sunshine Band. They both look at each other with painfully uncomfortable and uncertain glances. I thought they would have gotten their story straight in advance, but I was wrong about that. Finally, Von speaks up and says, "Get Down Tonight," so the DJ plays it. There are almost no background vocals, and what's audible is obviously not the Freeman Sisters.

The DJ has his back to us, so he can't see Rick lengthening his proverbial Pinocchio nose with his left hand while looking meaningfully at his wife and sister-in-law. We three stooges are all falling on the floor, our sides hurting with silent laughter. Then it's our turn for an interview. The questions seem to get more random and bizarre. He asks Sergio to compare Italy's soccer stars to Colombia's. He asks me if I believe in God. I'm shocked, but I collect myself enough to tell him that I do, but my relationship with the Creator is personal. Then he turns to Nick. Now, if we really were the Three Stooges, Nick would be Curly. Sometimes just looking at him makes me laugh. Nick is asked if he has played with any other famous bands besides the Freeman Sisters. He carefully considers the question, then decides to pick up on the exaggeration theme of the day, answering, "Sure, Barry Manilow and Liberace." After hearing Nick's answer, I'm laughing so hard that I'm in tears for the rest of the interview. As we walk back to our car, I'm thinking that I can't fathom how we're getting away with this, but we are.

CODA

At the end of this crazy two weeks, we're walking across the tarmac to our Avianca Flight, set to return us to the relative sanity of Miami. I have a brutal hangover, and as I look up at the jet we're getting ready to board, I notice there's a mechanic straddling one of the engines as if he's riding a bull at a Texas rodeo. He has what appears to be a sledgehammer in his hand and is banging both loudly and incessantly on the engine. And we're departing in twenty-five minutes? I've been up all night drinking Agua Diente and smoking fine Colombian. I think, "Just let me on this plane and get me away from this racket, so I can sleep! And if we do end up going down in the Caribbean somewhere, Lord, remember I do believe in God and just please let me sleep through it."

BO DIDDLEY

It's 1984, and I'm with the House Band at a club called Biscayne Babies in Coconut Grove, the epicenter of late-night tropical partying in Miami. Most weeks our group, called Richie and the Rockets, just plays our own show, which is based on our attempts to rehabilitate music from the 50s and 60s, rearranging and breathing life into songs that are quickly becoming musical artifacts.

My contributions to these arrangements, though at times creative, mostly come across as overly contrived. Oh, well; I'm still learning. This group is by far the strongest show band I've played with to date, and they're a lot of fun to work with. Once a month, though, we put our show aside and back up national acts such as The Drifters, Chubby Checker, The Shirelles, and the Belmonts (without Dion). These groups are organized (or disorganized) to varying degrees. Some of them are able to communicate in musical terms (tempo, meter, key, form) with the band, and for some of them you have to use your ear and follow them with little or no guidance. Using my ear in all situations is a lesson I've learned while playing talent shows on cruise ships. Even when amateur performers are able to explain what their musical plan of attack is, they rarely follow through once the spotlight is on them, requiring adjustments on the fly by the pianist. I got used to it.

This week, we're going to have to use our ears because we're playing for one of the fathers of Rock and Roll, Bo Diddley, and he definitely doesn't bring music with him. Bo arrives at the rehearsal, walks onto the bandstand, and plugs in his signature rectangular-bodied guitar. He fiddles a bit with the tuning, but it doesn't seem to help. It's one of the most out-of-tune guitars (or maybe any instrument) that I've ever heard. He then runs his rehearsal by starting a rhythmic vamp on an A-major chord using the Bo Diddley beat. He sings a bit; he plays a bit. He sings a bit; the band solos a bit. He sings a bit again, then he raises his guitar in the air and gives a quick and definitive downward thrust to cut us off. Song over. I heard him slip in a few stealthy D-major chords in unexpected places, so I ask him: "Bo, do you want us to play that D-chord with you or do we just stay on the A?" He looks at me with a disconcertingly serious expression on his face and says, "No. Just play the A-chord," he says proudly. "Just stay on A-major. I invented that one-chord shit." I smile, thinking about how jazz and classical musicians frequently denigrate Rock and Roll by calling it three-chord music. In this case, it's literally one-chord music.

Actually, I've come to realize over the years that classical music and jazz can be far simpler at times than Rock and Pop (Johann Strauss waltzes and the Dixieland style). The harmonies of artists such as Stevie Wonder and Steely Dan are as complex as those of the great classical and jazz composers. None of that matters because most of the public doesn't care about harmonic sophistication and Bo Diddley is planning to do nearly an entire show comprised of one-chord songs. He does pull out a ballad he wrote that uses two.

In the middle of our rehearsal with Bo, a well-groomed woman comes in carrying a clipboard and a microphone. She's accompanied by four men with cables, tripods, and cameras. They seem to be setting up for a video shoot. Bo stops the band and asks the woman what they're doing. She doesn't answer, but an officious looking, well-groomed man, approaches the stage and tells him that they're from the Today Show in LA and they're here to film Bo Diddley as part of a Whatever Happened To? series their show is doing. The man looks as if he thinks Bo Diddley should be really grateful to him for the attention. The conversation continues.

Bo: "I hadn't heard nothin' about a tapin' today."

Well-groomed man: "Our producer spoke with your people."

Bo: "I ain't heard nothin' from my agent 'bout this."

WGM: "Well, I'm sure it can be worked out, but in the meantime, we need to set up and start filming."

Bo: "You talk with my agent in LA. Then you get a signed agreement and have him call me when it's done. Then you can film. You're not filmin' nothin' till that's done."

WGM: "You can trust that we'll get that done, but right now we just need to start filming."

Bo: "Sorry, ain't gonna happen!"

Bo is staring him down. The well-groomed man looks like he just found one of those king-sized greasy South Florida palmetto bugs crawling around in his salad. He says nothing and the entire crew packs up and leaves.

Damn! I think. Bo Diddley just told the Today Show to go take a hike.

He turns to us and says, "Never let nobody use you. I don't care how important they are or how much money and power they got behind 'em. Back in the fifties, I had three number one hits and hardly saw a penny from any of it 'cause I was foolish enough to trust folks in the music business. Remember that!"

He starts back up on another one-chord vamp with the Bo Diddley beat, and the rehearsal picks up right where it left off. I spend the rest of the rehearsal thinking about how important it was for all of us youngsters hoping to make it in the music business, to witness how Bo stood up for himself.

It's show time, and we're all set up to back up Bo and the room is packed to capacity. He struts on stage to a hooting and cheering rowdy audience, carrying his geometrically unique guitar. He points his finger and waves it as if there's some unseen ghost or demon who's spurring him on. We do an entire hour-and-a-half show of nearly all one-chord tunes with him playing his out-of-tune guitar, but it turns out to be a blast. It turns out that Bo's a great showman, one of the best I've seen at working a crowd. Plus the beat is infectious. I notice that at least three or four of his songs have his name in the title (things like "Bo Diddley," "Hey Bo Diddley," "The Return of Bo Diddley," etc.) After what he's gone through, I can forgive him for being a little bit self-promoting. And yes, the Today Show crew is back, filming his every move. So I guess they must have gotten things squared away with Bo's agent. They also got his message loud and clear.

POLYGRAPH

Richie looks me directly in the eyes from across a circular table in what seems to be a conference room. The atmosphere here is much more corporate than anything I'm accustomed to. I'm not comfortable. For more than one reason.

"Are you 100 percent certain you put the keyboard away and locked the closet up that night?" he asks.

Two weeks of hell come flooding back to me all at once. I've been waking up nightly with thoughts such as:

Do I really remember every detail of that night? Maybe I forgot to lock the closet? Maybe I have some type of split-personality disorder, and I regularly steal without conscious awareness of it? Do I really know myself? What is truth? What is reality? Will my good friends in this band ever truly trust me again? Maybe they're just saying they trust me, without really believing it, just to make me feel better? etc., etc., etc.

Mary has reassured me numerous times that I'm essentially a good person and certainly not a thief.

This all began a few weeks ago when Richie, club manager and bandleader of Richie and the Rockets, called me the day after our show backing up The Drifters. I remember how he apologetically asked me if I'd take a polygraph test because an expensive, new keyboard belonging to the club was missing. It was a keyboard that I used on the gig, but I wasn't being singled out. The entire band and all club employees were being asked to take the "truth" test.

I agreed without hesitating. Following the attachment of a number of electrodes to what must have been the truth-revealing spots on my body and the administration of approximately five minutes of well thought out questions, the polygraph expert had sworn by his professional reputation that I was the villain. The wretched thief. The criminal. At the time, I immediately recalled an old friend who admittedly lied a number of times to polygraphers about drug use but was never caught. I suppose he must have convinced himself of his own innocence. Unfortunately, I haven't been able to do the same.

I look directly back at Richie. He's a nice and ethical guy, very much a straight-shooter. I'm sweating a bit. This meeting room seems very close. "Yes, Richie," I say. "I'm 100 percent certain. You've been great to me, and this is the best show band I've ever played with. I wouldn't do anything to screw that up or jeopardize my friendship with you and the rest of the guys. Even if I was really, really desperate for the money." I'm practically in tears now, but I realize that I am finally 100 percent sure of my own innocence.

Richie stares at me for what seems like a long time, and finally says, "It's all good with you and the club and the band. Diana (the club owner) told me that as long as I'm satisfied that you're being straight with us, that everything's cool. Our faith in you trumps Mr. Polygraph's professional reputation." Human contact over fuzzy science.

I leave Biscayne Babies with a renewed awareness of the decency of human beings. I hope and expect it won't be the last time I feel this way. I go home and make a few calls to the friends and family that I've been harassing with my troubles and tell them the good news. I give Mary a big hug and we go out for one of our limited budget celebrations.

CODA

It's now two weeks later, and I tell Richie and the rest of the group that I'm leaving to go and work for El Puma, having been offered what will be by far the highest paying gig I've ever done. I'm worried how Richie and the band will react, given my recent polygraph adventure. Richie and the rest of the guys just congratulate me on the new gig and swear that we'll stay in touch and remain great friends. I'm feeling really lucky to be a member of this brotherhood of musicians.

FRED

I'm riding on a bus in south Miami, fighting back tears on my way home from my piano lesson. I don't think anyone can tell I'm crying on the inside but I am. I've seen piano students brought to tears a number of times (myself included), but today my tears are from both a sense of loss and joy rather than shame. I'm grieving because I just told Fred Coulter that I'm leaving his studio and moving out of Miami to return to college to work toward a master's degree in piano performance. Fred has been my piano teacher, mentor, and great friend for the last four and a half years. These tears are tears of joy because all the love and respect I've developed over the years for Fred has proven to be justified. From my previous experiences, piano teachers tend to be a possessive and egotistical lot when it comes to their students. They want to take credit for the students' successes while distancing themselves from their failures.

Fred has proven that impression wrong time after time, with today being the ultimate repudiation. When I told him at the end of my lesson that I was leaving, his first reaction was, "When I used to teach piano in universities, I would send my students to another studio after three years with me, so they could get a different perspective and approach. You've been with me now for four and a half years, and you can probably benefit from a change. I know you want to go to New York, but let me call my old friend Lucien at the University of Kentucky to see if he can offer you something. He's a brilliant musician, and he'll be great with some of your technical issues." Fred immediately picked up the phone. Within minutes, I had an offer for a teaching assistantship at Kentucky, accompanying opera workshop and graduate recitals. This means I won't incur any debt while working to get my master's degree, and I'll even receive a small stipend for a minimal amount of work.

But the most important thing to me is how Fred reacted to the news. He knew I'd be emotional about leaving, and his matter of fact way of handling the situation was the best and easiest way for both of us to deal with it. Fred's attitude convinced me that my leaving is just one more inevitable step in my growth as a young adult pianist. His lack of ego, his kindness, and the knowledge I've gained from our years working together are the reasons for my quiet tears on this bus.

In 1980, when I started studying with Fred, you might say I was a bit directionless. I went to UM to major in classical piano performance, but what I secretly really wanted was to be a rock star. Although I'd been part of a few really creative rock bands, they'd all fallen apart due to psycho-dramas perpetrated by group members, myself included. As a student at the university, I'd found myself drawn to the music and musicians of the jazz department, but even more so, to the great tradition of the solo classical concert artists. Some of my peers were performing Prokofiev concerti, difficult Beethoven sonatas, and Chopin etudes. In my four years at the university, I had improved a lot in this area and covered lots of repertoire, but I was still not playing at a level where I'd realistically be competitive for a performing career. I wasn't sure I'd ever get there, and I still held out hope to make it as a rock star.

I met Fred in a counterpoint class he was teaching at the University of Miami and later, I studied composition with him. I learned that, as a young man in the early 1960s, he'd had a tremendously successful career in Europe, playing more than two hundred concerts annually including appearances with some of the world's greatest orchestras. I decided to try taking lessons with Fred after graduating from Miami, working in a cruise ship show band for four months, then trying my hand unsuccessfully at a pretty prestigious piano competition in Pittsburgh. Fred was teaching privately in his home because for some inexplicable reason, he was denied tenure at the University. I don't think I'll ever understand that. We had established a good rapport during my composition lessons, and I wasn't inclined to return to my piano teacher at the University after graduating.

I think back on how during a composition class at the University, I once asked Fred to explain a difficult concept not once or twice but four times! He kept at it until it sunk in. I realized at the time that type of patience was a rare gift in a teacher. As long as Fred was sure you were interested and putting forth effort, his patience was nearly limitless.

While watching through the bus window as the palm trees, stucco homes, and canals of Coral Gables go by, I try to remember all the things Fred has done for me in the last four and a half years. I recall how when I arrived for my very first lesson with him, he was listening to a brilliant recording of the Brahms Second Piano Concerto with the Berlin Philharmonic. Fred was the soloist. Looking back now, I realize that it was no coincidence that particular recording was playing when I arrived. Fred knew I loved Brahms, and he also knew that I felt performances like the one we listened to were probably not an attainable goal for me. But here he was, showing confidence in me, someone who'd performed professionally himself. My dreams of becoming a rock star diminished significantly that day.

Over the course of a year, while preparing to compete in the National Chopin Competition, I worked up three and a half hours' worth of Chopin's music: etudes, preludes, ballades, etc. Then during two consecutive studio classes, Fred had me play all of it! By the end of the second class, I was sure my fellow student pianists were tired of Chopin, but no one complained, knowing that soon their turn would come. This was just one example of how selflessly Fred gave of his time.

He was also constantly helping me and a number of his other students make audition recordings for these competitions. He had lots of experience with electronic music; he had written award-winning electronic film scores. He had also engineered audio recordings, and we all benefited from his knowledge in this area. At one point during my second year of lessons with him, I told him I'd need to discontinue my study because money was too tight (during 1981, I was constantly in and out of gigs). Fred responded by telling me to keep coming to the lessons and that I could pay him back when I won my first big competition, again showing unqualified confidence in me.

About a year ago, Fred finally came out and directly expressed his feelings about my potential. It came in the form of an admonishment. At the time, I was once again preparing for a competition. I came to a lesson having learned the first short section of the Schumann Humoresque, a huge, challenging set of character pieces. I told Fred that I wanted to use this piece for a competition in a little over a month. His response, with just a hint of impatience was, "Bob, I know what it takes to have a career as a concert artist, and I'm sure you're capable of doing it, but you've got to be patient! A lot of this music takes a long time to absorb, and you can only rush it so much." Despite the small reprimand, Fred made me feel that my potential was limitless. And he had the personal experience to convince me. The amount that he taught me about balancing chords, projecting and shaping melodies and inner voices, understanding and clearly presenting a sense of musical form, and the legacies left to us by the world's greatest pianists was huge. He had met piano legends including Cortot, Horowitz, Rubinstein, and Gould. But none of that was as important as this brilliant and compassionate man's faith in me.

Somewhere along the line, Fred also taught me that being a genius or having a special gift was no excuse for behaving like an egotistical jackass. I've had plenty of first-hand experience with classical and some jazz musicians who believed their abilities and expertise in their art somehow placed them above the rest of humanity, a sort of get-out-of-jail-free card for selfish and unethical behavior. Not Fred. His tremendous intellect and powers of concentration had equipped him to teach college courses in eight different subjects. I never saw him talk down to people, even though his amazing memory made it possible for him to learn an entire Mozart piano concerto mentally while traveling by train across Europe, playing the piece for the first time at the dress rehearsal on the day of the concert! Fred's pride in his students always seemed to be greater than his pride in his own performances. When I once asked him what his favorite thing about teaching was, he responded, "Watching you all get better."

At two on a Monday morning in the winter of '84, I pulled into my driveway following my steady Sunday night jazz quartet gig at Stefano's on Key Biscayne to find Fred and his wonderful wife, Beverly, waiting for me in my driveway. Beverly is a superb pianist who was a classmate of mine at UM, and she's one of my best friends. She and Fred had important news for me, but they didn't want to wake Mary up because she had to work the next morning. So, they just sat in their car in our driveway, waiting. They practically jumped out of the car and ran over to me the moment I parked to let me know that Beverly and I had both been accepted as participants at the Bachauer International Piano Competition!

To a non-pianist, this might not seem like much, but to a young musician who has been trying to launch a performing career by breaking into the upper echelons of the competition circuit, it was certainly worthy of a late night trip out for a snack and a few beers in celebration. Beverly and I were two of sixty-three semifinalists accepted out of 188 applicants. In this competition, first prize was a Steinway B seven-foot grand piano and 75,000 dollars' worth of touring and recording contracts, basically a launching pad for a career as a concert artist. Contestants came from literally every corner of the globe.

As the three of us sat over our French fries and beers talking about the programs we would present in Salt Lake City, the pros and cons of Beethoven sonatas versus Haydn, Brahms variation sets versus Chopin ballades, and Chopin's études versus Liszt's, it occurred to me that as excited as Beverly and I were, Fred was even more so. He was acting like a kid who'd just been told that he'd soon be taking his first trip to Disney World. To me, there was nothing surprising about Fred's reaction. Nothing at all.

CODA

It's early November 2011. I've just finished eulogizing Fred Coulter. He passed on after a long battle with cancer. I barely made it through my speech. There were a fair amount of long pauses to collect myself and lots of tears. In his later years, Fred became an ordained Presbyterian Stephen's minister, helping numerous shut-ins and hospice patients. He told me that he memorized and used prayers for the dying in all the major faiths and in a number of different languages. Ironically, his life ended with Beverly beside him in a hospice center.

Others at the memorial service spoke of his selflessness and love in the Lord's work. I spoke of the gifts he'd given to his students and of his great reverence for the creative process. I referred to the brilliant late works he'd written for me to perform, as well as the vocal works he composed for Beverly to perform at the college where she teaches. I also read a three-page letter sent as a eulogy by Bill Dobbins, a former composition student of Fred's, currently Director of Jazz Studies at the Eastman School of Music. His eulogy was possibly even more glowing than mine.

Fred died in relative obscurity, a pianist whose European debut had been compared favorably in reviews to that of Vladimir Horowitz fifty years ago. But I know that accolades didn't concern him; in fact, he had purposefully shunned the performers' spotlight upon his return from Europe. He was completely content to positively affect the lives he touched and to explore the mysteries of the human creative process. As I look at this gathering of Fred's family, friends, students, fellow clergy, and parishioners, I know my grief is not just for my own loss, but also for the lessened place our world is now with Fred Coulter gone. I know that nothing lasts forever in this dimension, but I'm quite certain that the positive effect Fred had on this earth will be passed forward for generations.

EL PUMA, PART 1

A few weeks ago, Hector, Puma's musical director, called to offer me the gig as second keyboardist for Jose Louis Rodriguez, also known as "El Puma." I had to labor over the decision more than anything that's ever involved my career. I had already accepted a teaching assistantship at the University of Kentucky, which was scheduled to start in less than three months. The university is counting on me, and my friend and teacher, Fred Coulter, had pulled some strings to arrange the assistantship for me. I decided to return to graduate school after six years away from academia, mainly for idealistic reasons. I wanted to try to spend a few years not dealing with music mainly in the context of dollar signs.

On the other hand, taking the gig would mean traveling to South and Central America, as well as the Caribbean, playing stadium concerts for thousands of frenzied fans. I'd also get paid really good. I called Fred, my parents, my brother, and a few close friends. I spoke with Mary. Everyone I asked helped me to weigh the decision and eventually all came to the same conclusion. They all told me that I'm a big boy now (twenty-seven), and I just had to decide for myself. I finally took the idealistic route and called Hector back. I told him that unfortunately, I was already committed to returning to school at the end of August, so I couldn't accept the job.

To my surprise, Hector said, "Bob, we start rehearsals for this tour in less than a week, and I'm running out of time to find someone good. Would you be willing to take the gig until it's time for you to move at the end of August?" I didn't have to think too long about it. I could have my cake and eat it, too. I accepted the gig, worked on the music, spent two weeks rehearsing almost every day with the band, and now I'm playing my first "Puma" show in Panama City on the evening of my twenty-eighth birthday.

My friend Steve (first keyboard) warned me that these shows get crazy, but nothing he told me could have prepared me for this. A Panamanian girl who looks to be about sixteen years old jumps up on the stage and glues herself to El Puma who is 1985's number one selling recording artist in Latin America. She's dressed in a tight chiffon blue dress with black high heels, and she's wearing a shit-ton of make-up. Her legs are wrapped around his hips, her arms around his shoulders, and her face is pressed up against his neck. She's so in love with him that she's crying, dripping tears mixed with make-up, and smearing large skid marks of purple-red lipstick all over the collar of Puma's impeccably pressed tuxedo shirt. He has his left arm around her waist and with his right hand, he's still holding his microphone and singing one of his biggest hits, "Dueño de Nada."

Puma's used to this. After all, this is the fourth girl who's managed to crash the stage and make it to him, and I guess that we're only seven or eight minutes into the show. Tony, the tour's stage manager, runs onto the stage, grabs the young lady, and with more than a little effort, extricates her from her adhesion to the love of her life. He drags her, kicking, screaming, and crying, off the stage and I'm guessing out the stage door. I don't give it much thought because I need to follow my music closely, this being my first show with Puma. His records were made in Italy, and I'm replacing the forty-piece string section on Puma's recording. String parts on a synthesizer are what I have to play to make this gig, including Puma's closer, a backbeat shuffle version of Beethoven's "Ode to Joy." I definitely feel like a musical prostitute, despite my unsuccessful attempt to turn down the job offer.

My first show with Puma ends, closing with our blasphemous Latin-pop version of Beethoven's 9th Symphony, complete with screaming fans holding up lighters and swaying back and forth. The band is so loud that I swear I can still hear the echoes from our last chord bouncing around in the rafters a full thirty seconds after it's been played. We're responsible for packing up our own equipment at the end of each show, though we don't have to move it. By the time I'm done, Steve is also finished and has gone off to call his pregnant wife who's back in Miami. Hector, the music director, is gone, too. No one says a word to me. My first show could have been the best or worst ever played in the history of Puma-dom, but I'll never know. No one's complaining, so I guess I'll just assume that no news is good news.

PUMA PART 2 - CHICKEN SALAD SANDWICHES

Damn. I know it doesn't seem like such a hardship, but it looks like I'm not going to get to eat before the show tonight. I can put up with nearly anything but not on an empty stomach. Right now, Jose Luis Rodriguez's backup band is being herded into a locker room in a soccer stadium in Cali, Columbia, that reeks of horse dung. South American flights are notorious for running late, but today's flight was worse than usual. We arrived at the airport at eight in the morning and were told our flight was delayed. Imagine that. I dozed off and woke up at eleven. I waited a few more hours. At one thirty in the afternoon, our nine thirty flight took off. As we collected our bags in the Cali airport, Tony, the road manager, informed us we didn't have time to check into the hotel or get anything to eat. He said they'd bring in some takeout for us at the concert site.

As a vegetarian, I'm quite sure they won't bring us anything I can eat, and we usually don't get back from the show until sometime between eleven and midnight. By then, all the hotel restaurants are closed. I'm not dumb enough to walk the streets of this cocaine cowboy city with limited language skills, looking for a place to eat in the middle of the night. Oh well. I guess I'll buy a few bags of banana chips from the hotel vending machine and eat them while drinking thick homemade espresso in Fofi's room. Fofi is El Puma's drummer. These guys make their espresso so strong and thick that I can pretend it's food.

We're waiting in the aromatic locker room for the gear to finish being loaded in when Tony arrives with two large bags stuffed with sandwiches and some syrupy sweet cans of soda. He says, "Sorry guys, but this'll have to do for dinner tonight."

I don't even look inside the bags, but I hear the guys saying they're all chicken salad sandwiches ("chicken" and "salad" being two of the only Spanish words I can recognize). There must be at least twenty-five sandwiches in these bags. Every band member who has one in their hand is looking at it suspiciously. Fofi finally digs in and quickly eats a half a sandwich, kind of the same way I'd drink cough syrup. Renee (the guitarist) takes two bites, rolls his eyes, and puts the sandwich down on a bench. No one else is brave enough to even try. I just have to see what's up with these sandwiches, even though it could give me nightmares. I open the wrapping on one of them and pull back the wax paper. They consist of white bread, a combination of chicken fat and gristle, and some dangerous-smelling dressing that might possibly have once been mayonnaise. I'm happier than usual to be an herbivore.

While the guys are discussing our dinner, I notice a few of our extremely youthful military escorts peeking around the corner of the entrance to the locker room. These guys have been with us since we got off the plane in Cali. There are about twenty of them and their job seems to be to intimidate the general public into staying away from us, especially from El Puma (Jose Louis Rodriguez). They all have beautifully groomed uniforms and shiny automatic weapons that they carry drawn at all times. One of them asks Julio a question and he answers, "Seguro." The next thing I know, eight or ten of these military security guards come streaming into our locker room and start eating some of the sandwiches and stuffing the remaining ones into their beautiful, immaculate uniforms at the same time. One guard pauses long enough to ask Julio another question. They talk for a bit, and when he leaves, I notice a tear or two in Julio's eye.

"What were you guys talking about? What's the problem?" I ask. Julio is our bass player and is usually my first choice within the band for translating Spanish. He tells me that the young guard has five children and wants to know what his prospects would be like if he makes it to the US. Not only does his military salary not pay enough for his kids to go to school, but it barely pays enough for him to feed them. The guard wants Julio to help him. Julio very much wants to, but there's absolutely nothing he can do. I recall that years ago in the early 60s, Julio's dad came to the US as a refugee to escape the tyranny of Fidel Castro, so he very much understands. But none of us can help. I suppose the guard will just go home and tell his wife that the Puma Show Band couldn't do anything to help as he empties the chicken fat sandwiches out of his pockets. Maybe his commanding officers think that he'll just console himself with his nice shiny uniform and the cool automatic weapon he gets to carry. Or maybe they just don't think about him and his family at all.

PUMA, PART 3

We've been bouncing from city to city and country to country with the Puma tour for about a month. Bogota, Cali, and Medellin in Colombia. Santo Domingo in the Dominican Republic. Oranjestad in Aruba, and now San Juan, Puerto Rico. We don't get many days off and we rarely have time for tourism. All the same, we're generally put up in the nicest hotels these places have to offer. Here in San Juan, we're staying in the Condado section of the city. This area is all hotels, restaurants, casinos, and beautiful beaches with crystal blue Caribbean waters. We were supposed to go back to Miami for a week, leaving tomorrow. But we just got word that we've been held over in Puerto Rico for another week. Our show in San Juan went great last night in terms of crowd response. Now they've booked us for two additional shows in Ponce and Mayaguez for next weekend. I hated calling Mary to tell her it'd be another week until I'd be home, but if we're going to be stuck somewhere without having to work for three days, Condado isn't a bad spot.

Most of the band members decide to celebrate the news of our unexpected four-day beach holiday by crossing the street to a little pizza joint to throw back a few beers and pies. A couple of my fellow band members turn down the offer to go eat so they can keep their places at the blackjack and poker tables. The word is that our percussionist has already lost two weeks' salary during our first three days in San Juan. Living the dream. The five of us who've decided to make it a pizza and beer evening sit down at a table and begin considering the catalogue of toppings featured on the menu.

When I look up, I notice that Luisa, Puma's personal valet, has come in and is placing an order at the take-out counter. She's a slightly heavy-set, jovial girl of about twenty. I ask her, "Why isn't Puma gonna come down and join the band for pizza and beer?" I'm half joking, but Luisa looks at me in all seriousness and says, "Are you kidding? Didn't you see the hotel lobby? When we're on tour, he usually doesn't go anywhere unless he absolutely has to."

I think about it for a second and remember the fifty to sixty girls camped out in the lobby of our hotel since we arrived, all waiting for a glimpse of Jose Luis Rodriguez. They're mostly not interested in the band, unless to use us as an avenue to gain an introduction to Puma. Personally, I never talk to any of the fans. I'm mono-lingual.

We joke around with Louisa for a few more minutes until she leaves to take the pizza up to Puma's penthouse suite. And then I get to thinking: Puma is the biggest pop star in Latin America. He owns a Mercedes and a Rolls Royce. He's adored by millions of fans, but he can't walk across the street to go and have pizza with the band. He can't go to one of the nice jazz clubs they have in Old San Juan. Even when I saw him on the beach in Aruba, he was surrounded by staff and a couple of bodyguards. Then I have a minor epiphany. I realize I no longer have any desire to be famous. Ever since I was twelve or thirteen years old, I've felt my life's goal would be to play music I love for huge adoring audiences, to be the next coming of the Beatles. But not now. I still aspire to make a comfortable living while making great music. But the fame stuff? You can keep it.

SUMMER, 1985

LESTER

Lester has a pretty sweet life. He lives in San Juan, Puerto Rico, and he plays drums four nights a week with an excellent jazz trio in one of the Condado section's finest hotels. That in itself isn't enough to pay his bills, so a few times weekly, he'll arrange and serve as a guide for horseback riding trips for tourists. The ride begins at a ranch located at the base of the beautiful mountains of El Yonqui, Puerto Rico's rainforest. Then it passes through grasslands and farmlands, eventually arriving at Luquillo Beach, where the horses are prone to take off into a serious gallop. Following the excitement of the gallop, Lester lets the group dismount and buy coconut milk, pineapple drinks, or souvenirs from vendor huts near the beach. He rounds everyone up and rides back to the ranch in a more direct line, taking a sparsely trafficked road. From there you can see some of the most beautiful landscapes and beaches on the entire island.

Today, I'm riding for the second time with Lester. The two of us have become friends during my tour with "El Puma," and we're staying in the same hotel where Lester works. I sat in a few times with his group, and we had good chemistry playing jazz standards together. We've got a lot in common, starting with our love of music. We're also both Jewish guys from the northeast, and we have similar likes, dislikes, and a slightly cynical yet sentimental world view. So besides hanging out at the beach and playing a bit too much blackjack in the hotel casino, I go riding with my new friend.

I notice that Lester keeps looking over his left shoulder, which shouldn't be surprising, given that he's responsible for all these tourists. But instead of watching the fifteen or so awkward-looking mounted tourists, he seems to be spending more time looking at the eleven-year-old, dark-complexioned Hispanic boy whom we picked up at the ranch as an additional guide. The boy's name is also Lester.

Lester Sr. was told just two months ago that he's a father, but he thinks the kid doesn't look a whole lot like him. The boy's mother showed up in San Juan back in May and told him, "This is your son from eleven years ago when we had one wonderful night together. He's a problem in school and at home and I can't seem to control him. It's your turn to try." Lester confided this whole account to me and told me he agreed to have Lester Jr. stay with him at least through the summer. The mother went back to New York. So far, Junior has done well as a "working man" with tending to horses and riding shotgun for the tours, but Lester Sr. tells me that Junior is really itching to go back to New York and his homies. He's not sure he should let him go back. He's not sure how much authority he can assert over Junior. He's not even sure if Lester Junior is related to him. A little trouble in paradise, I guess.

I'm anything but a skilled rider. To me, horseback riding can be alternately aggravating and satisfying, as well as painful and exhilarating. It all depends on the horse's personality and its attitude toward me. Today, Lester lets me ride a horse named Silver that he trained himself. This animal's been clocked at thirty-five miles an hour. I immediately find that Silver responds to the tiniest movements of the reins or pressure from the rider's legs. He also spares me excessive butt bumps. I already feel like this horse is a friend for life and that this ride is definitely on my top ten list. But then—we hit the beach. With a small release of the reins and a tiny click of my boots on his sides, Silver breaks into a gallop. Thirty-five miles an hour wasn't an exaggeration. As we gallop full throttle, I notice a sea grape tree with its branches stretched across the beach about a hundred yards ahead. My choice is to either pull in the reins and walk Silver through the ocean or duck low onto Silver's neck and gallop under the tree. I choose poorly. After passing "under" the tree, Silver is unscathed, but my tee-shirt has three tears in it, and my head has a few gashes, one of which is causing blood to drip into my left eye. At least I did manage to stay on the horse. Lester comes up to me quickly and seems really concerned. Only the gash on my forehead looks like it might be serious. The bleeding doesn't stop easily, but Lester tells me he's going to fix me up. We ride over to one of the little concession stands under the shade of some palm trees behind the beach, and he buys a small towel and some pure coconut oil. After wiping off the blood, Lester slathers some oil onto the wound and tells me to take a walk into the sea and dip my head into the salt water. It burns like hell, but when I get out, the bleeding has stopped. Lester puts a little more oil on the wound and my other cuts. I apologize a number of times for causing concern and for not setting a good example for the tourists. I had warned him that I'm not a highly qualified cowboy and that I don't know what I'm doing. And I was right. The two of us find a bench and sit, drinking fresh coconut milk. The vendors sell these, and are highly skilled at opening the tops of the nuts with two swings of a machete.

Lester obsesses over his new son, watching him tie up the horses so the tourists can relax and take a dip. He asks me what I think about his situation and what I would do if I were in his shoes. I tell him that it's true that the boy doesn't look anything like him, but he seems to be a good kid, so I would do exactly what Lester's doing: treat him like my son and see how things play out. But I know advice can be a dangerous thing to give. Lester's a good man, and as we ride back to San Juan on our tourist bus accompanied by a technicolor Caribbean sunset, I'm hoping the advice I've given him is good, and that he gets to hold on to his little piece of paradise for a while longer.

PUMA, PART 4 - RENEE

Renee is a remarkable guitarist. He plays Puma's show with tremendous ease and musicality. It doesn't matter whether he's playing with heavy rock distortion or using subtle vibrato on classical guitar passages; every note he plays is superb. Right now, I'm sitting next to Renee, waiting for sound check to begin, and I decide to ask him a question that's been bothering me for a while.

"Renee, if everything's so great in Cuba, why did you leave and come to Miami?"

Renee crossed to Key West in the 1981 Mariel boatlift. He was a classical guitar teacher at the Havana Conservatory, seemingly a pretty good gig. Since I've been working with Renee, I've heard him speak of Cuba's great universal education system, the lack of drugs and crime in Havana, and the virtues of their national health care system. So why leave?

"Two reasons, Bogie," he says. "I was listed on a government register as a teacher at the Havana Conservatory. I wanted to play, not teach, and they didn't give me a choice. Also, I wanted to come to America where I could buy Jimi Hendrix records."

I guess that sums up capitalism: Lots of problems, but freedom to pursue whatever career you choose (and excel as Renee definitely does), and freedom to buy whatever records you want to. It may be puzzling to some that Renee, who's such a brilliant classical, jazz, and Latin player, would also be so interested in playing hard rock and heavy metal. But he's also brilliant at that style. Renee, Fofi (drums), and Julio (bass) often do power trio jams at sound check that are as good as any I've ever heard. At one point, I asked Renee why the three of them didn't start their own group. All of them are tired of the Puma show and hoping to find other work soon.

Renee responded in his thick Cuban accent, "Bogie, look at dis face. Could you see dis face on MTV?"

It's 1985, and the days of rock musicians performing for years without anyone ever getting a good look at their faces are over. Renee is heavyset, has a ruddy complexion, and a large nose. I look at him for a moment and try to think of something tactful to say. "I guess not, but you guys still sound ridiculously good." That's the best I'm able to come up with.

CODA

It's the late 1990s, and a friend of mine just saw the amazing Cuban born jazz trumpet player Arturo Sandoval at Blues Alley in Georgetown. He tells me that Arturo's guitarist was brilliant, someone named Renee Toledo. I'm guessing Renee is happy he took that boat trip some seventeen years ago, and I'm just really happy to hear he's getting the recognition he well deserves.

PUMA, PART 5 - PERU

I'm having dinner with my friends, Julio and Oscar, in the Starlight Room of the best hotel in downtown Lima, Peru. We're on the top floor, and we're surrounded on all four sides by glass, so we have a great view of the city. I thought I was done with Puma shows after doing a few run out dates in Atlantic City, Caesar's Palace in Vegas, and the Colorado State Fair last year. Surprisingly, there was a large enough Hispanic population in Colorado that we had an audience of nearly ten thousand.

It's now the summer of 1986 and for the past year, my attention has been focused entirely on musicology readings about Stravinsky, Bartók, and Schoenberg, style analysis of Haydn and Brahms, and working up Rachmaninoff's Rhapsody on a Theme of Paganini to perform as soloist with the University of Kentucky Symphony Orchestra.

But then I got another call a few weeks ago from Hector, Puma's music director. He needed a keyboard sub for a three-week tour of Ecuador and Peru. School was out of session, so I didn't have to think about it for very long. No rehearsals involved and the show is pretty much the same as it was when I played it last summer. But this tour is turning out to be even crazier than last year's.

Our first stop was Guayaquil, Ecuador. When we got off the plane, the scene resembled the Beatles arriving at JFK in New York. Puma produced constant number one hits in Ecuador and Peru for the past five years but had never performed live in either country. The currency exchange in Ecuador was so poor that no one could afford to sponsor his tour until now. In Peru, I think the incessant terrorist attacks by the Shining Path communist guerrillas have kept the country on the brink of civil war, which just made things too dangerous.

It was Puma's first time arriving in Guayaquil in the flesh. Literally, thousands of frenzied fans streamed toward us across the tarmac as we deplaned. I've always been uncomfortable in Latin American countries with the way police and the military casually patrol the streets with drawn weapons (usually automatic or semiautomatic). During my cruise ship days, I remember seeing police patrolling with drawn swords in Caracas. But when we landed in Guayaquil, I was thankful for the intimidation factor and our police escort. Otherwise, I don't think we would have made it safely to our airport holding room, complete with a first class buffet and an open bar.

During the flight, the road manager took our passports and immigration documents to get us cleared so we wouldn't have to stand in line. Instead, we waited, eating cheese, crackers, and a local ceviche while drinking some nice red wine. I thought about how nice it would be to receive this treatment every time I arrive at an airport. But I don't kid myself. If I wasn't with Puma, the only greeting I would have received would have come from a dour customs agent asking me, "Is your stay for business or pleasure?"

The tour lived up to my expectations. Three shows in Guayaquil, the last one a free public concert for an estimated 110,000 people. I felt like I was playing the Woodstock of Latin pop. At the concert, I was glad once again for the intimidating presence of the police and military. As our bus approached the city's central piazza, we were surrounded by a crush of fans. I'm certain they didn't know Puma was traveling in a separate limo. We couldn't move forward, and the Guayaquil crazies started to rock the bus from side to side. We were rescued by billy club wielding police who quickly cleared a path for us. I didn't see any of the swinging clubs land, but our fan club sure scattered fast. Even though it was dusk, I could clearly see the fear in the eyes of some of our audience as they lunged to get out of the way. I learned a few years ago on my first trip to Columbia that the average South American citizen sees the police more as an institution to be feared than relied on.

Eventually, we were able to make our way to an elevated stage, and when I looked out, the piazza was like an ocean of humanity with the overflow bleeding into all the side streets. The show was a blur. Tremendous crowd noise and terrible outdoor acoustics. I always feel a bit bad for Gary, our sound engineer, as he deals with different problems at every tour stop. But this concert had to be his biggest challenge.

Later on that evening, we were having an espresso party in Fofi's room, and I remarked how cool it was to play for a crowd that big. The rest of the band looked at me as if I had farted robustly in the middle of a wedding ceremony. I guess I haven't been doing the Puma show long enough to be that jaded, but I figure I may as well enjoy this crazy ride for the short time I'm on it. I'm pretty sure that I'll never play for over 100,000 people again.

Then it was on to Peru. The ride from Lima's airport to our hotel told the story. Armored military personnel carriers at every street corner. Razor wire adorned the fencing around every government building and every house that seemed even moderately affluent. We clearly heard the sound of distant gunfire. And to top it off, we saw a group of people in the street, gathered around what appeared to be a corpse. I'm not sure. But the man was definitely not moving, and no one in the crowd was making any move to administer first aid. When we arrived at our hotel, we were given permits that allowed us to be on the streets after the citywide midnight curfew. But we were told to be careful because sometimes the police shoot before asking to see your permit. Throughout South America, I've seen lots of seventeen-year-old police officers with their fingers on the triggers of drawn semiautomatics. Plus I barely know enough Español to ask for a men's room or order from a simple menu. Once I managed to get Julio and a waiter to double over with laughter by ordering "apple foot" when I meant "apple pie." I decided to make sure I was back at the hotel by midnight.

The hotel has armed guards stationed at every elevator door. Three weeks ago, a Shining Path bomb was detonated on the seventh floor of our hotel and it's still closed down. Our band even got into a small quasi-violent confrontation on our first night out to dinner. There were nine of us at a table in a typical mid-priced Lima restaurant. There were two men and a woman sitting at a table behind us. They were loud and, apparently, more than a little bit drunk. One of them asked Renee, "Eres Cubano?"

"Si," answered Renee.

"De Miami?"

"Si."

The three locals rambled on for a while in Spanish. To me, it was incomprehensible, but not to my friends at our table. The Peruvians were holding a battery and laughing. I couldn't understand so I didn't think much of it. But then everyone at our table turned to face the drunken diners. This was my best clue that something was wrong.

Turns out that our new "friends" thought it was amusing to joke about using their battery to make a bomb to use on the "Capitalist Pigs." Most of the musicians at our table were Miami Cubans who'd managed to escape Castro. They weren't at all amused. Eventually, the would-be terrorists got up to leave, and one of them laughed and said something to Renee. I wished I'd studied Spanish instead of Russian in high school. In a flash, Renee was in his face, yelling and pointing his finger and poking the Peruvian communist comedian on his forehead. The communist's glasses went flying and broke, but before Renee did any more damage, Julio and Oscar got in between him and the terrorist wannabe. The three Peruvians collected their things and left quickly, just as the restaurant owner came by to try and smooth things over.

I didn't know what was said, so on the way back to the hotel, I asked Julio to translate. He told me that all through dinner, the three communists at the other table had been mocking the US and the Cubans who deserted their cause by leaving their homeland. It turns out that during his face-poking tirade, Renee exclaimed, "Don't you tell me about Cuba! I grew up in Cuba! You know nothing about it! My family gave up everything to come to the US, and I don't need your horseshit opinion about it!" After thinking about it for a minute, I told Julio this city was the closest I'd ever been and hopefully the closest I'd ever be to a war zone. But bravo, Renee.

After two shows in Lima, it was on to Iquitos, a city of seventy-five thousand in the middle of the Amazon. This so-called city had only one paved road, and the only hotel was a Holiday Inn that had regular electrical outages, leaving the guests with no AC in the middle of the Amazon. While we explored the town, people tried hard to sell us turtles, monkeys, and even a baby pig that a teenage boy held up to each of our faces as we passed by. I considered going for a jungle tour, but the last boat left the hotel an hour before we arrived. Instead, I decided to take a walk by myself through the jungle on a path behind our hotel. I made it about a quarter mile and decided it was probably smarter to turn back. I heard what sounded like thousands of insects and reptiles scurrying about under my feet. I opted instead for a few hours exploring Iquitos with all the other band members and sitting at a sidewalk café drinking a Cerveza next to the Amazon River. Puma, as usual, was sequestered in his luxury suite. The entire place was teeming with life. It was remarkably beautiful and seemed to have a deep, spiritual power that somehow made its way into my dreams after the show.

We were at the airport at eight the next morning and were told our flight would be very late. The city didn't have lots of transportation choices. No roads and no trains went there. You came by boat or by the one daily flight that comes and goes from Lima. That flight, which was supposed to arrive in the morning, got there at seven in the evening. In the meantime, we paid a visit to a rather dismal local zoo, had lunch in town, and read every bit of print material we had. They finally allowed us to board the plane at eight. As we put our luggage into the overhead compartments, an authoritative voice came over the loud speaker and barked something incomprehensible in Spanish. I looked at Julio for assistance.

"We need to get back off the plane." He rolled his eyes and said, "Mechanical issues. They're gonna take a test drive and make sure everything's OK."

We finally boarded after watching the plane fly three big circles around the airport valley. I'm usually not afraid of flying, but I held on white-knuckled all the way across the Andes and back to the relative safety of Lima's simmering revolution.

The next day we left for Arequipa in the middle of the Andes and the desert. It's a fascinating city full of both Incan and Spanish colonial architecture. Machu Picchu, one of the world's Seven Wonders, was within driving distance, but as usual, there wasn't enough time to go there and get back for sound check. In my frustration, I reminded myself that I took this gig primarily for the money and I wasn't a tourist. With our flight back to Miami booked for the next morning, we returned to Lima. We walked around the city a bit, and I bought a cassette from some truly virtuoso pan flute street musicians.

In the daytime, Lima seemed like a pretty normal South American city. But now, at night, we sit and have dinner in the Starlight Room looking out over mostly deserted streets, watching those ubiquitous armored troop transports and hearing the echoes of occasional gunfire. I think that it'll be even nicer than usual when our plane touches down in Miami tomorrow. This trip has definitely made me more patriotic, and although the Puma tour's been a great adventure, it's an adventure I'll be glad is over. I'll be glad to return to my simple life of study and practicing back in Kentucky.

CODA

I got a last minute call to play a solo piano gig in a renovated art-deco hotel on South Beach during my one night in Miami before flying back to Kentucky. The hotel's in a part of town that when I first moved down here in 1975 looked like the depression era had never ended. It's now eleven years later, and South Beach is in the middle of an economic renaissance.

The hotel restaurant where I'm playing is beautiful and they have a wonderful piano. The place is full of young adults of every imaginable ethnicity. The thing they all have in common is their impeccable fashion sense. Everyone in the place has perfect hair, perfect makeup, and perfectly fitting up-to-date clothes. While looking around the room, the first thing that comes to mind is that all of them must have spent a substantial amount of time in front of their mirrors before leaving home.

The other thing they have in common is their unanimous obliviousness toward me. Not even a nod of the head or a small smile as they walk by. This lack of interest isn't unusual for me to deal with on solo gigs. If I really let it bother me, I'd have had to quit playing professionally years ago. But tonight, I can't help but feel a good deal of irony. Two nights ago, I was playing for twenty thousand crazed fans in a soccer stadium in Arequipa. A week and a half ago, my personal safety was threatened by over a hundred thousand screaming fans in Guayaquil. I'm still the same musician playing lots of the same notes. I'm still the same person. Context is everything.

VINCE AND VINNIE

Vince DiMartino is one of the world's great trumpet players and teachers. He's also a good friend and mentor of mine. Tonight, we're going to play a concert together for a national percussion symposium that's taking place at the University of Kentucky. For the past week, I've been the staff pianist for this gathering of musicians who live to beat on things. If I was living in New York or Chicago, there would be hundreds of competent pianists to play this gig, but, fortunately for me, in Lexington, Kentucky, I was the best choice.

During the first few days of the workshop, I accompanied Spyro Gyro, percussionist, Dave Samuels, Latin percussion specialist, Norbert Goldberg, and former Maynard Ferguson drummer, Dave Mancini, as they gave instructional seminars. All good times. But tonight's concert with Vince and Vinnie is the symposium's main event. Vinnie Colaiuta is universally recognized as one of the world's top jazz/rock/fusion drummers. On the afternoon of the concert, Vince and I are joined by Tony, a student of bass at the university and a good player. We're in the university's concert hall at the Center for the Arts. We go over a few tunes while we're waiting for Vinnie to finish up a master class in a different hall. We play through an original samba of Vince's and a tune I recently wrote.

Vinnie arrives a few minutes late. We shake hands as we're introduced. I can tell right away that Vinnie doesn't want to be here. He's sweating a bit, probably from demonstrating at his recently completed master class, and his complexion is pretty pale. His girlfriend (who, somebody whispers, is a recent Playboy centerfold) and his manager accompany him. Nobody introduces us to them. We're scheduled for an hour and a half rehearsal followed by a two hour dinner break and then the concert.

Vinnie sits behind the drums and asks what we want to play. Vince gives him the music to his original samba. The tune is structured so the entire group starts with an eight-bar melody and then breaks for an eight-bar drum solo. Vinnie gets four measures into his solo, stops playing and says, "This doesn't feel right. We play eight bars together, and then I'm supposed to just start bashing?"

Vince is a very nice guy, but I know him well enough to know that he's really fuming. Without saying a word, he just walks over to Vinnie and takes the music off of his stand. Three minutes into our rehearsal and already we're circling the drain.

I jump in with, "Well, Vinnie, what do you want to play?"

Vinnie's arms are folded, and he seems to be looking down at his snare drum. He finally looks up and asks, "You guys know 'Captain Señor Mouse'?"

"Captain Señor Mouse" is one of Chick Corea's most difficult fusion compositions. We have it in a fake book, and I've listened to it and read through it but never really learned it. We agree to give it a shot. (After seeing what happened with Vince's tune, I quickly decided to not even mention my original.) Our reading is good, but Chick's tune is really difficult. We have a few snags, and when we get to the end of the form, Vinnie says, "Maybe we won't do this one."

Now I'm getting frustrated and decide to speak up, "Vinnie, we're learning this on the fly, but I'm sure we can do this one tonight. Let's give it another crack." This was basically my way of asking him to please have a bit of patience. Vinnie looks a bit skeptical but agrees to keep rehearsing it. We spend the rest of our rehearsal time working on "Señor Mouse," and as the rehearsal ends, I feel like it's starting to sound pretty good.

But as Vinnie's leaving, the last thing he says to us is, "Guys, I think I don't really feel like doing that tune after all. Just bring some fake books tonight and we'll pick some stuff to play." Before any of us can respond, he's out the back door of the hall with his little entourage.

Jim, the UK percussion professor who hired me and a real nice guy, has been watching this whole scene. He comes up and tells us that Vinnie got food poisoning on last night's flight from Los Angeles to Kentucky, so that's probably the reason for his prickly attitude. Jim tells us that he's sure that the concert will be just fine. I hope so, but after this rehearsal fiasco, I've got no reason to believe that it'll be anything but a nightmare.

Twenty minutes before the concert, Vinnie arrives, and we all huddle around a fake book. We pick out jazz/rock/fusion favorites like Eddie Harris's "Freedom Jazz Dance," Miles Davis's "Eighty-One," and Wayne Shorter's "Pinocchio." Vinnie's attitude seems a lot better, and Vince is mostly quiet, so our planning session is painless.

When we walk on stage, we get a nice round of applause from our audience, made up of mostly percussionists and drummers. But when Vinnie is introduced and walks over to sit behind the drum set, the place goes crazy. This guy is both a hero and role model for much of our audience. We kick it off with Freddie Hubbard's "Red Clay," and the energy is intense from the first note. This hall was really designed for strings, and just a small tap on a ride cymbal echoes for what seems like a full thirty seconds. And Vinnie doesn't do small taps. He plays loud and "drives the train," leaving absolutely no doubt about where the beat is. He solos on every song and the ideas he plays are both rhythmically fascinating and highly musical.

Vince's solos are brilliant. They have a laser-like accuracy and an organic development of musical ideas. Each tune we play builds progressively in intensity until I find myself standing and playing a synthesizer solo on Wayne Shorter's "Pinocchio" with the drums thundering behind me. I feel totally disconnected from the physical world. I've heard that music has the power to do this. Vinnie's the thunder, Vince is the lightning, and I'm being carried to musical heights on a wave of energy they're creating.

We play two encores at the end. The concert has already run seventy-five minutes instead of the scheduled forty-five, but Vinnie is backstage rattling his sticks together, saying, "Come on, guys! Let's play one more! Just one more!" I think it's safe to assume that he likes performing better than rehearsing. Jim (who has already let us return to the stage for two encores when our time was up) tells him, "Sorry, afraid not," and he cues for the house lights to come on.

I shake hands with Vince and Vinnie, but unfortunately, I don't have time to hang out and talk. I'm late for my gig at the Bistro (so much for my recent lecture to my group there about punctuality.) The concert certainly far exceeded my expectations, and as I'm driving to my gig, I think about how people who have nothing in common, or maybe don't even like each other, can make something uniquely wonderful happen when pulled together by the common language of jazz. Vince and Vinnie.

THE FRIENDLIEST
AUDIENCE

It's 1988 and I'm on stage at Haverford College, just outside of Philadelphia. This concert is just my second paid professional solo piano recital. My first one was for a museum concert series on Miami Beach back in '86. I've played plenty of college recitals as well as a number of recitals at churches in Miami. Fred Coulter, my former teacher, was kind enough to set those up for me. Those concerts were really just preparation for upcoming competitions and were attended mostly by our tight-knit studio class and our families.

Tonight, I played Mozart's K.333 Bb Major Sonata and Ravel's entire Miroirs as the first half of my program. The second half consists of only one piece, Schumann's Fantasy, Opus 17. It's a long and very difficult work, appropriately manic in its changes of mood. Schumann struggled with mental illness, spending his last few years in an insane asylum. One moment this piece is triumphant, the next it's filled with quiet reflection, and the next filled with serious agitation. These mood swings, along with Schumann's ability to compose long, beautiful phrases, are the aspects of his compositional style that attract me most to his music. Right now, I'm on the last movement. I think I breathed an audible sigh of relief after completing the treacherously difficult March movement. That section featured lots of difficult leaps, and the last movement challenges the performer to execute very subtle gradations of tone control with the goal in mind of creating exceptionally long phrases with huge climactic arrival points. I generally don't use metaphors when playing, but for me, this music is probably the most overtly sexual of anything I've ever performed, classical or otherwise. Long sections of tender foreplay always leading toward an inevitable climax. Hmm. As I'm executing slow arpeggios with a gorgeous alto melody projecting from the thumb in my right hand, I'm aware of how quiet the audience is. Quiet not only in terms of noise, but also in terms of movement. They're like statues. I generally try not to be aware of my audience while playing, but I briefly realize that I've managed to capture them tonight, successfully inviting them into my musical vision of Schumann's world.

As a performer, it feels so different to play for an audience like this, as opposed to playing for an audition or a piano competition. I've been playing a lot of competitions recently, and I'm very accustomed to hearing the rustling of pens and papers as my jury of three to fifteen judges scrutinize everything I do. Extremely difficult circumstances for trying to make music.

About a year ago, I wrote a letter to John Davison, professor of theory and composition at Haverford College, a small liberal arts school just outside of Philadelphia. Davison was my brother Dave's composition professor, and one night during my last year of high school, I visited Haverford and heard him play a few of his own pieces. I liked his music very much. At the time, it seemed to me that he had his own unique musical language. I ended up playing a single movement sonata of his for my junior recital at the University of Miami. So ten years later, after receiving my letter, John Davison offered me a slot on Haverford's Guest Artist Series. This opportunity was even more exciting for me because I had never played a recital in the Philadelphia area where I grew up. So when lots of my family and old friends took an interest, my mom and dad really went overboard; they rented a bus to drive everyone to my recital. My dad's a wonderful family doctor and my mom's a friendly and gregarious lady. Sometimes it seems like they know everyone within a ten-mile radius of their home in South Jersey.

They had their misgivings about me pursuing a career in music. Dad would make me play for him when I was home for the holidays from college at the University of Miami to make sure I was making progress. But they've always been extremely supportive. They attended all my University of Miami recitals, my University of Kentucky Concerto Competition winner's performance, and financed my very expensive undergraduate college education. But busing in such a friendly audience is more than I could possibly have hoped for. That's also why I don't even take a peek at the audience. How distracting would it be if I were to make eye contact with Cousin Gordon? Or Aunt Bonnie? Or Doug? Or Mom and Dad? So as I reach the final climax of the Schumann Fantasy, I don't look up, but I know I've got them. They're in my world now. My world and Schumann's.

At the end of the concert, I take three curtain calls. As I'm walking back onstage for my last bow, I'm thinking I'll probably never again have an audience on my side the way this one is. But I can always hope.

Robert Boguslaw, 1985

BOBBY MCFERRIN

As I'm walking down one of the gloomy gray corridors of the Fine Arts Building at the University of Kentucky, a friend mentions to me that the great jazz singer, Bobby McFerrin, is speaking informally to students this afternoon at the university theatre where he's scheduled to perform tonight. Even though I've found his solo vocal recordings to be unique and creative, I've decided not to go to his concert and to play my steady gig at The Bistro instead. Our bills are being paid in large part by my six-night-a-week restaurant gig, so I have to be careful about taking time off from work. However, I think, why not go to his talk and see if he might sing something for us?

McFerrin's lecture is engaging, informative, friendly, and funny. But I realize at the end of the talk that he's not going to sing. I have the audacity (and poor taste) to ask him if he can sing a bit for us because I can't make it to the concert, given that I have to work. His cheerful demeanor makes a quick exit, and he gives me a deadpan stare, telling me that I can stick around and listen to his sound check if I want to. I'm definitely off of his A-list now. The sound check, though brief, doesn't disappoint. McFerrin must have one of the most flexible voices on the planet. Large intervals and sudden vocal color changes are executed with deceptive ease.

After the sound check's done and as I'm leaving the building, a distinguished looking African American woman wearing a dashiki asks me if I've changed my mind and decided to make it to the concert. I get the impression that she's his wife. I tell her I'd love to, but that unfortunately, I really can't afford to skip work. Then I reconsider and say that I could make it for the first forty-five minutes and still get to the gig on time.

She says, "Why don't you do that? He won't mind if you have to leave." It's decided then.

So I show up fifteen minutes before the concert begins, only to discover it's sold out. Someone sees my look of disappointment as I walk away from the box office and offers to sell me an extra ticket of theirs. I accept. The seat is in the fourth row, front and center. Not an easy place to make a quiet exit from.

The concert is great. I wouldn't have thought it possible for a solo voice concert to hold my attention like this. He sings everything from Charlie Parker's "Scrapple from the Apple" to "Freedom Jazz Dance" to the "Beverly Hillbillies" theme. I don't want to go, but when my time comes, I get up to leave and, of course, I end up awkwardly crossing over about a dozen or so audience members.

McFerrin's in the middle of a tune, but he interrupts the song, gives me a mock-contemptuous look, and proceeds to jump down from the stage and follow me up the aisle, pleading for me to stay, and wondering why I'm leaving, and didn't I enjoy the show?

I turn and attempt to explain that I have to go to work, but my explanation is drowned out by nearly universal audience laughter. I'm pretty amused as well. I guess the joke's on me. I'm the brunt. Did Bobby and his wife set me up to become a punchline for McFerrin's show? I guess I really don't mind being the subject of a joke (as long as it's not about my family or my piano playing.) Anyway, I've been in this business long enough to know better than to ask an artist like McFerrin for my own private performance. One hell of a nerve. I had it coming.

THE BISTRO

Norman called me about an hour ago and told me I'd better get down to the Bistro right away if I had left anything there that belonged to me. He told me that the gig is over and the Lexington police were impounding everything in the place: the furniture, the bar, the tables and chairs, and all the five star kitchen equipment. This was the best gig in town, and I lasted three and a half years on it. In my seven years of professional gigging in Miami, I never held a job for more than six months. I worked at the Bistro six nights a week, three solo, and three with a trio. We were joined by a singer on the weekends. The piano was positioned by the fireplace, which gave the lounge a comfortable, welcoming atmosphere. The entire restaurant was carpeted with a thick, plush, red tartan carpet.

Until today, the Bistro was the only true gourmet French restaurant in Lexington. It attracted a lot of wealthy horse farm owners. Women with mink coats, bloodshot eyes, and too much makeup. Men with an air of self-confidence and light southern accents, often discussing what kind of price a three-year-old filly might get. I even saw Liz Taylor and George Hamilton come in for dinner one night.

When Keeneland is up and running, Lexington's famous seasonal race track hosts the spring sales of thoroughbred foals. People come from all over the world. Besides the equestrians, we also get a reasonable number of locals, starved for jazz. Most of them are in love with the Sinatra and Bennett tunes, but some of them are interested in hearing my originals or the tunes of Metheny, Corea, and Hancock that we play from time to time. The third group of patrons are those who are bar hopping late in the evening. To them, the Bistro is just one more bar to belly up to before stumbling home. A number of them are Vietnam vets who could tell you disturbing stories of their deployments. Some of them don't want to talk about it.

Coming to work in the same place for years, I made a number of good friends. Frank is a doctoral student in policy studies who had worked previously in DC for the Carter administration. Flynn is a University of Kentucky computer science professor who would sit in occasionally, singing authentic Irish folk songs. Doug is a doctor of psychology from Duke University who was previously married to a Jewish girl from Long Island. Originally from the hills of eastern Kentucky, he had an accent so thick that you'd think he was talking with a big wad of cotton stuffed in his mouth. Usually, there was a table full of older women sitting near the piano who would pepper us with requests for their favorite Gershwin or Porter songs. The closest thing I've had to a fan club.

The bartenders, Scott and Judy, became friends of mine. Every night, they'd fill a brandy snifter with three or four shots of cognac, B&B, or Grand Marnier for me. I'd nurse it through the four hours of the gig, never becoming falling down drunk, but consuming enough alcohol to take a toll on my kidneys while keeping me warm and happy. The drinks were free. I discovered some time ago that it's always worthwhile to tip the bartenders well and often. There was so much revenue coming into the place that I don't think the owners knew or cared about the band's free drinks.

The bartenders and waiters frequently partied in the restaurant after the owners and customers went home. After last call at the bar, usually doubles, the wait staff made eggs back in the kitchen. Some smoked weed outside on the porch.

Rickie, the gay maître'd with the football player's build and a pink alcohol flush to his face, once told me: "Now don't you talk bad about Jim Bakker around me! I love Jim Bakker! If I was Jim Bakker, I'd have done exactly what he did. I'd have kept all that money and fucked everyone I could!" One of my favorite drunken barstool quotes.

I took part in a lot of the parties, but that pretty much stopped in July of 1987 when Nicole was born. The first time I experienced a hangover while trying to calm a screaming baby cured me of any inclination I may have had toward alcoholism.

Standing here now watching the police supervise the impoundment, it occurs to me that I'm more than a little amazed that I was able to keep this gig all these years and still regularly get up the following morning and work on a Brahms concerto, Prokofiev sonata, or Bach's Chromatic Fantasy and Fugue—or conduct a jazz band and ace a Style & Analysis exam. Mary and I have both been working on graduate level degrees, holding down teaching assistantships, and trying to be good parents to two babies. On top of that, I've been pushing hard in my attempt to become a classical concert artist, playing recitals and occasionally participating in nerve-wracking piano competitions.

But my favorite memories of this place will be of two great friends: Jeff, a violinist colleague of mine who lives up the street from the bar and comes in almost nightly, and Norman, the drummer I auditioned and hired for the last two and a half years of the gig. Jeff is one of the most considerate and overall nicest people I've ever met. He's a musician for all the right reasons. He has passion for the music he loves and the violin. He's also indisputably hilarious. He holds up his lighter at the end of any particularly burning numbers that we play. Also, I don't think I've ever met anyone who gets as much pleasure from telling a joke as Jeff. He rubs his hands together more and more vigorously, and his eyes widen progressively as he approaches the punch line. I could listen to him tell the same joke again and again—and I do.

Norman is an African American drummer, overweight and about seventeen years older than me. I love his playing. He's obviously listened to Philly Joe Jones, Max Roach, and Elvin Jones, but mostly I hear the influence of Art Blakey in his drumming. He plays every note with tremendous commitment, especially hard-bop and funk. I get a lot of meaningful looks from Norman when we see notable behavior from some of the characters that frequent the Bistro. He also occasionally does something that I've never seen a drummer do, or any musician for that matter. He'll fall asleep while playing. And keep playing! I was warned about this tendency of his when I hired him, so I considered it a compliment that we worked together for four months before I caught him nodding out for the first time.

"Norman," I'd say, then "NORMAN!" I'd yell.

He'd suddenly come to and rush the beat a bit, shaking his head with disappointment at himself. He'd lick a finger and make a fake mark on the wall.

"You owe me one, Norman," I'd say.

He's already had a heart attack, so he takes blood pressure medication that makes him sleepy, and he also has a day job working at a print shop. On top of all that, he and his son build and drag race motorcycles. Talk about burning the candle at both ends! Norman and his wonderful wife Jean have our family over pretty often for important holidays. Given that we live miles from either Mary's or my family, this is really a blessing. The two of them always have a large group of neighbors and family hanging out in their living room and kitchen with lots of country cooking going on. Crock pots full of stew, roasted chicken, casseroles of mac and cheese, green beans, home-cooked cornbread, and desserts. They have a way of making us all feel like part of the family.

This is all ending because Sandy and Lou, the owners, parted ways romantically about a year ago. They seemed to maintain a professional working relationship for a while, but all the employees knew that things were strained. Sandy eventually found a good-looking stud nearly twenty years younger than her, and the word is that she emptied some joint bank accounts and bolted for the Bahamas. With those funds gone and Lou left with nothing for the creditors, he had no choice but to close the place, with everything in the restaurant becoming collateral on his debt. Anyway, that's what the word is. Either way, it's time to get my sheet music and cords out of here and see what I can do about finding a new gig. Even the best gigs don't last forever.

CODA

It's 2008 and I'm playing solo piano for a typical White House bill signing job. But it's not typical for me. I'm playing Pat Metheny's "Last Train Home," a personal tribute to my great friend, Norman Higgins. When we worked together at the Bistro in Lexington, Norman used to say to me, "When I die, you gotta play 'Last Train' at my funeral."

Sadly, I didn't hear of Norman's passing until months after the memorial service. So I tell myself, "This one's for you, Norman. I'm so very sorry I didn't make it out to Kentucky for the service, but your memory is going out in this music today in the Grand Foyer of the White House. You're a great soul. God and peace go with you."

African American Museum Opening, Lexington, KY, 1988
Left to right: Bob, Al Hood, Kasi Harris, Jim Rankin, Duke Madison
& Norman Higgins

ON GOLDEN POND

I left Plymouth, New Hampshire at nine this morning, figuring I'd be home around midnight. That didn't happen. I'm driving through rural Kentucky. It's three thirty in the morning, and as I pull back onto I-64 West, I finally see the Quality Inn sign I've spent the last twenty minutes looking for shining through a fog bank that's as thick as molasses. I've been driving through this mess since about ten o'clock this evening when I was sixty miles north of Charleston, West Virginia. I don't think I've been able to crack thirty miles an hour since. I was still about a hundred miles from our home in Lexington when I finally decided to give up. The fog bank and the diffused oncoming headlights had been playing games with my mind, and in the last fifty miles, I'm certain I started hallucinating. I decided to finally leave the highway and check into a hotel.

I was trying to avoid the expensive luxury of a hotel room. Mary and I are living just a little bit above the poverty line. I'm on my way home from the New Hampshire Music Festival, and I need to spend the money I made on bills, not a hotel room. I finally surrendered to this surreal fog. But it looks like I have to skip the comfort of a clean bed and try and make it home tonight. Turns out I couldn't find the hotel once I got off the highway. There were no visible turnoffs and no signs to be found until I started to pull back onto the highway, but now it's too late. I've apparently driven right past the hotel entrance without being able to see it. So I resign myself to a few more hours of twenty-five miles an hour driving with a maximum of about seventy-five feet of visibility.

On this trip south through New England and the Mid-Atlantic states, I've had plenty of time to reflect on what was undoubtedly the best classical performance experience of my life. This was my second year performing at the festival. I was offered the festival pianist position on the recommendation of my friend, Dan, violin professor at the University of Kentucky. The job consists of playing for two of the festival's weekly chamber music concerts, as well as playing any keyboard parts that may be required with the orchestra.

My first year was wonderful, but this year was even better. This year, my stepdaughter, Hosanna, came with me. I talked to the festival orchestra contractor, Jack, and he was nice enough to help her get hired as a stage hand, a summer job and quite an adventure for a seventeen-year-old. Hosanna has been a bit of a troubled teenager. She's gay, and had to make an extremely difficult adjustment to life in Lexington, Kentucky. She was uprooted in 1985 when her mom and I got married and left Miami soon afterward. It's hard to imagine two more different places than Lexington and Miami, and it didn't help that she was thirteen at the time, probably the most awkward stage of adolescence.

But recently, I've been seeing signs that she's getting more comfortable in her own skin. And it's also encouraging that she seems willing to work hard and was able to make some good friends at the festival. We had some nice times canoeing and hiking. We shared a "dead car" adventure on the trip up. I made the mistake of destroying my little Toyota's transmission by running over a wood block in the highway. Thanks, Mom and Dad, once again for bailing me out! The bailout this time involved driving from New Jersey to Maryland at two-thirty in the morning to pick us up. I'm most grateful to Hosanna for her help with my first large ensemble composition, Variations for Orchestra. Tom, the festival's conductor and music director, agreed to give me a reading of the piece, using a half hour of the orchestra's valuable rehearsal time. Fortunately for me, Tom's very interested in new music, and he's also an exceptionally kind and unpretentious man (somewhat rare for conductors). As usual, I delayed too long in collating and taping the parts. At nine-forty-five that morning, I was still taping and checking notes and rehearsal numbers. Downbeat was at ten. Hosanna helped me, even though it made her late for work (what a bad influence I was that day). I had finished writing the piece over a month ago, and there was no excuse for my procrastination. At the very last minute, Hosanna and I finished distributing the parts, and we ran to a small recording booth in the rehearsal hall.

I didn't have any luck with the high fidelity tape-recording gear. As I ran out of time and left with the score for the rehearsal in the concert hall, Hosanna yelled to me that she got it working. Hallelujah! There's nothing more valuable for the growth and development of a composer than having a recording of one's piece played by a top-flight professional group. But it's nerve-wracking. Probably even more so than my recent performance of Brahms's second piano concerto. For that matter, I was probably more nervous for this than any of the international piano competitions I'd ever done. I hadn't thoroughly checked every part, so what if I'd left out or added measures? What if the computer had printed out a part in the wrong clef or the wrong key? Many of the orchestra musicians had become my friends. What would they say to me if my piece was simply dreadful? They'd probably just walk by me and avoid direct eye contact.

But my fears proved unfounded. I sat in the hall with the score and answered a few questions about dynamics and percussion doublings, but fortunately, there were no musical train wrecks. Tom had done his homework with the score, and he navigated the tempo changes and expressive rubatos just as I had heard them in my head while writing the piece. The piece puts a large emphasis on the cello section, and the cellists read it beautifully.

At one point, Tom told them, "Put a little more 'Boguslaw' into it."

There was some laughter, but I took it as a compliment. When the rehearsal ended, I thanked Tom a dozen times. In his gruff and understated way, he simply said, "A good piece. That's a really good piece."

Following the rehearsal, I was able to go out to lunch with my orchestra friends without wondering if they'd lost all respect for me. Hosanna had monitored the recording for me, but unfortunately, she was unable to join us. The stage crew always had work to do at the end of rehearsals.

The memory from my two weeks at the New Hampshire Music Festival that will probably remain the most indelibly inscribed in my mind and soul was getting to play a private concert, "On Golden Pond." Loon Lake was used for the filming of that classic Fonda-Hepburn film that so poignantly dealt with approaching the end of life. And although Loon Lake is not open to the public, it is circled by a number of homes owned by wealthy New Hampshire Music Festival benefactors. Most of these homes have large decks, bay windows, and French doors that open to give the owners access to the lake. All the homes have gorgeous views of the water and the densely forested background. Some of these benefactors allow the festival musicians to use their beaches for swimming, boating, and fishing. So I was able to enjoy the unique serenity of "Golden Pond."

But my last trip to Loon Lake wasn't for a beach outing. It was for a private preview of our upcoming festival performance of Brahms's Piano Quartet no.1 in g minor. This piece had been on my bucket list for years, and I suggested a performance of it. Carl and Sarah, the owners of one of the Golden Pond homes, were long retired US State Department employees who had traveled the world working for the diplomatic corps. They were both well into their eighties. They were enthusiastic lovers of classical music as well as good friends of Dan and Beth. Dan's wife, Beth, is a wonderful cellist and also a good friend. So Carl and Sarah were more than happy to have us come over for a dry run of the Brahms's quartet the night before the festival performance. My parents took a drive to Plymouth for a few days and accompanied me to Golden Pond. Our ensemble was completed by Caryn, a very nice but quiet lady who plays violin with the San Diego Symphony. She came to the festival in large part to get the opportunity to play her second instrument, the viola. She's also a world-class musician. I feel very fortunate to get to perform with these people.

When we arrived, I settled in to Carl and Sarah's beautiful Steinway B in the middle of the living room. I took one look out onto the back deck and quickly realized that it was the most idyllic setting I'd ever performed in. Large, silent blue spruces shaded the deck, and forty feet from the back of the house was Loon Lake, glowing in the orange light of a mid-summer sunset. I know there were other vacation homes nearby, but from where I was sitting, it seemed like we had the entire lake and forest to ourselves.

The strings tuned up, and Dan brought us in on the expressive, winding melody of the opening theme of the quartet. The first movement is, in turn, beautiful and triumphant. This is one of the true masterpieces in the chamber music repertoire. The entire quartet is brilliant, both in terms of compositional architecture and emotional integrity, but my favorite part is the slow movement. It has a gorgeous opening melody that evolves into an uplifting march. For me, it's much more than a typical military march. It's an inexorable march of one's soul toward redemption, similar to the Turkish march of Beethoven's ninth symphony. I felt emotionally exhausted at the end of the movement, but I had to maintain focus to have any chance of making it through the hellaciously difficult final movement. This last movement is Brahms at his best in his use of Hungarian folk idioms. When we completed the piece's final rousing cadence, the fifteen or so people who made up our little private audience all jumped to their feet, applauded, and congratulated us. We were rewarded with some nice finger foods, wine, and beer.

I was talking with Beth while downing a glass of Cabernet when I overheard my mom talking to Sarah.

"What a beautiful deck you have! I just love it here!"

Sarah responded, "Is that my deck?"

There was an awkward silence, and my mom changed the subject to the Brahms. I had heard that Sarah suffered from dementia, and that it was becoming a struggle for Carl to take care of her, but I hadn't realized how severe her condition really was until now. Sarah and Carl's home was filled with beautiful artifacts from the Far East and Africa. They had a framed letter of gratitude from the Secretary of State. They have this wonderful home and they fill their lives with some of the greatest music mankind has ever created. But age is now taking its toll. This concert, which I hope to remember for years to come, might possibly be completely forgotten by Sarah tomorrow.

It's five-thirty in the morning when I finally stumble through the front door of our tiny Lexington house. Finally, no more fog banks to drive through. Mary's asleep on the living room couch, trying to wait up for me. I wake her with a kiss, and we manage to make it down the hall toward our bed. Before turning in, I take a quick look at our beautiful babies sleeping peacefully in their cribs, Nicole and Gabrielle. Mary trying to wait up for my return. The debut of my orchestra piece. A supportive Dad and Mom who've been there for me. Hosanna growing and maturing. The serene beauty of New England. The friendship of Tom and the wonderful festival musicians. And Brahms's g-minor piano quartet performed "On Golden Pond." Quite a list of things to live for. As I gratefully climb into bed, I promise myself that I won't forget this feeling of peace.

THE SENSATIONS

Is this going to be my career? Keyboard player for the Sensations? I'm in Lexington, Kentucky, on my way home at nearly two in the morning and I'm exhausted. After teaching a section of class piano earlier today, I practiced for a few hours, played my Brahms Sonata in studio class, went for a swim at the campus pool, grabbed a sub, and eventually drove myself and my keyboard to the downtown Lexington Radisson for a four-hour Sensations gig.

When the Bistro closed, I spent nearly a year doing solos and duos at the Gratz Park Inn. When that dried up, I joined one of central Kentucky's most successful party bands. I needed the work and I'd run out of nice restaurants and hotels. That list was pretty short. The Sensations play a combination of classic Motown, current Top 40, and some standards. The band sounds pretty good when playing anything with a rock backbeat, but when it comes to the standards, well, I'd just prefer to stick with Motown.

Even though "Word Up," "Sugar Pie, Honeybunch," and "Brick House" aren't my favorites, it's not the music that's primarily the problem with this group. It's the leader. When I joined the group, I was warned he would try to underpay and generally take advantage of me, and the warning was justified. One time, our fearless leader told a brilliant drummer friend of mine that he wouldn't pay him a hundred to play a gig that was a three-hour drive away because "You're not worth a hundred dollars."

I've had more than one conversation with him that became unpleasant. One time, he whined to the band that he was paying us too much. I offered to compare tax returns if he felt we were being overpaid. He instantly changed the subject. A few of the guys in the band are talented, but the effort it takes to be constantly vigilant to defend against our shady leader's efforts to cheat us takes away any fun I might have out of the gigs. Anyway, my hearing is not what it used to be, and this band is much too loud. A mind numbing, bleeding eardrum kind of loud.

This Radisson gig was intended as a showcase for the Sensations to attract more lucrative private parties. In this band, I stand up to play the keyboard and dance around a bit as I play. Get "in character." I do move a little when I feel the spirit, but by now, I've accepted the fact that dancing is definitely not my strong suit. I suppose I'm not much more awkward looking than our plump front line, made up of our male vocalist and trumpet player (the fearless leader). Next to them, the female singer wears a short, tight skirt which crosses the line from cute to slutty, but she does the little girl Madonna kind of voice pretty well for what this music requires. The drummer is a good guy with a dry sense of humor who lays down mean funk and rock grooves, and he's the main reason the band's so loud. Just don't ask him to swing. Our sax player is also a nice guy who plays well and has a day job as an insurance salesman. He told me once that he goes to church regularly, just in case there really is a God. He plays it safe, so I guess it's no coincidence that he sells insurance. Dave, the guitar player, is my best friend in the band. He's got a great sense of humor that makes our breaks go by quicker, and he's the only other jazzer in the group. We talk a lot about Pat Metheny, Herbie Hancock, and Miles Davis. He also writes some really nice tunes.

Tonight, our crowd is what you'd expect in a Radisson lounge in downtown Lexington, a fair number of college students mixed with a number of youngish hotel guests. I'm sure they're in town for tomorrow's matinee University of Kentucky basketball game. It's across the street at Rupp Arena. UK games are by far the biggest regional draw in central Kentucky.

As we start the gig tonight, I think about a relatively new trend in the bar/nightclub scene. Multiple TV sets strategically placed around the room. They don't turn them off, even when we're playing. I'm sure that no disrespect to the music and musicians is intended. My guess is they're left on to give the people in the bar who aren't having any luck with the pick-up scene or the dance floor something to do.

Tonight I notice that a movie about the Vietnam War is playing. Now there's something to party to. We're playing Kool and the Gang's "Celebration" and the dance floor is full of drunken, sweating, and screaming twenty-somethings, doing something that approximates a conga line. I glance across the room at one of the TVs. A US soldier has just shot and killed a woman, and he's being talked out of blowing away her newborn baby. I think it's *Platoon*. But that's just background for the partying in the Lexington Radisson. The foreground is us, The Sensations, keeping the dance floor full and the place jumping with one of those carefree 80s party nights.

Now I'm finally on my way home from the Radisson. I'll be up early tomorrow with my beautiful baby girls because Mary needs to go to the university in the morning to both teach and take a class. As I come to a traffic light, I notice a sedan in the left turn lane with a young woman hanging her head out the window. It doesn't look promising, so I move to the right and stay back. She begins throwing up, and I can hear the sound effects even from back here. I intentionally look away. I've seen this before, and I wouldn't mind missing it this time. Another car passes me in the middle lane and pulls up next to the hurling girl. Two college guys stick their heads out the window and start to cheer her on. "Go, Go, Go!" I try even harder not to look and listen. The light turns green, and I speed through the intersection, telling myself, "I will not be doing this when I'm sixty! I will not be doing this when I'm fifty! I hope and pray I won't be doing this when I'm forty!"

CODA

It's four months after the Sensations' Radisson gig. I'm still with the band, and I also play a few nights a week at a Hilton Hotel. The piano is probably the worst-maintained piano on the planet. I guess that's to be expected when the instrument is positioned directly in front of a faux waterfall where it constantly absorbs moisture.

Right now, I'm checking my university mailbox. As a teaching assistant, I don't get paid a lot, but at least I get my own mailbox. I find a note from my wonderful teacher and friend, Lucien Stark. "Bob, I saw in the Musicians' Union paper that there's an opening in the 'President's Own' Marine Band," he writes. "You might want to take the audition. I know that ordinarily you probably wouldn't consider the military, but this is a great job. No boot camp. You play at the White House a few times a week, sometimes for the Marine Corps commandant and also for high quality classical concerts. I have a former student in the band. Why don't you give him a call?"

Let me see, concerts and gigs at the White House or a career with the Sensations? Tough call.

JOINING THE CORPS

We get a wake-up call at four in the morning. We roll out of bed, throw on our clothes and stumble down to a waiting bus in front of the Days Inn. The US government has been kind enough to spring for a room for us as a last-day-as-a-civilian gift. My roommate is ten years younger than me, and this is the second time he's joining the Army. He did two years, got out to work as a mechanic, lasted six months, and then lost his job. He's from rural Indiana, has a high school diploma, and going back into the Army is his best option. I'm here, in southern Indiana on a travel day for *Cats*. I'm playing second keyboard. I'm taking a pay cut of about forty thousand a year to join the Marine Band—at four in the morning. I'm on this bus with mostly eighteen year olds who are getting ready to sign on to fight the Gulf War. I'm beginning to question my judgment.

I'm taking this job so I can get to see my two-and-three-year-old daughters grow up and also spend at least some time with my wife. I'm tired of being on the road. As I get on the bus, I realize it isn't one of those luxury Greyhounds I've been riding recently with the *Cats* touring company. This bus seems to press metal posts and panels into your flesh, no matter what angle you're sitting at.

We arrive at the MEPS center. This is my first exposure to the military's fondness for acronyms. I have no clue what MEPS stands for, but I do know I'll be questioned, tested, examined, poked and prodded by doctors, and eventually asked to swear the oath of allegiance that will commit me to being a marine for the next four years. I'm a vegetarian, a pacifist, a borderline hippie, and a third generation American liberal of eastern European Jewish descent. Is something wrong with this picture?

We shuffle off the bus and into a foul-smelling cafeteria. Even the odor of the brewing coffee is somehow nauseating. Maybe that's just because it's 0500 hours. The fried eggs are practically liquid and are gushing across the plates of most of the recruits, eventually merging with the bacon grease to form one hell of an unappetizing puddle. I stick with coffee, toast, and a cup of instant orange juice. I'm guessing this breakfast would probably be considered a luxury, if we were at boot camp. We're eventually herded into a waiting area with a grumpy looking staff sergeant sitting behind a desk. He tells us to sit and that we'll be called individually for our interviews. At 0700, when no names have been called yet, I begin to understand that this entire day is going to be a "Let's-show-'em-who's-boss" day. How surprising that they're not trying to make things convenient or comfortable for me.

The staff sergeant loudly announces that he's going to give all of us Marine Corps recruits something to watch while we're waiting for our interviews. He slips a video into the VCR. I'm tired, but I decide to try to stay awake and watch, thinking maybe I'll learn a little bit about the Marine Corps while I'm waiting. It's *Full Metal Jacket*. I drift off to sleep while a brutal drill sergeant is berating and humiliating his new recruits, which makes me glad the Marine Band doesn't require boot camp. I wake up to the sounds of gunfire on the screen. Apparently, one of the would-be marines has decided to blow away the drill sergeant and then eat his own gun. What a great first impression.

Finally, at around 0915, I'm called in for my interview. I've been awake for nearly half a day, and the process is just beginning. The interviewer is the first friendly person I've met today. He asks about my family, and really seems to focus on my step-grandfather, George, a wonderful old British gentleman who spent years working for an English oil company. My best guess is that they're concerned about allowing anyone into the US military who has a familial relationship with a foreign national. George is nearly eighty years old and is starting to have problems remembering where he left his keys and sunglasses, so I seriously doubt that he could remember any of the fifteen- or twenty-digit secret codes he would need to be an effective spy.

Then the interviewer gets to the really important stuff. "Have you ever been arrested?" No. "Have you ever been a member of the communist party?" No. "Have you ever smoked marijuana?" No. "Have you ever been a member of any organization that advocates the overthrow of the US government?" No. "Have you ever been treated for any psychological conditions diagnosed by a mental health professional?" No.

Suddenly, he spins toward me on his ergonomic chair and in one motion, brings his face a matter of inches from mine and says loudly, "Are you sure you've never even tried marijuana, not even in college?"

I calmly answer, "Yes." I guess he thinks my answer is unlikely coming from a musician who went to college in the late 70s. I let him think so.

Fortunately, I pass my interview and my new-found friend, staff sergeant interviewer, tells me where to go to take the ASVAB test. Seemingly another incomprehensible acronym, but I soon figure out that this is the military's version of an IQ test. The test proctor also turns out to be unpleasant, a thin and brusque older man. He acts as if he must have drunk the same sour coffee and runny eggs that we did. He talks to us all as if we must have tremendously limited language skills. His attitude is pretty consistent with the mood of the day.

We're asked to fill in a block on the PERSONAL INFORMATION section of the test, indicating whether we're left- or right-handed. I make the serious mistake of asking, "What if we're ambidextrous?" After all, I dribble with the left and shoot with the right. Also, my piano teachers have unanimously thought more highly of my left hand than my right. The unhappy proctor gives me a disdainful look and says: "There's always got to be one idiot who asks that question." He pauses a moment for dramatic effect, then continues, saying, "Whatever hand you write with!"

The military says I'm right-handed, so it must be true. I spend the next few hours taking the ASVAB test, and the most challenging part is trying to stay awake. It's kind of a simplified version of the SAT, but there's one section that I have some fun with that seems to be designed to determine my ability to decipher codes. I imagine myself sitting in an isolated station somewhere north of the Arctic Circle, breaking incredibly complex codes and single-handedly saving western civilization. When the test is done, I return to reality, and they send me to the part of today's activities I'm looking forward to the most—the medical exam.

Now I'm standing in line with a group of new recruits. We're all in our underwear. We've already donated both blood and urine. I'm getting my first indication that my bodily fluids no longer belong to me. One by one, we're asked to turn our heads and cough while the unfortunate doctor gets to check numerous pairs of testicles. I'm assuming that mine passed muster as I'm brought into an examination room for a private check-up and interview. The doctor seems very interested in the knee surgery I had ten years ago, and I realize the US government doesn't want to end up paying for my pre-existing healthcare issues for the rest of my life.

The doctor looks a bit puzzled and asks me, "No boot camp? Joining the Marine Corps at age thirty-three?"

I explain that I'm joining the "President's Own" and that basic training isn't required. I then push my chest out a bit and tell him, "I exercise regularly, swimming or running about five times a week."

He looks at me, shakes his head, and says, "You'd never make it through basic." That's pretty deflating. I guess he can tell I'm really disappointed (I really thought I could have made it to infantry if I wanted) because he tells me that Marine Corps basic training is designed for eighteen-year-old bodies, not thirty-three. "Even twenty-five year olds have a hard time making it through," he says. Somehow I don't find a lot of comfort in that. At least he gives my physical his stamp of approval.

I find myself back with the interviewer from this morning. He's very impressed because he has the results of my ASVAB test and he tells me that I'm "highly qualified to do any job that the Marine Corps has to offer!"

"Even mechanical engineering?" I ask. I've become convinced after years of failure with my attempts to fix even the simplest things on my own cars, that engineering is a lifelong shortcoming of mine.

"Even mechanical engineering and code reading," he says. Hmm...let me think. I decide to stay with music. As I said, no boot camp.

My last stop on the day's odyssey is a meeting with an army major who will have me sign documents and swear the oath of allegiance which will make me a marine for the next four years. After signing and dating my enlistment document (probably the seventeenth signature today), the major tells me that he'll give me a head start on military etiquette, and I receive instructions on how to come to attention and render a hand salute. I can already tell I'm not going to be very good at this.

The major then tells me to repeat after him: "I, Robert Boguslaw, do solemnly swear to protect and defend the Constitution of the United States against all enemies foreign and domestic, and to obey orders."

I'm thinking maybe I won't go through with this. I'll be taking a 65 percent pay cut. I'll be giving up my freedom to come and go as I please for at least four years. I'm feeling pretty dehumanized by this whole process.

The major comes to, "So help me God."

I pause, and in a flash, my wife and two small children come into both my mind and heart. I think about the prospect of playing *Cats* eight times a week for the foreseeable future. "So help me God," I repeat.

"Welcome to the Marine Corps," says the major. I'm committed. I'm a marine.

PART II

THE WHITE HOUSE YEARS

PRESIDENTS BUSH AND GORBACHEV

It's the summer of 1991, and I'm heading over to the White House by myself to play for the first time in the private quarters of the president of the United States. The guest of honor is Mikhail Gorbachev. He's no longer president of the Soviet Union, but he's currently on a lecture tour, discussing the dissolution of the Soviet Bloc and its foreign policy implications for the future of world peace.

I'm pretty uptight as I sit in the White House Usher's Office, waiting to be escorted upstairs. Once I pass through security, I have freedom to move through the house, with the notable exceptions of the private residence upstairs and the West Wing. A wonderful older gentleman in a tuxedo and a white tie has the job of taking the first family and their guests up and down the elevator. His name is Mr. Wilson, and he's been working at the White House since the Johnson Administration. As I wait in his office, Head Usher Gary Walters answers a phone call, says thank you, and then turns and tells me they're ready for me upstairs.

Mr. Wilson and I head for the elevator and, as we come to the second floor, I hear voices through the door. The elevator opens, and there I see President and Mrs. Bush talking with Kathy Fenton, the assistant social secretary. The president immediately comes over to me and shakes my hand, saying, "Thanks for coming, Marine."

They're all very nice and welcoming, but I certainly don't feel at my most comfortable. Kathy offers to show me to the piano. I don't really need an introduction to the piano, but I take her up on her offer, grateful she's giving me something to do during my short wait for Mr. Gorbachev's arrival. I notice that Kathy's hair is perfect. Her dress is perfect. Her makeup is perfect. All this perfection doesn't make me feel any more comfortable. She shows me to the instrument, and I immediately seek my personal musical sanctuary, sitting down and playing songs from Guys and Dolls, Oklahoma, and My Fair Lady.

Part of my audition for the Marine Band consisted of being asked to simulate a performance of cocktail piano music at the White House with the president in close proximity; the idea was to create a quiet atmosphere of understated elegance. When I was younger, I used to look down on this kind of playing, but as I've grown a bit older, I've come to the conclusion that there really is an art to doing this well. It's probably a good thing that I now take it seriously because Presidents Bush and Gorbachev are walking toward me. They stop and stand in the well of the piano, close enough that I could reach over the instrument and touch them with my right hand. There are a lot of conversations going on right now in the Yellow Oval Room, though I can't quite make out what they're saying, but I hear words like perestroika, disarmament, détente, and references to Germany, Poland, and Czechoslovakia. The Berlin Wall was recently demolished. It occurs to me that I'm sitting very close to the two world leaders who recently presided over the end of the Cold War.

I'm remembering air-raid drills where we learned to duck under our desks to escape nuclear winds in 1963. But the threat of nuclear annihilation I had grown up with is seemingly over because of the leadership of these two men who are talking casually only four feet away from me. After about forty minutes of ridiculously soft piano music and cocktails, the guests drift toward the elevator and go back down with Mr. Wilson.

Kathy Fenton comes over with her perfect smile and says, "Well, I guess we're all done for this evening. Thanks so much. I'm sure we'll be seeing you again soon."

As Mr. Wilson shepherds me back down the elevator, I'm thinking, another twenty years of this might not be so bad. Even if I do have to get weekly haircuts and learn the proper uniform ironing technique.

Bob with President George H. W. Bush

THE MEDAL OF FREEDOM

The Medal of Freedom has to be a lot of fun for the president. Most of the national awards and medal presentations considered to be important enough to take place at the White House are not selected directly by the man in charge. One exception is the Medal of Freedom. This one is completely and totally at the president's discretion. He can give it to a war hero, a distinguished public servant, his favorite movie star, or even his best friend. Today, President Bush is giving this medal to his predecessor, the great communicator, Ronald Reagan. We're only two days away from the inauguration of Bill Clinton, and I'm certain that today's festivities are basically going to be one last big celebration of the conservative Republican domination of American politics during the '80s and early '90s.

Unfortunately, I'm running late. I'm pretty new with the Marine Band, but when I first arrived at Marine Barracks Washington, DC, I learned quickly that the three most important keys to having a long and successful career with the "President's Own" were playing well, not exceeding the weight standards, and never, ever being late, especially when it involved the White House. I could write an entire chapter on DC traffic, as it has unfortunately become a prominent part of my life, but suffice it to say that this morning I took three alternate routes to try to escape the congested areas...and each one got progressively worse. That's why I'm running up to the front gate of the barracks just as Colonel Bourgeois is coming out to get on the bus for the White House. He looks at me, gives a slight frown, and tells me that he'll hold the bus for me. At least I'm not going to miss the job. I run to the locker room, throw on my uniform (without even pressing it!), then run back down to the bus, knowing the entire time that tomorrow I'll be "counseled" on punctuality. Oh, well. I knew what the deal was when I swore the oath.

After arriving and clearing security, we're set up with the orchestra in the Grand Foyer of the White House. We know this event is a big deal because they've asked for the orchestra. For lesser events, we usually send a pianist, a small jazz group, or a chamber ensemble consisting of strings with piano. On these high-profile jobs, I have some parts to play in the orchestra book, mostly pops numbers, but I also give the orchestra breaks by playing either jazz trios with the bass player and drummer or doing solo piano, mostly classical. The orchestra needs these breaks, as repetitive motion injuries among musicians are pretty common. Especially when required to play non-stop for three or four hours. Today, I'm playing a lot of Bach, Preludes and Fugues from the Well-Tempered Clavier and select movements from his first partita.

As I'm halfway through the "Prelude in D Major" from the second book of the Well-Tempered Clavier, I become aware that someone is standing behind me and looking over my shoulder. Whoever it is has walked around to the back of the orchestra to watch what I'm doing. I finish the prelude and turn around to find William F. Buckley, Jr. standing behind me in his celebrated pose, his nose a bit in the air and his face cupped by his left hand under his chin. "A lovely interpretation. Very nice energy. Have you ever played that one on the harpsichord?" he asks. At this point, the orchestra is going into Mozart's Symphony No. 26, which doesn't require piano, so I stand and begin to speak with him about performance practice with regard to J.S. Bach's keyboard works.

I remember William F. Buckley, Jr. as the foremost spokesman and advocate of the conservative philosophy of his generation. As a child, I would watch him on TV debating foreign and domestic policies with the best that the Democrats could find to put up against him. Whether or not I agreed with him, I always had the impression that he was very, very smart. But now, I'm wondering why he knows so much about Bach and Baroque performance practice. After we discuss the various approaches to performing the arpeggiated chords in Bach's "Chromatic Fantasy and Fugue," I'm convinced he must be a musician, so I ask him if he plays. It turns out that not only does he play, but he has an all-Bach harpsichord recital coming up next week in Palm Beach, Florida. I guess he must take his hobby pretty seriously. After our discussion, he tells me he'd enjoy hearing more Bach or Scarlatti. We shake hands and he leaves to go and join the scores of other prominent Republicans who have the run of the White House for just a few more days.

Besides Presidents Reagan and Bush, I also see George Shultz, Alexander Haig, Donald Regan, and James Baker, just to name a few. Eventually, as the event winds down, both presidents and their wives come over to the orchestra and warmly shake hands with Colonel Bourgeois, President Reagan greeting him as an old friend. They all give us a smile and a wave of thanks and recog-nition. When the guests are nearly gone, one of President Bush's aides walks by me and confidently says, "See you guys in four years." We'll see.

THE EMPEROR'S
STATE DINNER

In the past three years, I've played a number of state dinners. Black-tie for the men and competitive evening gowns for the women. Tonight, the Clintons are doing a receiving line in the house before they proceed outdoors to a tent. It's a "tent" in name only. This tent is more lavish than a typical Ritz-Carlton hotel. President Clinton has scaled back his tendency to converse with everyone in the receiving line, but it's still a lengthy process and runs a bit late. That's routine, but the thing that makes this particular dinner extra special for me is that the guests of honor are Emperor Akihito and Empress Michiko of Japan. They're special, not necessarily because of their royal bloodlines, but because my wife, Mary, is half Japanese and was born in Tokyo at a US military hospital. She still has aunts, uncles, and a grandmother living in Japan who are really excited that a relative will be performing for their emperor and empress. Mary's mom, Virginia, lives in Hampton, VA, and still keeps treasured mementos of her childhood and youth in Japan. She also has photos of her grandfather in a Japanese military uniform from the 1880s and wood-block prints he made that are quite beautiful. She has a chest made in Japan that I think she might have used to transport her personal belongings when she first came to the US in the 1950s with her three small daughters. At the time, she was a relatively new wife of an Army Medical Corpsman, and possessed almost no knowledge of American culture and the English language.

But tonight, I have with me one of her most prized family possessions: an original score of Variations on Urashimataro, a large-scale piano work written by my grandfather-in-law, Yuzuri Ike. It's penned in his own hand. My mother-in-law passed it on to me some ten years ago, probably in the hope that I might someday do a performance of it. Today's the day.

Mary has always described her grandfather as a "Renaissance man." He was probably one of the first Japanese nationals to ever go to Europe and study western classical music, sometime in the early twentieth century. Mary recalls him being an accomplished pianist, violinist, violist, and cellist. He taught all those instruments, did some high level conducting, and composed numerous film scores and symphonic works. My impression is that he made most of his living from scoring films and teaching. In his spare time, he became an accomplished downhill skier, sewed his own clothing, and built radios, so I guess "Renaissance man" is a good title for him.

But right now, I'm mostly concerned with grandfather-in-law's Variations. This piece is beautifully crafted, structured very much like a Brahms or Beethoven variation set. It starts with a simple folk melody accompanied by triadic harmonies. Each variation becomes progressively more complex and harmonically adventurous, though the phrase structure remains constant. It also gets progressively more difficult to play. I start when I see the president, first lady, emperor and empress come down the grand staircase and proceed to the East Room to begin their receiving line.

Because solo piano playing is used to give the Marine Chamber Orchestra a break during these long formal events, I've been instructed not to do any selections longer than five or six minutes. I play only the theme and first five variations of Urashimataro. I get a little more nervous than usual, maybe a hint of Grandfather's spirit hovering nearby, listening and watching over my shoulder. I breathe an emotional sigh of relief as I finish, but I don't think anyone really noticed anything unusual in my playing of the Variations. But then, I see a few Japanese diplomats who give brief applause and a small bow, and I find myself really hoping that Grandfather's pleased. I know that I am.

CODA

Mary just received a letter from her Aunt Yoko in Tokyo. Yoko was so excited because she had written to the Empress Michiko about how her nephew had played a piano work a few months ago written by her father, a prominent Japanese composer, at the US-Japan State Dinner. It's highly unusual for Japanese royalty to respond to communications from the citizenry, but Yoko had received a call from the empress's personal assistant to tell her that Michiko remembered having heard the piece, and that she recalled how lovely it was. Grandmother-in-law and aunts were all very, very happy. Actually, I'll never know whether the empress ever truly took notice of Grandfather-in-law's piece, but it sure meant an awful lot to my mother-in-law and my extended family in Japan that she said she did.

We never got to meet, but I have no doubt that Grandfather-in-law and I made a strong familial musical connection, even though we're separated by half a world and two generations.

THE ALIBI CLUB

It's a chilly November evening, and I'm walking west on I Street in down-town DC looking for the Alibi Club. I'm sure I must have passed it more than once, since this is my third time down this block. I expect to see signs or flags or some sort of doorman like you find in front of Washington's other prestigious private clubs. I eventually give up on trying to find any distin-guishing markings and instead, I start looking at the numbers. I finally locate it and discover I must have missed it because there's no sign in front and its appearance is similar to any other row home on the block. I knock, and a quiet, elderly butler comes to the door and ushers me in, telling me to wait in a smallish, dimly lit dining area with a slightly claustrophobic feel to it. I figure this place probably dates back to the nineteenth century because of the crown moldings and wooden staircases. The walls are covered with paintings of important and distinguished-looking older men. Some of them are black and white sketches, almost cartoon-like. Many of them definitely go back to the jazz age and even earlier.

I got called for this gig yesterday by a private contractor. He told me I'd be playing for a small group of senators and their wives as a celebration of tomorrow's midterm election. Turns out that I don't feel much like partying as the Republicans' "Contract for America" under Newt Gingrich was val-idated today at polling stations across the country. Democrats like to call it the "Contract on America," but mocking the conservative platform of Gin-grich, DeLay, Thurmond, and Helms does them absolutely no good today. Congressional liberals were subjected to a plain and simple old fashioned ass-whipping. I do find it a bit interesting that the Republicans were so confident of their victory yesterday that they hired a piano player for tonight's celebration before the votes were counted.

I'm starting to become restless and look at my watch when someone else arrives at the front door. In walks the US Senate minority whip, Alan Simpson, the senior senator from Wyoming. "Nice to see you," he says in a western drawl, seemingly recognizing me. I've seen him a number of times at the White House, serving under both Presidents Bush and Clinton, but I don't think we've ever spoken.

He shakes my hand and asks, "Have you ever been to the Alibi Club before, Marine?"

Figuring he must remember me from the White House, I tell him, "No. I've never had the privilege." He looks at his watch and says, "Well, we've got a few minutes before everyone else gets here, so let me take you on a little tour."

I don't object, and he does seem to be proud of the place. The senator points to paintings and drawings of John Foster Dulles, Henry Roosevelt, and George Marshall, among other prominent Supreme Court justices, cabinet secretaries, and members of the senate. He seems to know something about every former member of the club. I'm not surprised, as he has a well-deserved reputation for possessing one of the sharpest minds in Washington. I believe I've read that he never lost a case while practicing law in Wyoming. He comes to a portrait of Prescott Bush, and I ask him if he's any relation to our last president, George H.W. Bush. "Yeah, that's his dad," he tells me. Turning to me with a bit of a mischievous smile, he says, "You know, George is a club member, too. It's an all-male club, and he hesitated joining because of all this political correctness, but then he just said 'fuck it, I wanna be a member like my dad.'" As he chuckles a bit, there's a knock on the front door and I thank the senator for the tour. "Glad you enjoyed it," he says and goes off to celebrate with his Republican colleagues.

I start playing older show tunes and some country music on an old upright piano as the senators come in and take their seats for dinner. Maybe they had to get special permission from the club, but their wives are with them tonight. I hope the nineteenth century club founders aren't too appalled as they watch these goings on from Republican Heaven.

What's more shocking to me is that one of the guests is a prominent Democrat, Senator Bill Bradley from New Jersey. Not only is he here, but he seems to be really enjoying the food, the wine, and the conversation. On the one hand, I feel disappointed that he's partying with the "other side" on this ever-so-terrible night to be a Democrat. The press would have us believe that all the Dems are at home crying in their beers. But on further consideration, I decide this is probably a good thing. Maybe if some of these congressmen from opposing parties actually like each other, there might at least be a chance they'll be able to get something done. Here in DC in November of '94 that'd be pretty novel. I'll just hold onto hope that sometime in the near future, the two parties will start working together with the best interests of our children in mind.

CHICAGO KARMA, PART 1

I'm in Chicago for a tuba euphonium conference at Northwestern University. That's right. People come from all over the world to immerse themselves in a long weekend of low-brass camaraderie. Discussions of mouthpieces, new types of valve oil, and new tuba quartet arrangements, day and night. I'm here to accompany Mike, our principal Marine Band euphonist. I wrote "Fantasy for Euphonium and Piano" specifically for this performance in the hope I might be able to get my first classical composition published.

I have three very close old friends whom I like to visit in Chicago whenever I get the chance. Right now, I'm watching my old friend Bob play with a really fine jazz quartet. It's an outdoor gig in June, and they're playing on the patio of a very large and impressive office building that looks out over the Chicago River. I can see all the way to Lake Michigan—pretty nice.

Bob played drums with me at The Bistro in Kentucky for the first year of that gig. He and his wife were really nice to our family when we were new in town. He then moved to the big city to see how he could do in the jazz scene, and it's turned out quite well for him. He teaches at DePaul University, plays in one of the region's most successful big bands, and has done all kinds of high profile club dates and shows. I'm happy for him because he's one of the kindest people I know. Not a mean bone in his body. I always have to chuckle a bit when I think about Bob. He's from Owensboro, Kentucky, and has a pronounced southern accent. Yet, when he's behind the drum set, if you close your eyes, you'd swear you're listening to Elvin Jones or Tony Williams, two of jazz drumming's most formidable Afro-centric virtuosos.

Right now, Bob's quartet is finishing their first set with an up-tempo blues, and the tenor sax player is tearing it up. I feel the tiniest bit nervous when I look at him because I know this guy. His name is Marc Colby, and I unsuccessfully auditioned for his group around fifteen years ago in Ft. Lauderdale. Small world. At the time, Marc was well known in both South Florida and Chicago and had a number of pretty successful records on the market. It was commercial jazz, but it was definitely composed and performed with lots of integrity. At the time I played the audition, I had recently graduated from the University of Miami and had already been in and out of a number of gigs. I really wanted the job. So even though it's been years, seeing and hearing Marc play causes my stomach to flip a little. When they finish the blues they were playing, Bob comes over and gives me a hug. It's been at least three years since we've seen each other.

"How's the family?" "What kind of gigs you been playing?" "You getting good students these days?" These are the typical questions we ask each other.

When it's time to play again, Marc comes up to us to tell Bob the break's over. Bob introduces me to Marc, tells him I'm an old friend, that I play in the Marine Band, and asks him if I can sit in. I decide not to tell Marc about our having met fifteen years ago. He doesn't recognize me (maybe because of my considerably smaller amount of hair), and I might not have recognized him if I had passed him on the street. No need to prejudice him.

Marc says, "Sure, we'd love to have you sit in."

They go back and the quartet cooks hard on a couple of tunes. Then they invite me to come up. Observing sit-in etiquette, they ask me what I want to play. I suggest the standard, "I'll Remember April." I have a preference for tunes like this that alternate between Latin and swing sections. It allows the soloist to build a musical flow with a kind of built-in variety that some standards don't have. I kick it off with a vamp, then I solo on for a bit. When

Bob comes in behind me with the bass player, it's just like old times. Marc eventually comes in with the melody and follows it with a wonderfully crafted solo. I follow him, and although my solo isn't as noteworthy, I feel that it's respectable. At the end of the song, they ask if I'd like to play another. I say, "Sure," and we play one of Jobim's classic bossa novas. I wouldn't mind playing more, but that'd be poor sit-in etiquette, so I take a seat in the audience and listen to the end of the set. When they're done Bob and Marc both approach me.

"Nice job. Great to play with you again," says Bob. "Man, you sound great!" says Marc.

I look at him and smile and say, "I wish you'd felt that way fifteen years ago."

Marc looks at me with a puzzled expression on his face.

"I auditioned for your group in Lauderdale in 1980 when you needed a keyboard player."

Marc makes an effort to pretend that he remembers me, but I'm pretty sure he doesn't. I don't blame him. My audition years ago wasn't good enough to get me the gig, but it wasn't bad enough to go down as a "most awkward moment in music" story. Anyway, Marc thinks about it for a second, laughs, and tells me that he's sorry, that he made a mistake, and that he should've given me the gig.

As I get back into my rental car to head for my hotel in Evanston, I'm thinking that I'm really glad I decided to go directly from the airport to visit my old friend, rather than heading immediately for low-brass purgatory at Northwestern. I'm also thinking that tomorrow's the day of our concert and the debut of the piece I wrote. I'm becoming convinced my Chicago karma's pretty good.

CHICAGO KARMA, PART 2

I'm sitting in the Green Mill with a beer, listening to a great local straight ahead jazz quartet. The room is dimly lit, smoky, and smells of beer. There's a pretty good-sized audience and they're all quietly attentive as the tunes unfold. This kind of audience is one of the main things that I love about Chicago. Brad, a trumpet player I've been hearing about for years, is the leader and my friend Bob is the drummer. I'm here in town with the Marine Band for the huge annual Midwest Band Conference. I'm glad to have a free evening, so I can catch up with Bob and get a break from three solid days of immersion in band music and band directors.

It's been two and a half years since I last saw Bob. I sat in with him back then while in town for the national tuba/euphonium conference, and I'm hoping that maybe I'll get the chance to sit in and play with him again. We have really good chemistry. The piano player is off-the-charts burnin', and I'm thinking that maybe I shouldn't play if I have to follow him. He's also five or ten years younger than me. While checking out his McCoy Tyner caliber solo, I notice a familiar looking figure come in and sit at the other end of the bar out of the corner of my eye. He's got a saxophone case and a trumpet case with him. It's Ira Sullivan.

For my money, Ira's the Mozart of jazz. I've seen him trade eights and fours with Red Rodney (one of the world's great bebop trumpet players) and sound every bit as creative and inventive. Then, on the same tune, he put down the trumpet, picked up the alto sax, and sounded just like Charlie Parker. I don't make the comparison to Mozart lightly. Mozart was a natural genius of musical composition. Ira's a natural genius of jazz. What the two of them have in common is the gift of effortlessness. Ira's been known to pick up a new instrument, sound like an amateur, but within three months' time be playing it on the bandstand with some of America's finest musicians. Nobody else does that. Ira can play pretty much any instrument used in jazz at a level equal to or higher than any of the musicians who share the stage with him. Similarly, Mozart is known to have composed an entire string quartet in his head on a carriage ride from Salzburg to Vienna, and upon his arrival, to have copied out the parts without ever putting the piece in score form. No sketches. No editing. Effortless genius, which is quite a rare gift.

I know Ira from Miami. Fifteen to twenty years ago, I would go and listen to him play at Monday night jam sessions at a Unitarian Church in South Miami. He would mentor young musicians at these sessions, and you could hear them grow from week to week as his influence took hold. I'd go and listen if I wasn't working, but it took me two years to get up the nerve to agree to sit in with him. A guitar player friend of mine encouraged me to give it a shot, and when I finally summoned up the courage and walked up onto the stage, Ira had looked at me skeptically, picked up his trumpet, and began playing fast, up-tempo lines that seemed to be changing keys every measure. Part of the training for young jazz musicians at these jam sessions was learning to use their ears to figure out what Ira was playing and where he was in the tune. Eventually, a couple other players joined in, and I finally figured out they were playing John Coltrane's "Giant Steps," one of the most difficult jazz standards ever written. I had played it before but hadn't memorized it, so rather than make a really poor first impression, I decided to do the prudent thing. I just sat there and listened.

At the end of one of Ira's typically brilliant versions of the tune, he turned to me and said, "Well, what do YOU want to play?"

"Just Friends," I said and snapped my fingers at a nice medium tempo.

I didn't play well, feeling consumed by the tension of the situation. I was convinced I didn't belong on stage with Ira, even at a casual jam session. However, I did go back and sit in a few more times at the encouragement of the guitar player and a few other friends, and things improved. Ira even complimented me a few times on my musical growth, though I certainly didn't feel that I could hear it. In 1985, I moved away from Miami and that was the last I'd seen of him. What are the odds that both of us would come into the Green Mill in Chicago on the same night to sit in? Well, pretty astronomical, even though Ira was originally from Chicago and I know he returns to visit occasionally.

That's how we ended up on stage together. During the break, Bob invited me to play, and Brad, the trumpet player, invited Ira. Once on stage, we quickly discuss what to play and come up with "It's You or No One." Ira looks over at me as if he might remember me but doesn't say anything. During my solo, he looks at me again, giving me a small nod in the affirmative. We play one more tune together, and I leave the stage to let the group's brilliant young pianist return to finish out the last set. When the set's over, Ira comes over to the bar, and I ask him if he remembers me from my Miami days.

"Yea. You're Bog," he says, surprising me. I remind him of the number of times I went home from his jam sessions at the church with my tail tucked between my legs. "Well, you've certainly come a long way from those days," Ira says.

After the gig, as Bob's driving me back to the Michigan Avenue Hilton, we talk a lot about Ira's unique genius. I thank Bob for having me sit in and tell him that I'm sure glad that I didn't give up trying to become a jazz musician all those years ago just because I couldn't keep up with Ira.

THE "CRUCIFIXION"

I'm in the pit orchestra at the Mechanic Theater in Baltimore, playing a synthesizer part for the national touring company of Jesus Christ Superstar. This is a revival of Andrew Lloyd Weber's first Broadway hit. It's a few days after Christmas, and I just got the call yesterday to do two shows, one tonight and a matinee tomorrow. There was an emergency that made it necessary for the assistant conductor to return to New York, resulting in a last minute gig for me that'll go a long way toward buying Christmas presents.

This is pretty unusual when doing pit work, not having a rehearsal or getting to watch a show. This type of gig is a completely different animal from playing piano for classical or jazz concerts. Different sounds and effects are synthesized electronically in digital "patches." I'm expected to simultaneously read and play the notes, watch the conductor out of the corner of my eye, kick a pedal with the right foot every time there's a patch change (sometimes more than three hundred in the course of a show), and use the other foot on a pedal that's connected to a digital screen with numerical readouts indicating my volume level. The numbers for these levels are indicated in the part, the road map for the music. In some of the more lengthy and involved shows, getting all this prepared can take weeks of work. Fortunately, this part's not one of the more difficult ones I've played and the show is mercifully short.

I spent enough time with the keyboard before the show to go through some of the harder passages as well as some of the quick patch changes. The conductor spoke with me briefly about where my important solos were going to occur in the part. That's about all the preparation I got.

The curtain goes up and my heart's beating fast, but I manage to keep it together for the overture, and then I calm down a bit. A lot of what I have to play doubles the brass and woodwinds. There are synthesized French horns playing with real trumpets and trombones in the pit, or synthesized bassoon rounding out a woodwind trio with real live clarinet and flute. I don't think the other pit musicians much like playing with the synthesizer, but I just do my best to blend musically with them. Next comes "Jesus Christ Superstar," the bombastic opening, followed by a first act that contains "I Don't Know How to Love Him" and "Everything's All Right" (which uses the same rhythmic vamp as Dave Brubeck's "Take Five"). At least I'm familiar with some of the songs from this show.

We get to the intermission with no major problems. I'm not paying much attention to the dialogue or plot that's coming from the stage above us because I'm too busy trying to make sure that there are no disasters caused by me, "Keyboard 2." But I am aware that as the second act has progressed, there's been more and more impassioned yelling, cursing, screaming, and even crying coming from the stage. I realize that the Pharisees have just called for Barabbas, meaning that Jesus is now marching to Calvary, carrying the cross, accompanied by a loud, hand wringing, overacting entourage.

Following one of the more difficult and turbulent sections in my part, I turn the page and find a patch change followed by sixteen of the easiest measures I've ever played. Each measure has an A quarter-note followed by three beats of rest. I could teach a monkey to play this in his first fifteen-minute lesson. But I also note that it's marked "solo." I vaguely remember seeing this when I first got the part yesterday, but I just skimmed it because it looked so easy. On the conductor's cue, I play the first quarter note. I'm shocked by the sound of the patch. It's the resounding crack of wood striking on wood. I've played quite a few percussion patches before, but never this one. The conductor cues the second measure. I play again and this time, an anguished cry comes from the stage. I do it a third time and this time the cry is louder. And then I realize: I'm hammering the nails that are pinning Christ to the cross. Lord, help me. I finish out the scene and switch to the next patch (viola and cello). The show ends without any more blasphemy emanating from Keyboard 2. Thank you, God.

On the drive home, I'm surprised by how guilty I feel about having taken part in musically nailing Christ to the cross. I know it's only a show. I know I'm just playing what's on the page. I was raised in a family of rational parents, grandparents, and siblings. But I still wonder briefly whether I'll come back tomorrow and play it again or if maybe I'll just call in sick to head off the possibility of eternal damnation. But deep down, I know that it doesn't matter whether I'm being berated on the bandstand by a sociopathic bandleader, playing "Feelings" for an incompetent cruise ship act, dragging my keyboard a quarter mile across a field in a state park in ninety-eight-degree heat while wearing a tuxedo, or nailing Jesus to the cross. I'll be back for tomorrow's show because that's what a gig warrior does.

WHITE HOUSE
PARTY BALLOONS

Every year, there are three picnics (barbecues) on the south lawn of the White House, usually on consecutive days. The congress, press, and senior staff alternately come over and party from late afternoon into the evening, usually taking advantage of Washington's best weather in mid-June. There's generally a bit more to these events than burgers, hot dogs, and picnic tables decorated in red, white, and blue. For one, the Marine Band usually provides part, if not all, of the entertainment. This year, we've got the Country Band and the Dixieland Band playing.

The Clintons' picnics differ in the sheer scale of the party. There's usually a carnival ride or two and maybe a few clowns making balloon animals for the kids, but this year there's a veritable county fair set up on the lawn. A merry-go-round, a gentle Tilt-A-Whirl, and yes, a hot-air-balloon ride. This ride doesn't have the traditional basket for three or four riders, but instead, carries one passenger up in a harness. The balloon is released by two pretty muscular attendants who also wear harnesses with heavy ropes attached to them. Once the ascendant rider is attached, they gradually let the balloon go until it reaches what I'm guessing is about one hundred and fifty feet.

Yesterday, I watched President Clinton exit the West Wing at the end of what I'm sure was a busy and long work day and head directly for the balloon tetherers. He spoke with them for a moment, then removed his sport coat. Before he could get the harness on, three lightning-fast Secret Service agents came running across the lawn and had an animated discussion with the president and the balloon carnies. At the time, I wondered if they were afraid that the wizard would fly back to Arkansas on their watch. President Clinton just put his coat back on, hung his head a bit, and walked back into the White House. It made me appreciate the fact that no one thought of me as important enough to prevent me from riding in a balloon. Then it also occurred to me that having President Clinton dangling over the White House lawn from some ropes and a large balloon would've made a really easy target for some would-be assassin. Once again, the Secret Service ruined the president's fun. But, of course, they were just doing their job.

That was for the press picnic. Today's the congressional picnic, and we're setting up the Dixieland Band. Laura, one of the assistants to the social secretary, comes over and is giving Kent and Ron (our two group leaders) a rundown of the event. Pretty typical. Our groups alternate sets, the president makes a few remarks, works a rope line, and then we alternate a few more sets. We'll get to eat a bit at the end after the guests have departed. While Laura's going over all this, she notices a few of us are intently watching the balloon men set up. She kindly comes over and says, "It's still forty-five minutes until we open the gates. If any of you want to try out the balloon ride, I'm sure they'll let you."

I say, "Thanks, Laura, but I think I'll skip it because of the uniform."

"Suit yourself," she says.

We're programmed to think of our uniforms as something sacred, to always consider how dignified and distinguished we look. But then I reconsider and say to myself, the hell with it! I'm not turning down a once in a lifetime chance to do a balloon ride over the White House lawn.

Three of us feel that way, so we go over to the tether attendants and ask for a ride. They're happy to oblige. They harness me, let out the ropes, and as I'm ascending and looking down at my spotless Corfam shoes at the end of legs dangling underneath my harness, I think about the possible headlines if the balloon guy's ropes happen to break: "Marine Band Pianist Becomes First Balloonist Musician to Escape Earth's Gravitational Pull" or "Dramatic Rescue of Marine Band Pianist by F-16s at 17,000 Feet!" Fortunately, it's just another innovative carnival ride, but I do get to see the White House roof for the first time, and I'm able to actually count the Secret Service agents stationed up there. That makes me think of another reason not to be president: Who wants to go to sleep at night knowing there are people walking on your roof with scoped sniper rifles, trying to keep you safe from probably thousands of people who'd like to kill you?

The tether attendants are highly skilled, so they provide me with a nice soft landing. As I remove the harness, Amy, our country band vocalist, shows me a photo she took of me while suspended high over the White House lawn. In uniform. Not surprisingly, I look exceptionally undignified. And this time I force myself not to care. After all, it's just a picnic.

RICK, PART 2

Mary (voice), Dave (bass), Robert (trumpet), and I just finished recording Leonard Bernstein's "Some Other Time," a beautifully reflective ballad I chose to end my first CD. It's the summer of 1997, and it took me until now, the age of forty, to feel I had enough quality original music and the right group of musicians to do this recording project. With the exception of this final tune, all the other tracks we recorded were original instrumental compositions.

Twenty years ago, when I first started playing steady gigs, I realized no one was interested in paying me a livable wage to play my eclectic original jazz tunes. At the time, I made a promise to myself that I'd keep writing, and I'd always try to do my best to keep the creative part of my spirit untainted by the drudgery of a seemingly endless conveyer belt of Donna Summers, Kenny Rodgers, and Lionel Richie tunes I played to meet my bills.

It took a long time, but my first CD is finally done. It's been a tremendously satisfying, yet nerve-racking four days for me. When the sound engineer told us we were rolling, I knew there were a limited number of takes we could do and still have any hope of completing ten tracks in four days. But now as I say goodbye to Robert and watch my old friend Dave load his bass into his car, it really sinks in how truly blessed I am to have been able to see this project through to completion. The performers on the CD are all great musicians, and a couple of them border on genius.

My brother Dave (guitar) has been staying with Mary and me for a few months while playing a show at the National Theater. Probably not his first choice for living accommodations, but his steady gig on Broadway, Sunset Boulevard, closed. He's not sure whether he and his wife, Debby, will move to DC where there seems to be more work for him, or if he'll just hold tight until he gets another road show. He played *Cats* for five years with one of the national touring companies.

Anyway, the arrangement's been good for me because the two of us were able to rehearse the guitar tracks almost daily for the last two weeks. Consequently, he sounded great on his three cuts. And obviously, it was real convenient for Mary and me to rehearse. Our musical connection can't be put into words. That leaves the drum parts, played by my old friend from Boston, Rick. My great friend, Pete, who'd been working with me ever since I arrived in Washington, contributed an intense creativity to the sax parts.

Over the years I'd see Rick once in a while when he was in DC for business. Besides continuing to play great, he went into the wholesale grocery business with his brother. We also hung out a bit together in '93 while I was in Boston, playing Symphony Hall on the Marine Band's annual fall tour. At the time, I played a few of my originals for him and told him I was close to being ready to record the CD we'd talked about years before. He immediately added brilliant drum parts that were exactly like what I'd heard in my head while composing the songs.

Now, years later, Rick and I have finally realized this project that took seventeen years to see through to completion. I'm hoping it's not the last time we do something creative together. But if it is, we at least have The Way, a CD that's finally come to life, born out of the friendship and collaboration of two young, aspiring freelance musicians in the excitement and craziness of Miami in the 70s and 80s.

CODA

It's 2006. A year ago, my second CD, Gabrielle's Hand was released on Summit Records. I had friends call me from Chicago to tell me they'd heard it on local radio stations. I received a playlist from Summit, my record company, that indicated it was getting substantial play on radio stations in California, Texas, and Ohio. I also got favorable reviews from *Jazz Times* and *Cadence* magazines, as well as *All About Jazz* online.

Three months ago, I was shopping at the huge Tower Records store in the Foggy Bottom neighborhood of DC. Every six months or so, I was in the habit of paying the store a visit to buy five to ten new CDs, trying to give myself an infusion of fresh musical ideas. Anything from classical, to jazz, to blues, to the geezer rock I still listen to occasionally in an attempt to relive my youth. I decided to look in the jazz stacks to see if there was a "Bob Boguslaw and The Way" CD bin divider. And there it was, right between "Blakey" and "Brecker," a "Bob Boguslaw" file card. I'd finally arrived! But now, a few short months later, I just read that Tower is bankrupt. The DC store's closed. My moment of fame is over. Pretty short lived. When I give it some thought, I'm sure people will still buy music electronically, but I don't have a clue how to market my music that way. A few people have told me my CDs are available on iTunes, but I don't even know what that means. I guess I better join the new millennium. I'll have to just throw myself in and sink or swim.

HAPPY BIRTHDAY, MARINE

Today's our birthday. Two hundred years as the oldest professional musical organization in the US. I think we predate the New York Philharmonic by about thirty-five years. I'd barely heard of the "President's Own" when I auditioned and joined in 1991. I've been with the Band for seven years now. We're frequently reminded by the Marine Band directors of our historic significance, probably to both encourage dedication to our mission and to boost morale. After all, we were nicknamed the "President's Own" by Thomas Jefferson. Not only that, but we also accompanied Lincoln to Gettysburg, were led for twelve years by the March King, John Philip Sousa, and have played for virtually every inauguration and state dinner in our country's history. In our spare time, we tour different regions of the US every fall and also frequently play for national and international band conferences to the great delight of the college and high school band geek communities. I have to admit I became impressed with my new gig once I learned its history.

Every five-year anniversary is celebrated by the Marine Band, which spends a large slice of its performance budget to rent the Kennedy Center Concert Hall for a gala celebration concert. At one of these concerts, I was recruited to slam on a bass drum in the upper balcony during Tchaikovsky's 1812 Overture. Colonel Bourgeois was disappointed that the fire marshal wouldn't permit us to set off actual fireworks, so numerous bass drums was the next best thing. A half dozen of us were strategically positioned around the hall to strike fear in the hearts of our enemies by mimicking cannon fire. It was a great effect as the drums (faux cannon fire) boomed throughout the hall. I couldn't help but feel sorry for the startled-looking audience members who were unfortunate enough to be sitting next to me as I brutalized that drum.

This year, we're not only doing the Kennedy Center concert with the brilliant Boston Pops conductor and composer John Williams, but we've also been invited to a party at the White House. Our families have been invited, too. This is something I was told would never happen when I first enlisted.

"You'll play a fair amount at the White House, but don't expect to ever go there as a guest," my section commander Charlie had told me.

Well, I guess he was wrong about the "never" part. Not surprisingly, we've been told we're going to have to perform at our own party on the South Lawn of the White House. There will be a lot of prominent current and former marines present, and it's really important that we make a good impression. So to a large extent, this birthday party has become another gig. I was put in charge of the combo that's been ordered to play Gershwin's "S'Wonderful."

As we're standing on the lawn waiting for President Clinton to arrive, I feel pretty pessimistic about our chances for a good performance. I wasn't thrilled about playing "S'Wonderful." It's a nice, cheerful tune, but to me, it doesn't lend itself terribly well to soloing. I suggested "Oh, Lady Be Good," and amazingly enough, the directors vetoed my idea because the title might be a reminder of the president's recent infidelities. It's 1998, and the president's notorious affair is recent history. We're playing our one song instrumentally, and when my idea was rejected, I thought, you've got to be kidding me. They weren't.

Even more troublesome to me is that we haven't rehearsed. I've been put in charge of a group where I'm outranked by everyone except for the bass player. I tried suggesting that we do a nice Dave Grusin arrangement of "S'Wonderful" to make things more interesting for us and the audience, but the senior member of the jazz combo told me that we didn't need to rehearse,

"We all know the tune."

I decided not to argue with him. We were uncertain as to whether or not we were performing a concert presentation or just doing background music. We finally found out just two days ago that people would definitely be listening, including the Marine commandant and the president. I decided to rehearse during sound check yesterday, but the White House Tech Crew was late running electricity to our mini-stage on the lawn. Sound check consisted of playing the melody to "S'Wonderful" one time through, so the engineer could make sure everything was working.

"Time's up, guys." It took all of forty-five seconds.

So today we did a short talk-through and now here I sit, preparing to lead my first Marine Band jazz combo at the White House. I feel thoroughly unprepared. Great.

Presently, we're waiting for President Clinton. It's July 11, and we're all getting a nasty sunburn. These uniforms are very hot, and the fabric doesn't breathe. I don't dare complain to the horn players and drummer as these guys deal with this practically on a daily basis in the summer months, constantly performing for outdoor ceremonies and parades. The president is more than a half-hour late, and by now, I've run through most of my repertoire of jokes to try to keep us entertained (great material like: "A skeleton walks into a bar and asks for a beer and a mop," and "What does a trombone player say when he gets to work? Would you like fries with that?"). Anyway, we're used to this with President Clinton, so no one's surprised when we pass the forty-five minute mark.

Finally, the president is announced and we get the cue to begin. We're the first of three representative Marine Band ensembles to play, and we don't sound any better than I expected. Not quite a complete embarrassment, but close. It's some consolation that the strolling string group doesn't sound much better. They're all wonderful players, but there are acoustical challenges involved in playing an outdoor performance. The performers are separated from each other by a significant distance, which doesn't lend itself to rhythmic and intonation accuracy. It's also just plain difficult for the audience to hear who are seated at picnic tables not terribly close by. The third and final ensemble is the marching band. They do the best job of the three ensembles, but even they don't sound completely at the top of their game, just because of the nature of an outdoor performance and the long, hot wait.

Thankfully, the performance part is over and the speeches begin. Our director, Colonel Foley, the Commandant of the Marine Corps, General Krulak, and President Clinton all speak. General Krulak's speech is probably the best of the three as he includes the historic significance of the Marine Band and its importance to "The Corps." President Clinton is his usual charismatic self, and he begins his remarks with a joke about how he always keeps the Marine Band waiting.

Standing at attention with a nice sunburn and sweat seeping through my uniform, I don't find it as amusing as he seems to. But his speech is good. As angry as I might be over the scandal he's immersed our government in during the past year, it's still very hard not to like him when I see him speak up close. He's definitely well-informed and articulate, and the accolades he gives the "President's Own" seem to be heartfelt and sincere.

When the speeches end, I rush over to Mary and two of my daughters, Nicole and Gabrielle. They're sitting at one of the picnic tables and I ask, "Anyone want to go shake hands with the president? He's doing a rope line!" The rope is used to keep the president from being overrun by the audience, but it allows him to shake hands and have a little personal contact. The White House ushers and Park Service employees put it in place. Nicole decides to go with me to shake hands, but Mary and Gabrielle prefer the hot dog/hamburger line to the rope line. I do wonder how much of Gabrielle's lack of interest in a presidential handshake is due to all the sordid details of President Clinton's affair that have been coming out in the press recently. I know that's why my wife isn't interested. My girls are nine and ten years old, just old enough to follow the news and understand what the president has done.

We make our way to the front of the rope line. I introduce Nicole to President Clinton, and he gives her his winning smile and says, "Well, very nice to meet you, young lady!" Then, glancing over at me, he says, "Nice job. Thanks for playing today." He has a definite knack for making you feel like you're the most important person in the world when you meet him.

Following the meet-and-greet, Nicole and I grab some food and join Mary and Gabrielle at the picnic table. My brother, Dave, and his wife, Debby, are also there as we were even allowed to invite some non-immediate family. They're all really enjoying this party, and I figure I better enjoy it, too. It's probably the last time I'll ever be here as a guest. It's really a beautiful day as long as we stay under the shade of the large old elm trees that shelter the picnic tables.

The family and I get up to make an ice cream run, and I spot a lone older man sitting at a table by himself with just a burger and a soda.

"Girls, come with me. I want you to meet someone. Now this guy's a real hero."

It's John Glenn, the first American to orbit the earth in a rocket ship. I can still remember how in 1962, when he completed his historic mission, all my five-year-old friends and I decided we were going to be just like him when we grew up. A real astronaut! Senator Glenn doesn't seem too thrilled to be taken away from his burger, but he's cordial, shaking hands with the girls, greeting my wife, and asking their names. Afterward, as we sit back down at our table, I tell David and Debby about whom we just talked to. I'm glad that our family got to visit the White House and meet a real American hero.

And I do owe a debt of gratitude to President Clinton for throwing a real nice party for us.

NATO ANNIVERSARY

Tonight is the first of two White House jobs dedicated to the fiftieth anniversary of the North Atlantic Treaty Organization's (NATO) founding. The level of tension I feel coming from the social staff is far greater than that of a typical state dinner. While waiting to play, I even hear the social secretary hissing instructions to the butlers. I've never heard anyone on the social staff lose their cool, so I'm pretty surprised to hear that tone of voice here. It's surprising but understandable. The social secretaries and their assistants are hired in large part due to their ability to remain calm when the pressure is greatest.

I freely admit to having more than a few "butterflies" myself. I'm not concerned about the occasional wrong note, the unfortunate use of rubato, or the poorly balanced voicing of a chord. I'm mostly worried about tripping over my own feet when entering the room, unintentionally knocking the music off the stand, or catching the cuff of my uniform on the edge of the piano and tearing my most beautiful of red coats (I know this has never happened in two-hundred years of Marine Band history and, in all likelihood, never will). Maybe I'll just knock the stand light over, resulting in a resounding crash, and cause all twenty-seven presidents and prime ministers to pause over their entrées and glare at me contemptuously. I'm more uptight than usual: twenty-seven leaders of the western world, their spouses, a handful of translators, and a few veterans of the White House butler staff are my entire audience tonight. The Haydn "Sonata in F Major" is going fine, but then the unthinkable happens. One of the butlers comes over and asks me to change the angle of the portable stand light I'm using so it won't shine in the eyes of one of the prime ministers. Now I've gone and messed everything up. Haydn and prime rib aren't good enough. They need Haydn and prime rib with no poorly directed lighting. I continue playing, hoping I won't be fired the next day.

Actually, I know I'm overreacting, but disproportionate anxiety is in my genes. I'm struck by how quiet the room is. I guess most of these leaders are reserving their conversations for the interminable policy meetings they're obliged to attend. I'm finally relieved of duty as two marine violinists enter the East Room to serenade our distinguished guests. I quietly exit, thinking that sometimes it's best to complete a job, knowing that absolutely nothing unusual happened.

NATO dinner, Act II, is going to be different. The guest list is large enough that the Clintons have rented a mega-tent and installed it on the south lawn of the White House to accommodate the expected five hundred or so distinguished guests. The after-dinner entertainment is to be the Kennedy Center Opera Orchestra accompanying a few of the world's great opera singers, performing carefully selected arias intended to aid in the digestion of exceptionally rich desserts. I haven't been told who the singers will be.

I'm to play with the Marine Orchestra during the cocktail hour and then while the president and first lady greet the guests in a receiving line. President Clinton is notorious for long receiving lines and consequently, he's almost always running behind schedule. I truly think it's because he just simply loves talking to people. Eventually, the line thins out as guests make their way out to the tent. We break, the orchestra packs up, and the tech workers remove the chairs, music stands, stand lights, and conductor's podium. They all leave, but I stay behind as I've been tasked to play following the dinner as all the presidents and prime ministers exit from the front portico of the house and file out to a caravan of waiting limousines. I'm not hopeful that I'll see or be part of anything terribly exciting after witnessing the icy formality of the previous night.

I wait for a long while and finally hear lots of voices coming up the stairs, so I break into Jerome Kern's "Can't Help Loving Dat Man." It sounds like all our esteemed world leaders are finally loosening up a bit as they enter the Grand Foyer. Probably cocktails, a different wine with each course, and the after-dinner liqueurs have helped them. I hear President Clinton's voice in the midst of all the chatter, and he's definitely enjoying himself.

I go into Gershwin's Prelude no. 2, which I've recently learned so I can use it as an encore for an upcoming performance of Rhapsody in Blue. At about the halfway point in the piece, I hear the president comment on how much he loves this music. He's standing right next to me, looking over my shoulder at the score. I'm impressed he even recognizes it, but he also knows what year it was written, that it's part of a set of three preludes, and even what Gershwin was going through in his personal life at the time he composed it. I comment on how impressed I am with his knowledge of Gershwin. The president tells me he's been reading up on him because it's the hundredth anniversary of Gershwin's birth and he loves his music and anything I can play by him would be great. So, I play "Nice Work If You Can Get It" before playing "Somebody Loves Me," and "Oh, Lady Be Good."

As I start to play "Someone to Watch Over Me," I hear someone with a lovely quality to her voice gently joining in, softly singing the lyrics from behind me. Then I hear the president say, "Go ahead and sing with him. He won't mind." He's right about that, because I look up to find Renee Fleming walking toward me. By now, the Grand Foyer has cleared out with the exception of the president, the first lady, Renee, and her escort. They're all very cordial and relaxed. The formal performance part of the evening is over for both the diva and the president. I quickly go through a couple keys to find one she's comfortable with, and we settle on D major. As wonderful as she is as an opera singer, I know there could be issues with entrances, form, and rhythm if she's not accustomed to "faking." I make the introduction simple, and she enters with calm assurance, singing the entire form beautifully with a great sense of pathos and style. It's not unusual for an opera singer to overemphasize the glory of his or her own voice and vocal technique when singing Broadway and pop music, coming off as overly affected or even silly. There's none of that with Renee. It's truly beautiful.

She does throw me a curve though. After she finishes the form, I go into a piano interlude. Usually I'll play two A-sections (verses) and the singer will come back in at the bridge (B-section), thus sticking with the composer's original song structure. After playing only one A-section though, she comes back at the bridge. I have a moment of doubt, but convince myself quickly that she's not doing this because my solo is boring her. I make a quick adjustment with the chords I'm playing, and there's maybe a half-second where someone with a trained ear could tell that something unexpected has happened. As the song ends, there are handshakes and polite hugs, and I take photos with both Renee and the Clintons. I play some more Gershwin as the four of them are getting ready to leave for the night.

As they're walking out, Ms. Fleming's escort leans over and whispers to me, "Nice save." I quietly tell him, "More than glad to be of service."

After everyone's left and I'm packing up, my friend, Daniel from the ushers' office, tells me that Renee was absolutely brilliant during her performance over dessert in the tent. I'm not at all surprised. As I'm leaving the State Floor, I hear the echoes of tables being disassembled through the Cross Hall, and I can swear that they're mingling with other echoes of the short private performance I just got to do for the Clintons with one of the world's greatest opera singers.

Bob accompanied Renee Fleming in an impromptu performance for President and Mrs. Clinton, 1999.

NEW YEAR'S EVE

We're not usually called upon to play Marine Band gigs on New Year's Eve, but this year is different. It's Y2K, millennium night. Maybe the end of the world is at hand. Or it could just be the first night of the next thousand years. Whatever happens, I'm playing at possibly the biggest New Year's Eve party on the planet.

I'm walking down the hallway from the visitors' entrance at the East Gate towards the nineteenth century part of the White House. The smell of freshly cut flowers is strong, and everyone is dressed in either a tuxedo or a ball gown, even the tech workers. There's a bit of tension in the air, which is typical right before a big, formal presidential event, but my friends who work in the usher's office are very cool under pressure and, as usual, have things well under control. We have three different groups playing here tonight. I'm to play with the orchestra, usually a lot of elegant pop and show tunes with a few light classical pieces thrown in the mix.

But first, I'm going upstairs to play for a short reception that the Clintons are having for some thirty or so guests: senior staff members and some family and close friends. I'm taken to the elevator and Mr. Wilson escorts me up to the private residence. I don't play up here very often, but when I do, I'm always struck by how cool it is to actually be playing in the president's home rather than performing in the Grand Foyer, which is part of the museum. Though for that matter, I really can't complain about playing in the Grand Foyer either.

I'm playing a lot of show tunes with a jazz flavor to the harmonies, keeping it as soft as possible as the guests are right on top of me. Madeline Albright's here. William Cohen and his wife are here. The first couple and Chelsea are here. Everyone seems pretty upbeat, which is a bit surprising, given the scandal that the president and his family have recently been through. It's a short reception, and gradually the crowd is leaving, going down the grand staircase to join the rest of the guests for a receiving line and dinner.

Soon, the president, the first lady, and Chelsea are the only ones left upstairs, along with me and the photographer. I feel inclined to wrap up "For All We Know" before going down to the Grand Foyer and joining the orchestra; they're expecting me when this short reception ends. But it's always been Marine Band policy to keep playing while the president or the first lady are still on the same floor as we are.

The three Clintons come together for a group embrace, whispering softly to each other. I can't hear what they're saying, but I get an overwhelmingly uncomfortable feeling that I'm intruding on a very intimate family moment. The warmth between the three of them is genuine, and as much as I find their obvious affection for each other surprising, I'm happy for them, especially Chelsea, as they seemingly still have such a strong family bond.

After what seems to be a long time in their group hug, the president says, "Let's go down and say hello to the next millennium." As they walk by, he stops to shake my hand and thank me.

Hillary says, "Let's get a photo with him. He's been working here for years, and I don't think we've done one with him."

We pose for the photographer; I thank them, and the Clintons go down the staircase to get the "Biggest New Year's Party Ever" started. It's definitely going to be a memorable night.

Bob with the Clintons, New Year's Eve, 1999

I come down the elevator with Mr. Wilson and make my way quietly through the ushers' office, coming out to the piano, which sits in the back of the orchestra. When I settle in and start looking around, I can't believe the constant procession of famous people walking through the Grand Foyer. Actually, the word "famous" isn't strong enough. "Legendary" is more accurate. I'm used to being around politicians, but there are generally only a few events annually where the White House is full of guests from the film, music, and entertainment industries. We're frequently reminded by our command not to stare, but I do anyway.

One moment, I see Steven Spielberg walking by the orchestra with Quincy Jones, but my attention is quickly drawn to the other side of the room where Liz Taylor enters with a beaming smile. There's a small commotion over by the strings as Jack Nicholson orchestrates some practical joking with one of the violinists. A few minutes later, I'm really knocked out by the sight of Muhammed Ali shuffling slowly across the foyer. His hands are shaking a lot, but he walks under his own power, sure-footed and still with an almost royal air of dignity. I'm very surprised because the word has generally been that Ali probably won't be seen in public any more, due to his neurological problems. But he somehow managed to make it to this one. Then there's Itzhak Perlman, followed by Chick Corea, Edward Albee, Max Roach, Jessye Norman, Sophia Loren, and on and on. The theme for tonight's celebration is "The Best of America." I think they got that right.

They've been in the East Room for a good while now, enjoying one of those meals that require a lot of different-sized forks and separate wines with each course. The orchestra plays one of my favorites from the Pops Book. It's an arrangement of Gershwin's "Bess, You Is My Woman Now." Some of the orchestra music uses piano, but when that's not the case, I keep myself occupied by stargazing or admiring the bust of Lincoln or looking at the excellent detail work on the portrait of JFK. Kennedy's is the only presidential painting in the house that shows the subject with his head bowed, so you can't see his face. I suppose that makes sense, and it always reminds me of one of the saddest days in American history that I still have a vague recollection of from my early childhood.

Toward the end of "Bess," one of the ushers approaches Colonel Foley and whispers something to him as he conducts. I guess correctly that the time has come for the strolling strings portion of the evening to begin. The strings and bass player get up and take their positions in the Blue Room. They're ready to march in and play as the guests eat their desserts. Admittedly, strolling groups aren't my passion. We have world-class string players in the Marine Band, but my first choice would be to hear them play a Brahms symphony or the Bach Double Concerto.

Following the usher's brief message, the colonel cues me, and I begin to play Mozart's Piano Sonata in B-flat, K.333. I've been playing this one regularly since my piano competition days.

A few minutes into the first movement, I notice a young woman with long, black hair standing across the foyer, paying close attention to the Mozart. She remains for a good while until I've completed the slow movement. She gives me a nod of approval and walks back toward the East Room. I get to end of the final movement of the sonata, and she returns with another woman whom I instantly recognize. It's Renee Fleming.

They walk by Colonel Foley and come around to the back of the orchestra to greet me. Renee says, "My sister, Rachelle, told me a Marine Band pianist was playing a wonderful rendition of a Mozart sonata, and I thought it must be you." I recall that I met Renee at the NATO dinner just a few months ago. She introduces me to her sister, gives me a friendly hug, and we wish each other a happy new year. The colonel gives me a polite, "Please keep playing" cue, and I start a Chopin nocturne. But not for long.

A minute after I start, two Marine Band trumpet players begin a powerful fanfare to announce the entrance of the strolling strings. These guys can really put out some sound, but always with impeccable tone. My portion of the evening is done. It's ten at night (or 2200, as we gunnery sergeants like to say), and I'm feeling fortunate because I know a lot of my friends are scheduled to be playing at the White House until 0400 hours—four in the morning. I say good night to the colonel and head out as quickly as possible. My stomach's churning a bit because I've got another gig I'm trying to get to.

I arrive at the Country Club in Alexandria around 2245 hours to find that this gig's not going terribly well. I can tell by the looks of confusion on the faces of the bass and guitar players and the look of desperation on the singer's face. The singer is my wife, Mary, and although she's almost always happy to see me, I don't think she's ever been more so than tonight. The leader, who plays drums and sings, has a kind of serene smile on his face, but from what I know of Frank, he always looks like that. I think he'd keep that same expression whether having an uncomfortable proctologic exam or walking his daughter down the aisle in a wedding gown. The sax player looks mildly amused, but then again, he doesn't have to try and decipher pitches from the cacophony of chords and bass notes that are coming from the guitar and bass player. But the vocalists do.

How did this happen? You can be sure that all competent professional musicians are booked tonight. Actually, I've worked with this bass player and guitarist before, and they're both quite good, fronting their own bands doing rockabilly and blues. But this job is definitely outside of their skill set and knowledge of repertoire. The keyboard is already set up, so I just sit down and join in. Mary turns to me with a look of sublime gratitude on her face. The dance floor is empty, but we gradually manage to get a few dancers before the countdown at midnight. Things go a bit smoother as we go. I find myself calling out a lot of chord changes.

As our portion of the evening ends, I'm glad that I'm no longer compelled to accept gigs that I don't know how to play just because I need the money. Mary and I embrace and kiss at midnight as another band comes on playing classic rock, R&B, and disco. We enjoy a few dances together, then decide to head home. When we get home, we put on Stevie Wonder's "Joy Inside My Tears" and have one last New Year's dance. To me, this is one of Stevie's most beautiful and soulful songs. As we dance, I feel overwhelmed by a deep nostalgia for the beautiful things the two of us have shared in the years we've spent together and the simple joy of this moment. I've been really fortunate. For me, it's certainly been quite an end to a millennium.

SLIP A LITTLE STEVIE
IN THERE

Today, I'm playing at St. Elisabeth's Hospital in Anacostia, noteworthy as the US's oldest fully functional psychiatric medical facility. It's pretty run-down, and a lot of the buildings are closed, maybe even condemned. I'm playing with a blues-rock band in the maximum security ward. The criminally insane. Sociopaths and psychopaths. This gig is sponsored by the DC Musician's Union. Today is "Watermelon Day," and the inmates get to have some live entertainment. As I pull into the parking lot, it strikes me that recently, I was at the White House playing for the Pritzker Awards, a prestigious prize for excellence in architecture. I'm sure that the catering for that event was different from what we'll get today.

I remember that when I was first playing gigs in Miami, I hooked up with a group that did a lot of union trust fund jobs. At the time, it seemed like we played for every type of institution on the planet. For the emotionally disturbed, the mentally challenged, the homeless and nursing homes. Looking back now, I admit I was a bit uncomfortable at some of these places, but I eventually grew to enjoy those kinds of gigs. They were probably some of the most appreciative audiences I've ever played for.

I also think back to the time we played for the Forensic Psychiatry Division of the Florida State Hospital. This isn't the first time I've played for the criminally insane. At the time of that gig, I noticed that around fifty percent of the patients were pretty lucid. The other half didn't seem to be clear as to which planet they were on. One inmate calmly asked us if Bubba's Jazz Club was still up and running in Ft. Lauderdale. It occurred to me that maybe this guy had been sitting at a table next to Mary and me when we saw Stan Getz or Betty Carter there.

One of the disoriented fifty percent took a running start while we were playing a George Benson tune and tackled a speaker column. He was quickly restrained and escorted back to his room. The one other thing I remember from that day was asking Dick, our bass player, what the prisoners were thinking about us and the special event concert we had just done for them. Dick wasn't a psychic, but as a blind, accomplished jazz musician, I was quite sure he had more highly developed powers of intuition than anyone I'd ever met.

Dick said, "They're just wondering if there's any way they can use us to get out of here." I remember checking the trunk of my car twice before leaving through the three security gates.

When entering St Elizabeth's, we pass through a number of gates and metal detectors before a guard opens a two-foot thick iron door for us that leads into the exercise yard. They have a small stage set up directly across from a number of foldout picnic tables. The tables are covered with aluminum trays filled with watermelon slices. The administrator who greets us is very pleasant and surprisingly calm. I guess that kind of demeanor helps in a job like this. She's a tall, big-boned woman, and she seems to be genuinely grateful we're here.

The other musicians I'm playing with are all current or former Marine Band members. Kent, the leader, is a strong blues-rock guitarist and will call the sets and sing. He and the other members play together a lot, and I get a kick out of joining an established group and seeing how well I can use my ear and musical instincts to fit in. As long as there's minimal pressure, which there is today.

At any rate, urban blues is very soulful and expressive music, but it's generally not complicated. We do tunes by B.B. King, Buddy Guy, Eric Clapton, and the Allman Brothers (the irony of playing a tune called "One Way Out" doesn't "escape" any of us). I get a particular charge out of playing Jimi Hendrix's "Little Wing." After B.B.'s "The Thrill is Gone," a voice from the side of the stage says, "Can you all slip a little Stevie in there?"

I look over to find that the requester is John Hinckley, the man who shot Ronald Reagan at the Washington Hilton Hotel. I had heard that he was a longtime guest at St E's, but I wasn't sure if he would be allowed to attend Watermelon Day. He's a short, nondescript man with longish, stringy hair, wearing a faded cotton shirt and jeans. Of course, any self-respecting blues band knows that our assassin is requesting something by Stevie Ray Vaughn, so Kent calls up "Texas Flood." Hinckley gives us what seems to be a sincere "Thank you" and a thumbs up. This band generates a great groove, and the guards and many of the more lucid patients are bouncing a bit with the tune. The more confused patients mostly just stare at nothing in particular and talk to no one in particular.

Following our last song, the nice administrator lady gets on the PA and barks out, "Let's hear it one more time for "Tastes Like Chicken" (the name of our band). Most of them applaud, but a few just look confused. "Now time to line up for head count," she barks out. I'm surprised how quickly they all fall into line on cue. There's some kind of power that she has over all these prisoners/patients, many of whom are large and intimidating. I'd rather not think about what type of threats and conditioning keeps them in line like this. After they leave and as we're folding cords and loading drums and keyboards into cases, a strange thought comes into my head: Kent and I are probably the only musicians in the world who have played for both Ronald Reagan and the man who tried to kill him. I allow myself a small chuckle and shake my head at one more of life's little ironies.

CODA

It's now 2014, and James Brady died a few days ago. Brady was Reagan's Press Secretary, and he was also horribly wounded during Hinckley's assassination attempt. I've read that his life was terribly difficult following the shooting. Any dark and ironic humor I may have found in the circumstance of playing for both Reagan and Hinckley doesn't seem so funny anymore. The pain and suffering caused by the combination of Hinckley's insanity and his access to a gun isn't something I can laugh about.

YOU CAN'T TAKE THAT ON THE PLANE! PART 1

I'm standing in line at BWI airport to check my bags and pick up my ticket for an 0815 flight to Dallas connecting through Atlanta. I'm going to meet up with a couple of Marine Band friends when I get there and we're heading directly to Denton to perform for a National Saxophone Symposium at the University of North Texas. The recital begins at 1400, and we're on the first half of the program. We'll be playing an interesting piece of new classical music written by a local Baltimore composer, Phanos Dymiotis.

This is an official, government-approved concert, so we'll be wearing our uniforms. I've done a few of these concerts before, but today is unique in that I'm picking up two boarding passes, one for myself and one for a bari (baritone) saxophone. My friend, Greg (the sax player who booked us), asked me if I'd carry his instrument. He's traveling from Boston, and the government will only pay to ship the sax from the Baltimore/Washington area. I don't mind helping him out. Greg's been a great friend to me.

I get to the Delta counter at Baltimore/Washington International (BWI), give them my name and photo ID, and tell them I'm picking up two tickets. I have my suitcase, my uniform inside a garment bag, and my friend's bari sax. The nice but brusque ticket agent punches a few buttons on her computer and says with a slightly puzzled expression, "I'm only showing one seat for you, Mr. Boguslaw."

"Are you sure? This should have been booked through the Marine Band."

"Yes, I'm sure," she says. Her tone of voice indicates that she's more concerned with the passengers lined up behind me than she is with solving my problem.

"How about under the name of Greg Ridlington?" (the saxophonist).

"No."

"How about Lacey Reid?" (Our admin chief who booked the flight).

"No."

"How about John Barclay or Major John Barclay?" (The officer in charge of the trip).

"No! Sir, you're going to have to either proceed to board the plane now or step out of line and let the next passenger come to the counter."

I select the second choice, though what I really want to do is come around behind the counter, push her aside (hopefully she lands on her butt in a humiliating yet painless way), and scroll through the passenger list myself. But instead, I carry all my things to the nearest payphone and start trying to call Greg, Lacey, and Major Barclay. No one answers first time around, but then I reach Greg. Unfortunately, he's no help, and he sounds a bit desperate when I tell him his pianist and saxophone may not make it on time. Greg tells me that he didn't have a hand in our flight arrangements, and that I should call the major.

I try again and this time, Major Barclay picks up. He tells me to go back to the ticket agent (whom I'm really looking forward to talking to again) and use the government credit card to book an alternate flight any way they can to get me to Dallas. It's imperative that I get there and that we do our performance. I guess that's because government funds have already been allocated for this. Right as I hang up the phone, I hear a last call announcement for my flight. No way I'm going to make that one now.

As I return to my Delta friend at the counter, it hits me: "Do you have a seat under the name of 'saxophone' for this flight?"

"First name Bari?" she asks, looking down at her screen.

I look down at my shoes and shake my head. There's no way I'm going to find the right words for this moment, so I just nod in the affirmative.

"I'm afraid it's too late now for you to make this flight. Can I book you and the saxophone on a later flight?" Since I can't put my frustration into words and I don't have time to come up with a perfect response, I just nod in the affirmative. Again.

Amazingly enough, Delta finds a flight for Bari and me that connects through Chicago and leaves at 0930. I should arrive in Texas around 1300 with the connection and might barely make it for the 1400 concert. Obviously, it won't be my most relaxed performance ever, but at least there's a chance I'll make it. I board the plane at 0900, but now it seems we've been sitting at the gate for longer than usual, and sure enough, a disembodied voice comes through the speaker system informing us we're going to have a significant delay, as windy conditions in Chicago are currently making it impossible to land. At this point, I'm giving up. I tell myself that never, ever, ever again will I make the mistake of traveling on the same day I'm expected to perform. I guess that I'll probably spend the evening in Chicago hanging out with some old friends before returning to DC to face the fallout from this mess. An hour and a half later, the flight takes off.

Amazingly enough, when we arrive in Chicago, I discover there are hourly flights to Dallas and they have room for me and Bari on the next one. I quickly call Greg in Texas. He tells me he'll pick me up at the airport, and we've been told that we can perform at the end of the program. I do the math and figure that with some luck we'll be playing at around 1600 hours. So I run for the flight, shifting instantly back into stress mode and out of defeat/ futility mode. We land a few minutes before 1500, and Greg and Regino are there to meet me in the government rental car. I allow myself a small sigh of relief...at least until I discover that none of my luggage has come off the carousel, including my garment bag with my uniform. It's all probably still lying around somewhere in O'Hare. Performing out of uniform is a big deal with the Marine Band, but it looks like today I'm not going to have a choice. Fortunately, I've got my music with me. One thing I did right today was to at least put the piano part in my carry-on.

We drive the forty-five minutes to Denton in thirty-five minutes. We go directly to the backstage area and are directed to a student restroom to change. I just watch as Greg and Gino change, feeling grateful that at least I'm not wearing jeans and sneakers. This'll be my first (and hopefully only) Marine Band concert in a pullover sweater and khaki slacks.

Finally, we walk on stage.

The hall is huge. The echo of our footsteps is louder than the applause, and that's not because people aren't clapping. It's because there are only three of them. Three of them and three of us. One of them is Greg's old teacher. Another one is the sound engineer. The third person is someone I don't know, but I think maybe I'll nominate him for president of our new fan club.

This concert was supposed to end a half hour ago, and all the saxophonists have gone on to attend a master class scheduled at 1600. We play anyway. It's not one of my better performances. Not just my hand but my whole body is still shaking from today's excitement. I didn't have a whole lot of time to warm up either. But somehow, I made it to Texas and performed for a bona fide national saxophone symposium.

Following the recital, we go to the hotel and I check in with no toothbrush

216

or change of underwear. A little while later, we go to a butt-kicking Mexican restaurant. Greg went to school here, so he knows just where to take us. After some great food and a couple of beers, Regino (my brilliant violinist friend) and I discuss playing the Ravel Trio together sometime, a piece that's been on my wish list for years. I'm finally feeling better, and I go to sleep thinking about how at least the day improved as it went, and something good might come out of this trip after all.

CODA

I approach the Delta counter to claim our tickets (Bari's and mine) for the return trip to BWI. This time I'm prepared to give the correct name of my inanimate traveling companion.

I tell the agent, "One ticket under the name of Robert Boguslaw and another one for…"

She sees me carrying Bari, and before I can finish my sentence, she smiles and says, "Oh, you don't need a ticket for that; just put it in the overhead."

YOU CAN'T TAKE THAT ON THE PLANE! PART 2

The Make a Wish Foundation has really gone all out for this one. I've played a few shows for them before, and the production values have always been top-of-the-line: professional staging, lighting, sound reinforcement, and some of Washington DC's best show singers, mostly from the Army and Air Force Bands. This time, they've really outdone themselves, and we're headed for Puerto Rico for a Valentine's Day show and three days in a five-star resort. The show's going to take place on a private island around five miles off the coast. For one (I'm guessing rather substantial) price, the guests get three nights in a hotel, their flight, their meals, golf/tennis/swimming pools, and the ever-so-romantic Valentine's Day show we're going to play while they all enjoy a gourmet dinner. I think a large percentage of the fee goes to the charity. At least I hope it does, but either way, I'm glad to be along for the ride. I took four days of leave to do this, and I feel certain it'll be worth it. It pays well, and we're going to be right next to Luquillo Beach and El Yonqui, Puerto Rico's rain forest, all very, very beautiful and very tropical.

A few days ago, Bobby, the show's producer, made a reference to us carrying a keyboard on and off a skiff to get us to the island. At the time, I made it very clear to him that I'm being paid to play the keyboard, not to haul it on and off of boats. I've done that before when gigging on cruise ships, and I can clearly remember that it's not pleasant. While waiting for my flight, I'm really shocked when two men approach me with a luggage cart carrying something very large in a heavy anvil case.

One of them looks at an invoice, then at me and asks, "Are you Robert Boguslaw?"

I nod yes.

"We're from Drums Unlimited, and we're supposed to deliver this keyboard to you to bring on the flight to San Juan."

I realize that not only did Bobby decide to ignore my comments about carrying a keyboard onto a boat, but he's decided I should bring it onto a plane as well. I quickly consider the possibility of getting in my car and driving home, skipping the entire trip. But I've already committed four days of leave time and cleared a whole weekend worth of gigs off my calendar to do this. Instead, I cringe and sign for the keyboard adding a scribbled expletive halfway down the page. It doesn't make me feel any better.

BWI is having mechanical problems with its luggage conveyer belts today, so everything's running late. When I finally get to the counter, the nice lady looks skeptically at the huge keyboard case I'm carrying. "Dragging" would be more accurate. I'm traumatized by a minor lower back strain while lifting the case onto the scale.

"You can't take that on the plane. It weighs 146 pounds, and 100 is the limit for personal luggage."

"But I have to be in San Juan by this evening," I say.

"Sir, there's a special cargo shipping station on the other side of the airport. I recommend you try there."

"Then there's no way I'm making it onto this plane with this keyboard?"

She smiles and with the hint of a chuckle says, "No sir. That's not going to happen."

I'm walking at an agitated pace to a pay phone when an airport security guard shouts at me, "SIR, IS THAT YOURS?" The entire airport can hear our exchange.

"Yes, it is, but I'm just going to use the phone for a minute!" The case is only thirty feet from where I'll be calling.

"SIR, YOU NEED TO COME AND GET THIS CASE! NOW! OR IT WILL BE CONFISCATED!"

For a moment, I think that wouldn't necessarily be a bad thing, but my misguided sense of professionalism won't allow me to abandon it. I drag the case, squeaking across the freshly waxed floor and set it next to my phone, managing to block all the other pay phone stations. Now I know why Bobby left two days earlier than the rest of us.

When Bobby picks up the phone in his hotel room in Puerto Rico, the first thing he hears from me is, "Are you fucking kidding me?! Are you fucking kidding me?!" He deserved to hear it twice. I go on for a while, saying things to him that I've probably only said to one or two other people in my entire life. I'm generally a pretty patient person.

"I understand," is all he says when I finish my tirade. "The main thing is that we get you down here for this evening's rehearsal. I'm going to call a courier and make arrangements for another flight and shipping for the keyboard," he says. "Call me back in fifteen minutes." He hangs up before I can get in some parting shots. I'd go and grab a cup of coffee while I'm waiting if I didn't have this coffin-sized keyboard that I'm tied to.

The courier and I drive down to Reagan National Airport in DC, and he drops the keyboard at a cargo shipping bay. I'm not heartbroken to see it go. He then takes me to Departures, telling me that Bobby's booked me on a noon flight to Miami, followed by a nearly four-hour layover before connecting to San Juan. I do the math and determine I'll arrive at 1945 hours when my rehearsal starts at 1930. We're rehearsing with the San Juan Symphony. The orchestra's been contracted to add a touch of extra class to the show. I'm sure I'll make a great first impression on them and Arnald Gabriel (the conductor) by arriving about an hour late. Maestro Gabriel served twenty-one years as former conductor of the USAF Band, Orchestra, and Singing Sergeants.

Fortunately, the flights run on time. Bobby's there to meet me at baggage claim, but before I can spit out the choice words I've been planning for his benefit for the last twelve hours, I notice Jack and his cute little twelve-year-old daughter are here with him. Jack is the producer of the show, a banker who's one of the main benefactors of Make a Wish. His little girl is going to be one of the singers performing for the show, and she's very, very excited to be here in Puerto Rico for her big stage debut. So I hold my tongue. I sit quietly in the back of our taxi as Bobby indicates to the driver that we're in a bit of a hurry, implying that he'll make it worthwhile for him if he gets us to the rehearsal studio quickly.

As I rush in and take my chair behind the piano in the middle of an orchestra that's already been rehearsing for nearly an hour, the conductor, Colonel Gabriel, gives me a little bit of a sidelong glance that doesn't seem terribly welcoming. As he cuts off the orchestra, it occurs to me that Bobby hasn't explained to him why I'm late, and I'm probably already on the poop list. The colonel says, "Fugue from West Side Story, Letter K." I've heard this section before, but I'm going to be sight reading and it's not easy. We play four bars and it's just piano, bass, and drums. Eight bars and still no orchestra. Sixteen bars.

I've spent the last twelve hours struggling to try and get here, dealing with anger and stress, and literally running through the parking lot to make it to rehearsal. Oh, yes, and I didn't get to play one scale, or one note for that matter, as a warm up. And first thing when I arrive, the conductor has me show my ass (musically) by having me play the most difficult and exposed section of the entire program—in front of the San Juan Philharmonic.

At around twenty-four bars, the orchestra finally joins us. I've played worse, but I've also played a lot better. Ironically, I tried to get the music for the show a few weeks in advance but to no avail. On the way back to the hotel, I don't say much of anything to anyone, receding into grumpy and tired mode. All I want to do is go and have a beer and fall asleep.

Two days later, the trip has improved quite a bit. It's consisted of some rehearsing between hours spent at the pool and beach. We even had time for a horseback ride through a bit of the rainforest. The food is great, and the band I'm down here with are all great people and wonderful musicians. Bobby and I have talked very little, and when it's time to load the keyboard onto the boat for the island, I oversee while paid roadies do the heavy lifting. Maybe my message got through.

CODA

We're on the island and it's romantic dinner time. Everyone eats and drinks until satisfied. Now it's show time. There's only one problem. When positioning the stage, no one accounted for the near gale force winds blowing off the water, probably forty mile-per-hour gusts. I worry throughout the entire show that my music is going to end up flying frantically off the piano and go floating out into the Caribbean Sea. This despite the wind clips that were supplied by the librarian and are traditionally used to hold charts in place on outdoor gigs. Amazingly enough, though, there are no flying music disasters. Not one, even with a full orchestra. But the big problem with the show is that whenever the microphones are turned on, there's a huge rush of noise that courses through the PA. It's the wind. Even though I think the audience can tell that the singers are singing "My Heart Will Go On" (from *Titanic*) and "All I Ask of You" (from *Phantom of the Opera*), I'm pretty sure the overall impression they'll take away from the show is that of rushing air amplified by a really top-of-the-line PA system.

Later in the evening, I'm sitting on a wicker lounge chair by myself on the front porch of a bamboo cabana I'm sharing with the guitar player, sipping one of those relaxing fruity rum drinks with an umbrella standing up in it. The show's over, and it's our last night in this tropical heaven. Up here away from the sea, the gale has diminished to a gentle breeze. I silently make a private toast to the Make a Wish Foundation for helping to make the dreams of sick children come true and for providing this gig in a tropical paradise for me. If I can just manage to forget my "You-Can't-Take-That-on-the-Plane!" day from hell, what's not to like?

FLIGHT 93

It's been over two months since the 9/11 attacks. There's still a sense of gloom over everything we do. Even when I go out to eat, see a movie, or attend one of my daughters' school programs, it's still there. It's probably worse here in DC than most other US cities. The damaged Pentagon is right across the river, a reminder of the attacks every time I drive past. There's also heightened security: terribly serious looking secret service agents and park police are everywhere, some carrying drawn firearms. They've put up lots of barricades around the Capitol Building and the White House, and the security perimeters have been moved farther from prospective targets. My friend, Daniel, from the White House ushers' office told me that on the day of the attacks, all personnel working at the White House exited the building to the South Lawn to look skyward. Security was convinced another plane was about to be used as a weapon to attack the president's home. Fortunately, Flight 93 never made it to Washington because of the bravery of the passengers. They fought back that morning.

One of the blessings of my music career is that in my work, people are almost always having a good time, or at least trying to have a good time. Today is different though. Today at the White House, President Bush is receiving Flight 93 victims' families.

During this solemn occasion, I'm keenly aware of how seldom I've been asked to provide music when loss and grief are the audience's overriding emotions. What do I play for family members who have just lost a parent, child, or spouse to such a senseless act of terror? At the same time, there's an undercurrent of heroism and sacrifice by the flight's passengers, who probably saved both untold lives and one of our country's historic national treasures, the White House. If I play music that's too gloomy, I'll only remind the guests of their grief. If I play lighthearted show tunes, it will trivialize the entire event. I opt for mostly classical, playing sonatas by Mozart and Haydn, a Schubert impromptu, some short pieces by Debussy, and a Chopin nocturne.

A teenage girl comes over to me and asks if she can sing "God Bless America." She tells me that both her parents were killed on Flight 93. I tell her that I'll have to ask Gary Walters, the chief usher, but I'd be happy to accompany her. It's the first time in ten years of doing this that anyone has come over and asked to sit in. I ask Gary, and he tells me that as soon as the president finishes his meeting with the grieving families and leaves the State Floor, the young lady is welcome to sing. I suppose this policy is meant to avoid doing anything that will take attention away from the president.

I play for a few minutes, and an older woman approaches me and asks me if I can play Debussy's "Clair de Lune." "I'd be glad to," I tell her, and as I conclude this quiet yet beautiful piece, she approaches and takes my arm in a tight grip. There are tears welling up in her eyes. "My mother was on that flight, and 'Clair de Lune' was her favorite piece. As a child, I remember her always sitting at the piano and playing it. Thank you, thank you, thank you!"

Once the president finally leaves for the West Wing, I motion for the young girl to come over and sing "God Bless America." We find a key, and I give her a brief introduction, setting her up by playing the melody from the last four measures of the song. Some fifty or sixty guests are still milling about when she starts to sing, but within a few measures she's receiving everyone's undivided attention. She sings well, and by the end of the song, everyone in the audience has joined in. Everyone's also in tears, myself included. Although I've always found this song to be overly sentimental, I don't think

I'll ever be able to hear it again without getting emotional over Flight 93 and the tragedy of 9/11.

Afterward, a man comes up to me and asks if he can play a piece he wrote as an homage for his wife who was also killed on the flight. He tells me he composes music for films.

At this point I just say, "Sure."

He announces the piece and makes his dedication to his wife. The music sounds like music for a film. It's well written, heartfelt and sincere, and once again, everyone is moved. Afterward, as I sit back down at the piano to play for the grieving guests' departure, I find myself thinking about the Paul Simon lyric from the song "The Cool Cool River." "Sometimes even music cannot substitute for tears." Maybe not, but I'm convinced that it can help.

WALTZ OF THE FLOWERS

It's the first Sunday in December 2001. I'm at the White House with the "President's Own" Chamber Orchestra. But this isn't your usual marathon holiday reception. Typically, the orchestra cranks out carol medleys and Leroy Anderson's "Christmas Festival Overture," given short breaks by our jazz trio playing some pretty authentic Vince Guaraldi charts from *A Charlie Brown Christmas*. Those receptions are generally for political supporters of the president, executive branch workers, and their families.

This reception is for the Kennedy Center honorees. The honorees received their awards last night at the State Department, and today, they get to experience this year's exceptional White House holiday decorations, gourmet Christmas buffet, and optional eggnog. (Personally, I could never understand the appeal of mixing dairy products with hard liquor. To each his own.) This year, the trees are all decorated in sparkling white and silver. The White House is always done up beautifully during the holiday season, but this one's got to be my favorite. Mary saw a photo of the Grand Foyer decorations and dubbed it "Narnia."

The honorees include Julie Andrews and Jack Nicholson, but the one I'm really excited about is Van Cliburn. From the first moment I became aware of the giants of classical piano, my earliest recollections involve Van Cliburn and Arthur Rubinstein. And today, I'm going to play Chopin's "Fantasy Impromptu in C-sharp Minor" when I see Cliburn in person. We've been asked by the White House staff to play music associated with each of the honorees. So Chopin it is. Unfortunately, it'll be played on the mediocre upright piano because there's not enough room for the historic White House Steinway Grand in our setup. Fitting the grand piano into the middle of the orchestra, where we usually setup, is understandably impossible. There are nearly twenty fifteen-foot Christmas trees on the State Floor and four in the Grand Foyer. So today, I'll play solo classical piano on a less than ideal instrument.

Right before the downbeat of the last piece the orchestra plays, Jack Nicholson comes over and covers up one of the violinists' music with his hands. When our startled violinist looks up resentfully, Nicholson gives him that classic "Shining/Joker" smile and says, "It's just me!"

At the conclusion of Mozart's "Eine kleine Nachtmusik," Colonel Foley gives me a nod. I can choose to play solo piano or enlist the help of the bassist and drummer to play some jazz, Broadway, or pop. I saw Van Cliburn walking in the Blue Room a few minutes ago, so knowing he's close by, I dive into the Chopin. Regardless of the upright piano with sluggish action. Regardless of the large window right behind me leaking extremely cold air on my back and arms. And regardless of the restrictive collar I've worn to perform in for what seems like half a lifetime. Actually it's only been ten years. Enough excuses.

I just play the Impromptu and it's not very good. I get a small round of applause at the end, and I look up to see Van Cliburn smiling and waving at me from the other side of the orchestra. I give a nod and a wave back, but I'm more than a little embarrassed by my lackluster performance.

The Marine trombonist sitting in front of me turns and says, "Van Cliburn told the orchestra to 'Tell that guy he plays good.'"

Cliburn's shiny new Kennedy Center medal must be putting him in a very forgiving mood. I don't see him leave, as the colonel is calling up the next piece, one of the Christmas medleys that has a piano part.

The audience is thinning out a bit now as the guests depart for buses that will take them to the Kennedy Center for the big tribute show. Then the colonel gets a request. It comes from a distinguished-looking, silver-haired woman whose face I can't put a name to, but I'm sure she's a former recipient of the honors award for ballet. She's asked the colonel if we could play a waltz. We regularly play the "Suite" from Tchaikovsky's Nutcracker at most of our December White House jobs, so Colonel Foley pulls out "The Waltz of the Flowers." There's no keyboard part in this movement, so I guess I'll just watch and see if anyone decides to dance. As soon as this elegant and spirited waltz starts, the requester and her escort begin to dance with a grace and ease that confirms my suspicion that they're serious ballet dancers.

A minute or so into the waltz, there are six or seven couples, including Walter Cronkite and Betsy, his wife of over sixty years, dancing in the Grand Foyer of the White House. Standing to the side and watching this little impromptu ball are Van Cliburn and his partner. His partner is watching the dancers with a hopeful look on his face, and he whispers something to Van Cliburn who's smiling. When Cliburn shakes his head in the negative, I'm certain that he's just turned down an invitation to dance. I feel a bit of regret that Van Cliburn doesn't feel comfortable enough here to dance with his male partner, even though today is in large part a celebration of his remarkable career.

But then, two older women come to the rescue and invite the Cliburn couple to partner with them in the waltz. They must have seen the same exchange that I saw. Cliburn and his partner accept, and by the time the orchestra reaches the rousing climax that concludes the waltz, Van Cliburn, his partner, and all the dancers seem almost deliriously happy. A bit breathless, they all thank the colonel and quickly hurry out to catch one of the buses to the Kennedy Center for the tribute program.

As usual, at the end of the reception, we're invited by the butlers and ushers to partake of the refreshments. That's our cue for the orchestra members to quickly put away their instruments and descend on the buffet table. No point in throwing away leftovers; the Marine Band will make quick work of them. Some of the ushers even jokingly refer to us as the "red locusts." I don't mind. After a long reception, I'm just ready for a nice plate from the White House buffet and a glass of excellent Cabernet. This job has some serious perks.

CODA

It's 2012, more than ten years after Van Cliburn declined his partner's invitation to waltz in the Grand Foyer. Today, our Marine jazz combo has been tasked to play for an LGBT reception. I didn't know what the lettering stood for, and our operations Gunnery Sergeant told me, "Lesbian, Gay, Bisexual, Transgender," with a hint of a smirk. Although we have our fair share of gay bandsmen, the "President's Own" is generally a pretty conservative organization. Lots of Midwesterners raised on traditional American values. I know for a fact that some of the members of my group would have preferred that they weren't picked for this commitment.

But I don't feel that way today. I have a close family member who's gay. My last piano teacher was gay and was a tremendous mentor and friend to me. I can't help but feel glad for all the gay and lesbian guests who will be attending this reception today, no longer having to hide their dark secret from the rest of the world. Even "Don't Ask, Don't Tell" has been repealed, and when the guests arrive, I notice quite a few uniformed military with their partners, including a Marine Corps White House social aide whom I've worked with for a number of years. The closet door is open, and the White House has invited LGBT into its living room. If Van Cliburn had been here today, I think he probably would have accepted the invitation to the dance.

SWITZERLAND

This trip to Switzerland has turned out to be by far the best travel experience I've ever had with the Marine Band. The 1992 trip to England to perform at the Mountbatten Festival in Albert Hall proved to be a huge disappointment. Legitimate concerns about the possibility of an Irish Republican Army terrorist attack meant we were required to stay with the Band throughout most of the trip. We sat through days of joint rehearsals with the British Royal Marine Band, where the sole purpose seemed to be a trombone section volume contest. I think the British won, but our guys certainly made a nicer sound.

The tab for the trip was picked up by the British, and they put us up for five nights in a twenty-five-a-night retired-military rooming house in downtown London. None of us expected the Ritz, but we all thought adequate heat and windows that shut all the way in February would have been a nice touch. I was glad to get home.

I traveled the northeastern US in '93 on the "President's Own" annual national tour. Every night, we played a medley titled "From Ragtime to Swing" which was a piano feature. We played Symphony Hall in Boston, Carnegie Hall in New York, and the Academy of Music in Philadelphia. As a little boy, I'd heard the Philadelphia Orchestra play there often. The Philadelphia performances fulfilled a lifelong dream of mine. The hotels there were also much more comfortable than our accommodations had been in London. The music and the crowd response were great, but there was a sameness to the tour's seven-week routine that got to us a bit. The biggest problem with that tour was going seven weeks without getting to see my wife and two young daughters.

"Daddy, you've been gone for so long that sometimes it feels like I don't have a daddy anymore," Nicole said to me after the first three weeks on the road.

Ouch. Twist the knife after you stab me. And at the time, we weren't even halfway done. Trying to keep things in perspective at the time, I reminded myself of marines who dealt with deployments that caused year-long separations from their families. I'm also home far more than I would have been had I continued to play for the bus-and-truck tour of *Cats*, my last gig before joining the "President's Own."

There were a few short trips over the years to New Orleans and Chicago, and one to Cincinnati for the Marine Band's induction into the Classical Music Hall of Fame. The Hall of Fame was a short trip but very gratifying. It was the first year of the "Hall," and as we walked onstage, we received what seemed to be a five-minute standing ovation from an audience of some of the world's greatest musicians and composers—before even playing a note. But unfortunately, I was running a 102-degree fever, which gave the whole concert a surreal, dream-like quality. But nothing could measure up to this trip to Lucerne, Switzerland for "WASBE," the World Association for Symphonic Bands and Ensembles conference.

We arrive in Lucerne on a Tuesday, and I don't have to be anywhere until our rehearsal late Friday afternoon. That's a lucky break. The architecture of Lucerne makes it seem like something from a fairytale, something with gingerbread houses. We're scheduled to play four different programs, but the Wednesday and Thursday concerts don't involve any keyboard. So I decide to take a boat ride across Lake Lucerne, hike to the top of a mountain, and spend a night in a Swiss Alpine inn that looks down on the lake and the city from a dizzying height. I chose this particular inn because it's a famous viewing spot for watching the sun rise and set over Lake Lucerne. Glorious.

On Thursday, I go with the band to the capital city, Bern. I want to see the city and hear my friends in concert. I have the unique experience of watching the Marine Band take the stage by being raised up mechanically, all seated and in position, from a sunken orchestra pit. It's as if the earth had opened up and magically conjured a complete virtuoso uniformed military band that rose from some subterranean depths. It's a supernatural performance, a typically awesome "President's Own" band concert.

The best part of the entire trip (even better than lots of great beer, cheese, and chocolate) is this evening's concert, our last night in Lucerne. They have a beautiful new concert hall with two exceptional Hamburg Steinway nine-foot grand pianos. The onstage instrument might very well be the best piano I've ever played. As we take the stage, the extended thunderous ovation reminds me of our Classical Hall of Fame concert a few years ago. Most bandmasters regard the Marine Band as the world's finest wind ensemble, and the enthusiastic welcome they give us certainly reflects it.

I play on two pieces, Copland's "Emblems" (his only composition originally written for wind ensemble) and Joseph Schwantner's Percussion Concerto. The Copland piece doesn't give the pianist a lot to play. But the Schwantner has substantial and prominent piano writing woven in tightly with the percussion textures. I play my part reasonably well, but my role in the performance is negligible compared to that of our soloist, Chris Rose.

Over the years, I've had the good fortune to work with a handful of musicians whom I consider "musical forces of nature." When performing with these select few, a palpable, inexorable musical energy emanates from them. Virtuoso drummers Vinnie Colaiuta and Louie Bellson, trumpet virtuoso Vince DiMartino, jazz multi-instrumentalist Ira Sullivan, and singer Renee

Fleming. These are the artists who deliver the music, regardless of the circumstances. You could put them in a strait jacket in a padded cell and stuff a sock in their mouths, and still somehow they'd find a way to make great music. Chris is in that category.

Throughout the concerto, he plays seemingly every percussion instrument known to man. He creates distinctive and beautifully sculpted phrases on all of them, not an easy feat when many of the instruments are non-pitched. The concerto climaxes in the final movement with an improvised percussion solo, lasting close to five minutes. The musical energy pours off Chris, off the stage, and into the audience. The audience then demands five curtain calls from Chris, while the band stands receiving applause for what feels like fifteen minutes. It's so loud that the entire concert hall seems to shake at its foundation.

Now I'm back at our hotel, loading up my backpack. I've taken four days of leave tacked onto the end of this trip. My good friend Greg is one of the Marine Band's world-class sax players. The two of us are going hiking in the Alps for a few days. Then we'll make our way to Lake Geneva for the Montreux Jazz Festival, where we'll hear concerts by Wayne Shorter, Chick Corea, John McLaughlin, and Michel Camillo.

Inevitably, at some point soon, I'll be on a miserable gig. Maybe it will be an outdoor wedding in full tuxedo in one-hundred-degree heat. Maybe two drunks shouting at each other over the piano in a hotel lounge as I play a version of a beautiful ballad such as "These Foolish Things." Maybe even a military gig on the South Lawn of the White House, where we play for three hours in thirty-seven-degree temperatures with frozen fingers for a Stanley Cup winners' event, cranking out the dreadful Chicago Blackhawks' theme over and over. I really do appreciate the good gigs when they come along. The Lucerne concert is definitely on the top of that list.

CRASHING THE PARTY

It's New Year's Day, and I'm sitting in the marine commandant's home playing exceptionally soft cocktail piano music. As the guests arrive and the conversation level picks up, I'll be able to gradually increase the volume, but right now the most important part of my job is being aurally unobtrusive. The commandant has hosted New Year's Day receptions for well over a hundred years. According to Marine Corps legend, "March King" John Phillip Sousa showed up at the commandant's New Year's Day parties, played a brief outdoor concert for him and his guests, and was then invited into the house along with the band members to warm themselves by the fireplace, drink hot drinks, and enjoy the generous buffet.

The home of the commandant is the oldest continuously occupied residence in the city of Washington, DC. Designed by Thomas Jefferson during the War of 1812, the house was taken by the British, and rather than burning it as they did most of Washington, they used it as headquarters for just a few days until the American forces expelled them. With that kind of history, this house is a very special place to the Corps. It's a big deal for the band to be invited in to greet the commandant and join the New Year's party. We're forbidden to drink alcohol before any performances, but afterward, it's permissible. The "President's Own" is received as guests in the house only once a year. Band members may bring immediate family members to join the party following the frozen serenade. There's also a pre-serenade reception for VIPs only.

This year, Mary has decided to come. I don't play this job every year, but this time around, it's my turn, so I invited her and the kids. A party like this is understandably a bit tedious for twelve- and eleven-year-old girls, so I'm not surprised that Nicole and Gabrielle declined. But for the first time, Mary accepted the invitation. We played a New Year's Eve dinner-dance at the Ritz Carlton last night, and maybe she wanted our party together to continue. Anyway, I'm glad she's finally going to see this beautiful place where I frequently get to work.

But why is she leaning over the piano right now saying, "Happy New Year, Bog," and giving me a quick kiss? I don't remember her being on the VIP list, and we're at least forty minutes away from the band magically appearing in the backyard. My philosophy about being in the Marine Corps is generally, "Don't ever give anyone reason to give you grief about anything. Ever." The atmosphere within the Marine Corps is generally very professional and collegial, but I've seen a few marines both in and out of the band get dressed down by superior officers, and as a forty-five year old pianist, I want no part of that. So I immediately become paranoid about my wife crashing the party.

Mary has always been a bit on the uninhibited side. When I first met her, she was living next door to the band house where I would practice with my college jazz/rock/fusion band (see the chapter titled "Go Karts"). She would come over and hang out with us and dance herself into a frenzy when the music was sufficiently funky. Once we started dating, she would do the same thing in steamy Coconut Grove nightclubs, whether or not I was inclined to join her on the dance floor. She was also the one at Bubba's Supper Club in Ft. Lauderdale who would yell approval at the top of her lungs when a brilliant solo by Bobbie Watson or Wynton Marsalis in Art Blakey's Band had been concluded, and was equally vocal in telling people at the next table to put a lid on the loud casual conversation when Stan Getz was playing a beautiful ballad. You could hear her yell encouragement a half-mile away at Nicole and Gabrielle's sporting events. So I'm not really surprised she's here. I just had that "always follow the rules" paranoia kick in.

As I'm playing, I see her talking to a couple of generals' wives and then a few of the enlisted marine servers, and finally the commandant's wife. They both look over at me, Mary points, and they smile. Oh well, if there's a problem with all this, there's nothing I can do about it now. Fred, our operations chief, has Mary's name on his list to be escorted over here. I do wonder how he's going to take it when she doesn't show up and he discovers she's been here partying all along. I tell myself to just enjoy life. I tell myself this party is probably some kind of novel fun for her, hanging out with the VIPs. The hell with paranoia; Happy New Year to me!

Mary comes over to the piano as the guests are beginning to put on their coats to go and watch the "surprise" Marine Band Serenade. I play one of her favorite standard ballads, "But Beautiful." We manage to share a private tender moment, even though we're surrounded by all of these very important people.

Following the Marine Band serenade, Mary and I pass through a receiving line and are introduced to General and Mrs. Jones. When I introduce Mary to Mrs. Jones, she says, "Oh, we've already met. It's a real pleasure to have you here." Seems Mary made a good impression.

As we take an escorted tour of the upper floors of the house, I ask Mary how she managed to crash the party. It seems it was pretty much inadvertent. She just told the guard on duty at the entrance to the 8th and I Streets barracks that she was here for the commandant's party. She conveniently forgot to mention that she was a band member's wife. The guard told her where to go to enter the house, and once again on arrival, she told the greeters that she had been invited to the CMC (commandant of the Marine Corps) reception. No problem. They let her in, and she got to party with both the VIPs and the Marine Band. A foot in both worlds, that's us.

TAKE ME OUT TO THE WHITE HOUSE

I thought I'd done just about every kind of gig that a pianist/keyboardist could possibly do. But today's a first. I've never been a ballpark keyboard player. Not until today. Sometimes I think this is the Marine Corps' (or maybe God's) way of keeping me from becoming too self-important when I start thinking of myself as an artist. For example, I first soloed with the Marine Orchestra in 1992, performing Beethoven's fourth piano concerto, which had been a lifelong artistic goal of mine. The next day, I was tasked to play a sing-along for some pretty intoxicated marine generals. They were actually very nice to me and it turned out to be kind of fun.

This time, I'm remembering that a few short weeks ago, I got to perform Ravel's Piano Trio in uniform with a couple of brilliant Marine Band string players. The trio was another big item on my bucket list. But right now, as I finish loading a keyboard and amp into a government minivan, I'm preparing to play in a four-piece Marine Band combo for a tee-ball game for six-year-olds who, for the most part, need to be reminded of the appropriate base to run to.

President Bush loves baseball, and he's decided to use the South Lawn of the White House to promote the game. The social staff is kind enough to let us set up under a tree. These games are going to take place monthly between June and September, and the mid-summer Washington heat can be brutal. Otherwise, I generally like the events where the staff and the first family get casual. One of my good friends from the ushers' office is wearing an oversized pork pie hat, the president is in a short sleeve polo shirt, and the social secretary is wearing a sundress. A tiny baseball field has been constructed at the east end of the South Lawn of the White House. Portable bleachers have been moved into place for the players' families and some lucky press corps members.

The players are tiny. They represent communities that seem to have been randomly selected, one team from north Jersey and the other from a small town in central Pennsylvania. I'm sure the White House social office did demographic research to make sure that all races, religions, and socio-economic classes are represented in this summer's games. To look at the field and the players, one might think that this is just another tee-ball game in Anytown, USA. Except that President Bush is in the role of baseball commissioner. And Cal Ripken is here to sign autographs and shout encouragement. And Bob Costas, one of ESPN's most famous announcers, is doing a live play-by-play.

Our contact from the Military Office of the White House fills us in on what's expected of us. We don't need to play the National Anthem. That's pre-recorded. But between innings, we're to play "Take Me Out to the Ballgame." Good thing I came prepared for that one. After the game (consisting of one inning—everyone bats once and the inning ends), we'll be playing background music for a typical ballpark lunch out here on the South Lawn.

Bob Costas begins announcing: "Batting first for the Edison Tigers is second baseman, James Mendes. James is six years old and a first grader at Cooper Elementary School. His favorite subjects are math and recess. His favorite book is *Oh, the Places You'll Go!* And his favorite baseball player is Derek Jeter." By now, James has sized up the ball on the tee and taken a big six-year-old cut at it. He misses. He now looks even more determined. Concentrating hard, he takes another big swing and this time connects.

"Here's a hot shot up the middle," says Costas with seemingly genuine excitement.

Actually, the ball rolls between fifteen and twenty feet. And so it goes until the team completes all of their at-bats. I play "Take Me Out to the Ballgame" with a synthesized ballpark organ patch, and the Baltimore Orioles Bird, who happens to be in attendance, succeeds in getting a few people to sing along. The second team then takes their turn at bat with similar results and similar insightful commentaries from Bob Costas. When the game ends, President Bush and Cal Ripken stand for a while signing baseballs for all the kids.

I watch the president walk across the lawn toward the West Wing, escorted by secret service agents. Despite our political differences, I feel glad for him that today he got at least a short respite from the weight of the world. By now, we've started our picnic music set. I call "Sweet Georgia Brown," deciding that Dixieland is probably the right kind of instrumental music for this kind of party. I can smell the burgers and hot dogs cooking, and I see families with plates full of food taking their places at the picnic tables. I'm reminded how my mom and dad would come to all of my little league games when he didn't have to work, and how we'd often get ice cream afterward. Of course, there's also a very popular ice cream cart set up near the hot dog stand. We all feel connections to our homeland in different ways, and for me it doesn't get any more American than this.

Bob with President George W. Bush

JOANNE

Our family wakes up in our beachfront condo that we've rented for our week-long summer vacation. The semi-tropical sun glistens on the waves, the sound of crying gulls is in our ears, and the smell of sea salt is in the air. It's peaceful here. Atlantic Beach, North Carolina, is a very beautiful place, but none of this seems right. Our vacation was interrupted by the death of my sister-in-law, JoAnne.

Last night, we drove back from the funeral in the middle of the night, so we could finish out our vacation. Mary and I don't feel much like vacationing right now, but we decided to finish out our week of condo rental for Nicole and Gabrielle. Twelve- and thirteen-year-olds who work hard all year should get to have at least a few days at the beach. In reality, a few days spent sitting on the beach and reflecting on JoAnne will be good for me and Mary as well.

JoAnne was one of Mary's four sisters, the closest to her in age. She was very, very smart, very caring, loved to laugh, had a bit of a short fuse, and was an absolutely "no bullshit" kind of person. She also had a truly tough life. A rough childhood, a bad marriage, and two children with a dad who deserted them all. She was on and off of welfare and food stamps and did lots of menial jobs, most of which involved cleaning with chemicals that combined with cigarettes to destroy her lungs. She also had a stomach disorder that was misdiagnosed by a number of Medicaid doctors. Eventually, they figured out that she had a necrotic gallbladder and did emergency surgery. She developed pneumonia while trying to recover from the surgery and was on oxygen for the rest of her life. She died while waiting for a lung transplant.

I spent more of my adult life under the same roof as JoAnne than any other adult except for Mary. At one point, JoAnne nearly lost her kids because she didn't have a home for herself or them. We had her come and stay with us while Mary and I were living in Kentucky. Three adults and three children in a very small three-bedroom, one-bath house. Those were crazy times. JoAnne would care for the kids in the daytime and go off to clean offices at night. That situation lasted for a year and eventually, she and the kids moved out to return to Virginia.

A few years after I joined the Marine Band, JoAnne came and stayed with us again for a bit, and got some college credits knocked out while working part-time on a farm near us. But she couldn't make ends meet and once again returned to Hampton, Virginia. She loved science, had a natural intellectual curiosity about her, and wanted to teach biology. But by this time, we could see her health beginning to decline.

We held out hope until the end that she'd get a lung transplant, but it wasn't to be. We just visited her in the hospital on our way to Atlantic Beach (Mary had made numerous trips to Hampton to take care of her and drive her to medical appointments), and although she was weak and struggling to breathe, JoAnne made a point to give each of us a firm hug and tell us she loved us. She didn't look good and we all thought that it might very well be the last time we'd see her, though none of us said so.

On our second day in Atlantic Beach, Mary's youngest sister, Kathy, called to give us the news that JoAnne had died. Mary was devastated, though she put a good face on for the kids. I could tell though. She was on and off the phone with her sisters for the rest of the day, making plans for both a burial and a memorial service. The next day, she rented a car and drove to Hampton to help with the arrangements, and the following morning, the kids and I drove the four hours in our car so we could all be there for the service. When you pack for a vacation at the beach, you don't bring clothing suitable for a funeral, so we made a quick stop to pick up a few items.

Mary and her sisters put their heads together and decided on music to be played and sung as prelude, interlude, and postlude. There was an electric piano at the funeral home and they decided that I'd be playing it. I was skeptical that I'd be emotionally strong enough to play without having a breakdown, but I didn't bring that up to anyone. It's what the family wanted. In addition to some classical prelude and postlude, they wanted me to play "In My Life" by the Beatles and "Everything Must Change." Both are great songs with a lot of emotional impact, even when you're not saying goodbye to someone you love.

The chapel at the funeral home was modest but nice. Mary and her sisters did it up with floral arrangements. JoAnne's kids, Lita and Leon, were pretty much inconsolable. Leon cried and begged his mom for forgiveness while standing over JoAnne's open casket. Lita had to be dragged from her mom's side so the service could begin. I viewed all this from behind the keyboard, playing some of the more introspective pieces of Bach and Mozart that I have in my fingers.

JoAnne liked lots of different kinds of music. I found myself thinking back to my first solo with the Marine Chamber Orchestra, Beethoven's Piano Concerto No. 4. JoAnne and her kids, Mary and our kids, and both of my parents were all there. They all seemed to genuinely enjoy it (except for Nicole and Gabrielle, who at 3 and 4 years of age decided to take a concerto-length nap), and JoAnne seemed to be proud of me. I remember at the time wondering how often this would happen, where I'd be able to share the joy of a successful performance with all these people I love. I was a lucky man and those were good days.

My brother-in-law, Tom, got up to deliver a eulogy. Tom is one of my favorite people. He's a successful psychologist who probably understands human nature as well as anyone I know. His speech was loving and compassionate, yet calm. Tom grew up with the Keating sisters at Fort Monroe in Hampton. He knew JoAnne when she was in pigtails. The warmth he felt for her and for the entire family was apparent in every word. When he finished, there was a deep silence, punctuated by short sobs from the mourners.

Then Mary got up to sing "Everything Must Change." I didn't know how she was going to make it through this. I don't think I could have spoken right then, much less sung at full voice. But she did it with strength and conviction. At a few points during the song, I had to look down and watch tears splash on the keys. I tried not to make distracting noises. But I managed to keep my place in the tune. As we ended the song and I thought about it, I realized I hadn't seen Mary break down yet. She can be very strong, but she was definitely internalizing. Following another deeply moving eulogy by JoAnne's younger sister, Patty, the ceremony ended. As requested, I played "In My Life," maybe my favorite Beatles' tune. Its theme is a deep appreciation for those we love. By the close of the service, JoAnne's sisters (Julie, Mary, Patty, and Kathy), as well as her kids, seemed to be a bit more at peace, or maybe it was just resignation to the prospect of an emptier life without her. I hope and pray that the music helped, even if just a little.

CODA

Later that night, Mary had her emotional meltdown during the drive back to Atlantic Beach. I felt sure it was coming. Then we spent a few more days enjoying the calming effects of sea and sand, though we were still always aware of a big empty hole inside all of us. JoAnne's kids developed into fine young adults and every year, we all get together for a family reunion in Virginia Beach as a tribute to JoAnne.

BEETHOVEN'S EMPEROR

I'm probably more excited about this performance than anything I've ever done. My daughters, Nicole and Gabrielle, are both sitting in the string section playing the accompaniment on Beethoven's Concerto No. 5, subtitled "Emperor." Kevin, the conductor of the Howard County Gifted and Talented Orchestra, did me an incredible kindness when he invited me to play a solo with him and the orchestra. I've done a number of concerti with professional and college orchestras, but this is the first time I get to solo with my kids and I'm loving it. Nicole is playing principal cello and Gabi is assistant principal violin.

Following the opening majestic piano cadenza, the soloist sits through an orchestral interlude. Some sections within the orchestra are struggling a bit, but I notice with more than a little sense of pride that the violins and cellos are sounding good on what is a challenging, professional level piece. Not too many high school groups tackle music of this difficulty.

And, of course, I find myself doing what most parents do while watching their kids excel at something, which is to recall the path that got us all to this point. Diaper changing. Chicken pox comforting. Birthday party mayhem. *Chronicles of Narnia* reading at bedtime. Help with homework. Family vacations. And especially driving to violin and cello lessons in DC, given by my wonderful Marine Band colleagues, Diana and Claudia.

For me, the most satisfying thing about being a parent has been watching my kids grow, learn, change, and get excited about new things. And that growth and change has been significant in their development as young musicians. When they were small children, Gabi and Nicole would generally fall asleep when they came to my classical performances. Not surprising. But nowadays, I catch them at times humming or singing themes from "Rhapsody in Blue" and the exposition of this Beethoven concerto. They're both still probably more excited about the music of Beyoncé and other current pop icons (which I'm fine with), but who knows how their tastes will evolve in the future? I'm actually a bit envious of kids their age. Not so much because of all the years they have ahead of them, but more so because of all the wonderful things life has in store for them yet to discover. All these thoughts pass through my mind as the orchestral interlude progresses toward my second entrance.

As I'm playing the delicate music-box-like closing theme of the exposition, I happen to look over at Nicole and notice that she looks as if she might be crying or at least fighting back tears. Her pretty, round face is a bit flushed and her eyes are glistening a little. My first thought is that maybe she's just been moved emotionally by the beauty of this wonderful closing melody. But that's unlikely. Probably the concentration level it takes for student musicians to play a piece like this won't allow for that. Then the thought briefly crosses my mind that maybe she's crying because I'm embarrassing her. She knows this piece pretty well, and I'm sure that my handful of wrong notes haven't escaped her attention. But bad enough to make her cry? I don't think so. The cadenza's coming up and it's challenging, so I force myself to take my attention away from the orchestra, and I file it away to ask Nicole about the tears following the concert.

Mary set up a nice little reception in the lobby for after the performance, and now I'm shaking hands and receiving congratulations. It wasn't the worst solo I've ever played, but it was far from the best. Then I see Nicole and Gabi walking toward me, carrying their instrument cases and looking very pretty in their concert black attire. Gabrielle walks right up to me and gives me an assertive hug that lets me know she's proud of me. I'm grateful for that.

Looking over her shoulder at Nicole, I ask, "Did I see you crying? Did I play enough wrong notes to embarrass you?"

I was joking, but Nicole starts crying again, throws her arms around my neck and buries her face in my shoulder, saying, "Daddy, I messed up your piece!" Turns out that Nicole had missed an entrance following a long rest. Some of the other members of the cello section had come in correctly, and Nicole had quickly found her place. Funny how when you're performing and you miss something, a glitch that actually lasts around one second seems like a half hour. I hadn't noticed and the audience certainly didn't.

I don't say it, but secretly I'm gratified that Nicole became upset. It indicates that she's setting high standards for herself, a good thing if she ever has any interest in trying to become a great musician. Probably the only person who noticed it was Kevin, the conductor, and I'm sure the brief miss of an entrance by Nicole was the least of his concerns, given all he was dealing with. I comfort her by telling her that I hadn't noticed, congratulate and thank both Gabrielle and her, and tell them (honestly) that I loved getting to play with their orchestra. I know I'll probably never be lucky enough to do this again, getting to perform one of the greatest piano concertos ever written with my kids in the orchestra playing their hearts out and rooting for their dad.

GO FOR IT!

Tonight, we have a trio playing for the Kennedy Center Honors in the Ben Franklin Room on the top floor of the State Department. This year, we've come up with songs for Susan Farrell, Julie Harris, Robert Redford, Tina Turner, and Tony Bennett. We always arrive really early for this gig, so we won't be conspicuously wheeling a drum set up the red carpet at the same time politicians, Hollywood luminaries, and an assortment of Kennedys are trying to use it. We cram into the southeast corner of the room, leaving enough space for Condoleezza Rice to slip by with her entourage. She'll have the privilege of handing out the awards and shaking hands tonight after tribute speeches have been given for each of the honorees. This all happens after a five-star dinner has been served. We play during the dinner and manage to fit in a fair amount of people-watching. This is the gig where I've gotten to know Herbie Hancock a little bit.

We see the State Department protocol people open the doors, and a stream of tuxedos and evening gowns pour in. That's our cue to start playing, and we set out by swinging pretty hard with Stanley Turrentine's "Sugar." It's one of my favorites to start background jazz sets with because it's bluesy, but it also has some interesting chord changes to solo on.

I do notice in the distance that someone is wearing a tuxedo and a cowboy hat, and he looks from here like he's got a long ponytail. People start taking their seats and the ponytail dude makes his way over to the table next to us and stands over his chair, staring as if he's considering how to deal with us. It's Kid Rock. Kid Rock at the Kennedy Center Honors dinner. When he catches my eye, he decides that it's a good idea to yell at me, shouting out, "Come on, guys! Go for it! Rock on!"

Our job is to be pretty unobtrusive and Kid's admonishments are having the opposite effect. More and more guests are starting to look our way now, wondering what all this hell-raising is about. I do the opposite of what he's asking, and I tone it down by playing "Desafinado," a beautiful but sedate bossa nova by Jobim. Our ten-gallon hatted heckler shakes his head and strikes up a conversation with a stuffy-looking older woman seated next to him. I decide to try my best to ignore him throughout the dinner. I do pretty well at it, but he still periodically takes note of us and shouts out encouragement. I'm under the impression that he doesn't really understand the concept of background music. I think that to Kid Rock, music has to be aural testosterone or nothing.

At one point, I'm reading some sheet music for "Simply the Best" for the benefit of Tina Turner. She nods and smiles from across the room. But Kid gets up, walks over to the piano, and temporarily covers my sheet music with his hands, saying loudly, "C'mon, you don't need to be readin'! Just go for it!" Ironically, I rarely do read music on these gigs, but the Kennedy Center has requested songs associated with the Honorees, some of which are not everyday tunes for me. But once again, I just ignore him. The whole thing takes me back to my days at the Grove Club in Miami, 1983, where periodically, loud drunks would decide it was OK to get in my face and tell me what the band should be playing. A bit different from tonight's atmosphere.

Dinner's just about done now, and I see State Department aides setting up papers on the podium. In a few minutes, speeches will begin, and we'll be done. Then we'll quickly and quietly sneak out the door right behind us with our gear.

Kid Rock gives it one last try, "Come on, guys, cut loose! Go for it!"

A pretty, blonde, middle-aged woman has been sitting right in front of us with her back to me throughout the dinner. She turns around and says, "Yeah! Go for it! You can blame it on us."

It's Bo Derek.

I figure what the hell, dinner's nearly over, and this whole table seemingly wants our music to become an event. I just launch into a boogie-woogie blues, the kind with an active running pattern in the left hand. We groove hard and Kid Rock yells "Yeah!" more than once. Toward the end of the tune, I'm aware that someone has come up behind me and is watching me play over my right shoulder. I finish the song and look up. Tony Bennett is standing behind me. "Yeah, man, I really dig your playing," he says. I just mutter my usual awkward, "It's an honor to get to play for you." I didn't plan for this. We shake hands, and Tony returns to his seat to listen to the speeches and to receive his award. As we're quietly packing, I think that maybe Kid Rock was right all along. Maybe I could have spent the entire gig "going for it!"

THE BARNEY CAM

This is a new experience for me: Christmas music for a dog to run around the White House by. The subject of this bit of sophisticated filmmaking is Barney, the "First Pet," probably America's most famous canine. (The days of dog stars such as Rin-Tin-Tin and Lassie are long gone.) This film is destined for the White House website and is really designed to give families around the US a chance to see this year's Christmas decorations while children are entertained by the excursions of Barney, the Bushes' Scottish Terrier.

The video producers have literally strapped a camera to the dog's back and led him through different rooms in the White House. I know this for a fact because Barney is led into the cross hall where we're set up as a jazz group to play Christmas music. As we're playing, the dog sniffs around our feet for a minute or two, cocks his head sideways with a puzzled expression on his face, and moves on to the next room to search for some new smells. I'm thinking there will be a fair amount of editing. We were told that there will also be cameos for both the president and first lady, basically to wish America a Merry Christmas.

I was tasked for this gig a few days ago when the major (our second-in-command) told me the White House had asked for the Marine Band to do some jazz combo Christmas arrangements this year as a sound track for what's become an annual Barney Cam production. Immediately, the great Vince Guaraldi's *Charlie Brown Christmas* soundtrack came to mind. However, that was rejected immediately because of copyright issues. They wanted us to use public domain music only but in an upbeat jazz style. Of course, we wouldn't want any somber mood music to inhibit Barney's antics. That also meant we couldn't play anything written after 1900. I've always had a bit of an aversion to "jazzing up" traditional Christmas carols (I guess I'm a purist), but I had no choice. The Marine Band never argues when the White House asks for something.

We ended up recording a trio at 8th and I of three songs I suggested and arranged (including "It Came Upon a Midnight Clear" and "O, Tannenbaum"), but it was deemed too serious. The White House video producers rejected my suggestions and sent back instructions to try again. This time with more "gaiety and levity." For our second crack at it, I took the "upbeat" suggestion very seriously: "Joy to the World" reharmonized and done in a bright swing tempo, "Deck the Halls" played with a fast syncopated rock groove practically lifted directly from Guaraldi's famous "Linus and Lucy" chart, and "We Wish You a Merry Christmas" with a New Orleans second-line funky march beat. This time, the video producers were happy with their new soundtrack, so my arrangements ended up on the White House website. I like to think our music helped keep Barney's attitude positive and well-adjusted while he was learning to deal with the rigors of stardom.

NEW ORLEANS, PART 1

I'm playing a jazz gig on Bourbon Street during the French Quarter Festival. The band is great, playing a lot of Dixieland with an emphasis on the music of the great jazz soprano saxophonist, Sidney Bechet. We've got a packed room full of traditional jazz fans from all over the world. This gig I'm playing ends at 0200, and I have to check out of my hotel tomorrow morning by six to catch a flight back to DC. I've spent the last week working with a crew for Habitat for Humanity. We'd been demolishing homes ravaged by the flooding that followed Hurricane Katrina. Every morning for the entire week, I got up at six, put on my funkiest work clothes, and drove my rental car from the Navy Lodge in Algiers to a ferry that would carry me across the Mississippi to St. Bernard Parish, one of the hardest hit areas. The crossing was always a little bit eerie because the river was invariably cloaked in a thick fog bank at that hour of the morning. We couldn't see the St. Bernard side until we were nearly on top of it. The only sign that we were closing in was the occasional sighting of a pair of refinery smokestacks poking up through the mist.

Contrary to the popular perception that the hurricane only destroyed the more impoverished areas, St. Bernard was very middle class and reminded me a lot of the neighborhood in South Miami where we used to live. Following Katrina, there was no electricity, no running water, no grocery stores, and outside of a few homes with determined souls relying on their portable generators, there was no one living here. Nothing was growing. All of the trees, gardens, and lawns were killed after being subjected to days of submersion under a toxic cocktail of Lake Pontchartrain overflow, backed up sewers, and lots of rain.

I asked myself, "Why are we here?" These homes seemed to be completely uninhabitable. There was a soup of rotted carpet or flooring with chunks of mildewed drywall underfoot everywhere we went. We had to wear masks at all times to avoid becoming sick from mold spores. The smell was awful, even with masks on, and I undressed and had to hose down my clothes at the end of each day before going back into the Navy Lodge. I was usually in the shower for a full half hour at the end of each work day.

I took leave from the Marine Band and signed up to work with Habitat. At our orientation, they explained that for every house we gutted and cleaned, there was a displaced homeowner who was going to save about six thousand dollars by not having to pay someone to do it. Once that was done, the owner could either rebuild or more readily sell their property. Habitat had asked all throughout the community (of those who could be found) whether the people wanted help with the cleanup, and pretty much everyone said yes.

So they put me in a group with a leader and eleven other volunteers. We all spent eight hours a day for five consecutive days smashing dry wall, tearing up carpet and flooring, hauling out ruined kitchen and laundry appliances, and mopping or sweeping up the refuse that Katrina had left behind. Anything that remained of family mementos, such as children's little league photos or high school graduation portraits, were stacked in a separate pile at the front of the driveway. Those piles were really small. The mildew had destroyed nearly everything.

On our third day of work, we had a visitor. A kindly-looking sixty-something woman drove up and started going through the memento pile. It was time for our lunch break, so our work group all gathered around her to see what was up. It turned out that the house we were working on belonged to her eighty-eight-year-old mother. When the hurricane hit, her mom had gone to Seattle to stay with her other daughter. She wouldn't be coming back. Our visitor had traveled to Lafayette to ride out the storm with friends, but her husband had remained in New Orleans for the duration. He still runs a local St. Bernard newspaper, and a good journalist doesn't leave town during a crisis. The nice lady told us that it was much more than houses, strip malls, and yards that got washed away. It was the entire St. Bernard way of life. She got choked up and her eyes welled with tears as she talked to us.

She thanked us more than once, saying, "My mom's much too old to deal with all this, and there's no way my husband and I could have done what you all did with this house. We're just so blessed that so many of you have come down from all over the country to help us." I looked at the skeleton of her mom's home as she carried away her few salvageable mementos and realized this was the reason I'd come.

The next day, we had more visitors. While we were starting to demolish a new house, a trash truck pulled up and two men got out to talk with our team leader, Jessica. After they left, surprisingly, Jessica came over and told us that we were all invited to a party after work. It seemed that one of the St. Bernard councilmen had moved back into his home, and he wanted to extend his gratitude and southern hospitality to some of the Habitat workers by inviting us to a barbecue. At the end of the day, we got our showers, changed clothes, and eight of us accepted the invitation.

The councilman's home was absolutely surreal. There was one other occupied property on the block, and that person was living in a trailer parked on a desert that had once been their front yard. The councilman's whole bottom floor had been gutted, so only the support beams remained standing, but the second floor was completely intact, and the bathrooms, refrigerator, electricity, and swimming pool filters all ran on two large generators.

But most surreal were the flower gardens in the back yard. I would never have guessed that something as ordinary as flowers could be a sight so welcome and yet so astonishing. We'd been working in this wasteland for three days at this point, and this was the first cultivated plant life any of us had seen. The councilman and his wife told us that they had returned so quickly following Katrina so others from their community would see that St. Bernard was still habitable. They were certainly determined to make sure their community came back, even though the nearest grocery store was probably a twenty-five minute drive. But that didn't stop them from serving us barbecue ribs and chicken, potato salad, coleslaw, and lots of cold beer. It seemed incongruous for us to be in the middle of all this devastation and yet be reaching into a refrigerator for a few welcome cold ones. We thanked them for their hospitality but were told that they're the ones who should be thanking us. Real nice downhome folks.

On Friday, after finishing our last day of work, our Habitat group decided to take a ride into the French Quarter and have a farewell dinner together at the Gumbo Shop. As we walked toward Jackson Square, a few of the women decided it was time for a souvenir stop. We all came out with some trinkets to bring home to our families and all the women bought feather boas. One of them remarked about how nice it was to not be covered in filth, to take their hair out of the hair-nets, and to dress up a bit to go out, topped off with the classic New Orleans feather boas.

The group was pretty interesting and we worked well together. There was a mother and daughter who were probably doing this as a kind of emotional therapy following mom and dad's divorce. There were a few college students, psychology and education majors. Carl, a fellow musician from San Francisco, probably became my best friend on the crew. He formerly helped run one of Bill Clinton's campaigns for the governorship in Arkansas.

Robin is an accomplished competitive long-distance runner from Lafayette. She is married to an emergency medicine doctor who had been flown in to work in the Superdome right after the storm. She confirmed that the conditions in that dome were actually even worse than the press had led us to believe. She showed us emails that her husband sent her, which she had then forwarded to a number of members of Congress on the third day after the storm. I suspect that by publicizing these first-hand accounts, she and her husband were in large part responsible for getting the US military involved in the rescue effort and for getting the Washington bureaucrats to finally get off their butts and take some decisive action.

But I think the most interesting member of our work crew was Bill. Bill was a highly successful broadcast journalist for most of his life. His number one hobby was flying and aircraft, particularly related to WWII. He had been the producer of the taping of Richard Nixon's resignation speech and was also in on the ground floor at the inception of Turner Broadcasting, where he worked until his recent retirement. Bill was seventy-four years old, and he drove himself and his tools down to New Orleans all the way from Bethesda, Maryland. He worked as hard as any of us all week, ruling out only the lifting of large appliances. He was twenty-five years older than me, and I was the second oldest member of our team.

A few speeches were given following our meal of classic New Orleans cuisine, but the last one, given by Bill, is the one I know I won't ever forget. He started by pointing out that he's a man of few words and rarely gives speeches. Bill had experienced all the positive momentum following our victories in World War II. He said that in recent years, he had started to despair for the future of the US, the country he loves so much. But we had made him change his mind. He said that watching the enthusiasm and energy all of us youngsters demonstrated while working toward a common cause made him think that possibly our generation could fix what was broken in our country. His speech somehow made my dinner of red beans and dirty rice taste even better.

After dinner, I bid farewell to most of my new friends, and a few of them said they'd come by and hear me play at Fritzel's, one of the only traditional jazz clubs left in the French Quarter. I'm playing with Mike Flaherty, bandleader of Dixieland Direct. Mike and I have a great rapport, both personally and musically, through all our years working together at the Market Inn. It's strictly a coincidence that he's in New Orleans scoping out the possibility of moving down here.

Ryan, a brilliant clarinetist/saxophonist who leads the house band at Fritzel's, called me for this gig mid-week. Ryan knows me as a member of Dixieland Direct because he lived in the DC area for about six months following Katrina. Ryan was flooded out and had to wait to go home. Our Dixieland band referred him for some gigs, and he worked with our group a few times. I think he hired us partly out of a debt of gratitude, but I'm also certain that he enjoys playing with us.

As I'm sitting here cranking out stride piano on "Please Don't Talk About Me When I'm Gone," I'm really glad I took the gig. Ryan and Jacques (another woodwind player) are both brilliant at playing the old tunes, interpreting them with a fresh and creative approach. A short time ago, we had a brilliant banjo player named Orville sit in and play "After You've Gone" as a duet with me at a hair-raising tempo. The audience isn't the largest, but it very well might be the most enthusiastic I've ever played for. I've also had a few mixed drinks. What the hell. Who cares about exhaustion and sleep deprivation? I'll catch up on my z's tomorrow on the flight home.

PRESIDENT BUSH
AND IRAQ

I'm playing solo piano for a corporate dinner at the Corcoran Gallery of Art. The piano is beautiful. There are huge stone pillars throughout the first floor foyer, and one of DC's most prominent caterers has set places for dinner for around seventy guests. The tablecloths are a gold color and the centerpieces have big, beautiful roses and hydrangeas of different colors. It's all very elegant and I hope I'm adding to the atmosphere by playing Debussy compositions, the Gershwin Songbook, and some Chopin. After a four-course dinner (they throw in a sherbet course somewhere for palette cleansing), they serve up the crème brûlée dessert, and the CEO comes to the podium for brief remarks. It turns out that they're brief because his main job is to introduce the guest keynote speaker, Bob Woodward. It so happens that President Bush recently gave Woodward three hours of interviews for his book and now Woodward is sharing insights on what he discovered.

It's late 2006, and things aren't going terribly well for the US in Iraq right now. IEDs, roadside bombings, the daily arrival of the remains of American troops at Dover, and the sight of maimed soldiers learning to get by with artificial limbs at Walter Reed National Military Medical Center—these are all commonplace.

Woodward starts his speech with a simple question, "How many of you here think that invading Iraq was a good idea? Raise your hand if you think so." Not one person raises a hand.

Not one.

This line of questioning brings back memories of jobs I've played in uniform at the White House rather than in a tuxedo like I'm wearing tonight. The first memory that comes to mind is January 2005, standing at the piano in the private quarters of the White House, preparing to play a brief reception.

Before the guests arrived, President Bush entered the room, extended his hand as he walked by, and said, "Thanks for being here, marine."

I shook his hand and gave one of my typical answers, "Always a pleasure for me." I'm sincere when I say this. No matter who's president, it truly is a pleasure to play White House jobs.

Then the president added, "It's a great day. A great day for democracy."

As he walked away, I thought about the tremendous number of deaths, the amount of violence, and all the destruction there had been leading up to today's elections in Iraq. I remember thinking, I hope at least something good is coming out of this mess. This democracy is certainly pretty damned expensive for both the US and Iraq.

I then remember a White House reception I played when the guests were all family and friends of deceased US troops, those who returned from Iraq in coffins. The president greeted all the family members privately after his speech, giving them thanks from a grateful nation. He later remarked to the press corps that it was one of the most difficult things he had ever had to do as president. I'm sure that was true, but I'm also sure that it wasn't as difficult for him as it was for the husbands, wives, and children of those who never made it home. As much as I personally struggled with the ethical choice of the war in Afghanistan, I finally came to the conclusion that it was a necessary military action that our country needed to take. I always felt that Iraq was a completely different story. I've denied myself the freedom to protest out of loyalty, plain and simple. Loyalty to the Marine Corps, to the commandants I've served under, to Colonels Foley and Bourgeois who helped my career thrive, and loyalty to the marines who are currently on their second and third tours of duty in South Asia. These are the people I really haven't wanted to embarrass or disappoint.

My attention turns back to Bob Woodward, who's getting ready to close his remarks. He just made the point that President Bush has a quasi-messianic complex; he isn't just a puppet of Cheney or Rumsfeld, as some would have us think, but rather he thinks that his true calling in life is to bring democracy and even Christianity to other parts of the world. As he concludes his speech, I go into Bach's "Sheep May Safely Graze" while thinking, Lord, please, please just get us through the next two years.

THE MARKET INN

The Market Inn in southwest DC is finally closing down. It's been open for fifty years, and I've been working Sunday brunches here for the past fifteen. In my first six years as a professional freelance musician, I never kept a gig for more than six months, so I'm more than surprised to have played with the same band in the same restaurant for this long. I came to the Market Inn as a sub in 1992. By the end of that year, John, my predecessor, had moved on to better things and the gig was mine. We wore red vests and played a lot of Dixieland jazz with some swing-era tunes thrown in.

When the original sax/clarinet player retired to Florida in 1994, we hired Henning Hoehne, a brilliant clarinetist who'd had a highly successful career with the Naval Academy Band. Henning plays with a fire and commitment to every note that I've never experienced in traditional jazz. He speaks with a tremendous amount of enthusiasm about three things: music, food, and fishing. Over the years, his musicianship has spurred our group on to become a world-class Dixieland/Swing ensemble. I've also ended up learning lots of songs, so I could keep up with him.

Mike Flaherty leads the group, takes care of business, and plays drums with a comfortable swing feel and lots and lots of energy. When everything's locked in with this group, Dixieland Direct, I sometimes find myself wishing I would never die because of the musical express train we're all riding on. But all things do come to an end, and like much of the rest of this part of DC, the Market Inn's been sold to government or corporate interests that have other ideas for this property. There's quite a bit I'll miss about this place, though I have to say it might be nice to finally stay home on Sunday mornings.

I'll miss Linda and Carl, the minority owners who've been forced to sell due to an expired fifty-year lease. They've taught me that club and restaurant managers can be your friends as well as your employers. She bakes us cookies at Christmas, and he always encourages us to try new items on the New Orleans style seafood buffet, complimentary for the musicians. I appreciate the fact that neither of them is afraid to get their hands dirty helping out when the place gets busy, and I get a strong feeling that they really care about their employees. Some of the servers have worked here for over twenty years, which is pretty much unheard of in the restaurant business.

I'll also miss the Episcopalian minister who comes in nearly every week but won't sit in the bar area where we play. Instead, he reserves the table directly outside of our room. For years, I couldn't figure out why he just wouldn't come in. I know he loves the music. Then it dawned on me: The bar is full of gentleman's club photos and portraits from the 40s, 50s, and 60s. Very tame by today's standards, but soft-core porn nonetheless. The most famous one is a full nude photo of Marilyn Monroe from the 50s. It sits behind me so that when the audience tires of watching my disturbing facial contortions while I play, they can look up and see Marilyn in her demure magnificence. A little different from the White House, where I might have a beautiful portrait of George H.W. Bush or JFK hanging on the wall behind me. From where he sits, our friendly clergyman can hear all our music, but he's not going to allow himself to be corrupted by any unsettling renderings of the female form.

I'll even miss Rhoda who, even at the age of sixty-eight, is still our resident wild woman. Rhoda lives nearby, so she walks to the brunch in her high heels and sun dresses, taking full advantage of the "all-the-mimosas-you-can-drink" part of the brunch deal. The more she drinks, the more she yells at the ends of our songs. Sometimes she'll shout out that the music just "gave me an organism." If she has enough to drink, she'll wander around to other tables, grabbing the shoulders of any well-built man she sees (no worry if he's 40 years younger than she is), or cuddling cute babies who can't escape their high chairs to avoid her smeared lipstick kisses. This got her into serious trouble at least once. One irate parent decided that he didn't want Rhoda grabbing, squeezing, and kissing his eighteen-month old. He asked her to cut it out, and when she didn't, he called the police. Carl told her it might be a good idea for her to leave before they arrived to arrest her. She took his advice and stayed away for a few weeks, but she eventually came back and jumped right in again with the crazed dancing and baby squeezing. She especially loves to hear us play Duke Ellington's "Caravan." The Latin groove literally gets her dancing in a frenzy, and there's not a lot of room for her to strut her stuff between tables.

I've talked to her a few times though, and I'm convinced she has a good heart and that her Sunday mornings at the Market Inn fulfill some sort of emotional need. Music has lots of different functions, but only Rhoda knows what it is about the Market Inn and Dixieland Direct that helps set her spirit free.

I think that I'll miss my old friend Dennis the most of all. Dennis has recently turned eighty-nine, but he still comes outside with us when we take a break, so he can smoke a cigarette. The front of the restaurant has a nice little patio where we usually eat during our breaks. Dennis is an African American who remembers seeing Louis Armstrong play when he was only nine years old. He told us that he was tasked by his father to sell beer at a concert, and he failed because he left his post to get closer to the music. He still remembers that his father whipped him for leaving free beer for the crowd to decide what to do with. He also remembers that it was worth it because he got to hear Louis play.

Dennis loves jazz as much as anyone I've ever met, and it seems that he's had personal relationships with nearly every important musician in the history of the art form. He tells us stories about Teddy Wilson, Art Blakey, and Miles Davis. But he has the most stories about Duke Ellington. It turns out that he escorted most of these groups on their famous Jazz Ambassador State Department tours in the 1950s. He can tell you how difficult it was to keep the entire Ellington band out of prison in Africa after some pot was found on one band member. He claims (and I believe him) to own every vinyl record ever made by the Ellington band, numbering somewhere in the 120s. He was employed by the State Department for years as an editor and did a lot of high-quality writing for them. I've even seen an outline for a history of jazz he was working on at one time. Very thorough and well thought out.

Dennis and his lovely Austrian wife, Brita, met in Trinidad while working for their respective embassies. She comes to the Market Inn every week, and I frequently try to convince them both that Dennis should write an autobiography. He always seems to change the subject when I bring this up, and finally Brita tells me (while Dennis is off to the restroom) that he just doesn't feel that he has the energy to write any more. I even try to get him to record an oral history through a colleague of mine at the Smithsonian, but he declines, saying he's "just too tired." We've watched Dennis's health decline over the years. The concern on Brita's face as she helps him to eat or to get in and out of a chair is more than obvious.

The signs of aging are apparent among our group, too. Henning is now almost seventy, still playing great but occasionally forgetting cues that he never would have forgotten ten years ago. Mike is putting on some weight, and my hair is falling out. Amazingly enough, this is a gig on which we've gotten old together. One last time, we play "Just a Closer Walk with Thee" and "The Saints Go Marching In" to end our very last set, with a dose of pathos followed by a serving of joy. I say goodbye and good luck to all my friends who work here, then go out and take one last long look at the marquee in front of the restaurant that will soon be demolished by a wrecking ball. Nothing lasts forever, but I know that seventeen years' worth of positive sound waves originating at the Market Inn's Sunday brunches are still floating around somewhere out in the ether.

ALASKA

I'm staring up at a cliff wall that must measure over 150 feet. It's nearly sheer, though there are lots of ledges and cracks in the rock for hand and footholds. I'm very grateful that I made it back down without a disastrous fall. The climb down was more frightening than the ascent, but it's well worth it to have the opportunity to explore the Mendenhall Glacier, complete with radiant blue caves. We didn't go far into them, as we'd been warned that large slabs of the blue ice commonly break off, and pristine streams run underneath the ice. Although Mendenhall and many of the other glaciers in the area are receding, we were able to still walk on top of it and feel the natural force and power of thousands of years of ice compression beneath our feet.

On this tour, the Marine Band Jazz Quintet arrived in Juneau and spent four days playing free public concerts and school programs for the Juneau Jazz and Classics Festival. All of our concerts were free and open to the public. Greg, the saxophone player who set up this trip, put together a lot of varied music for our programs, ranging from Chris Potter to Bud Powell to Duke Ellington.

The majority of school students were Tlingit Indians. All the schools had totem poles in front of them. One even had a taxidermy grizzly bear in a glass case as its mascot. When we presented our school programs, it seemed we connected really well with all the kids, whether or not they were music students. Some days, we did as many as four performances, which is a lot, given the time needed for setup and tear down of gear on each gig. One school program was scheduled so tightly that Chris, our drummer, didn't have time to set up his kit. Instead, he just took his sticks and played on any hard surface he could find, to the great delight of a classroom full of kindergarteners. The last concert was in the library at the University of Alaska. We were the featured group following a small festival of school jazz bands. It wasn't our best attended concert, but the audience seemed to love it.

Even with the tightly packed schedule, we somehow still managed to make it to the nightly parties held for us and the other festival artists. Lots of grilled wild salmon, wine, and sitting on outdoor decks to watch eleven o'clock sunsets over lakes, quiet evergreen forests, and snow covered mountains. Linda, the festival's artistic director, got us free tickets for some of the classical performances and made sure we made it to her home for a beautiful reception that she hosted for all the performing artists.

Everyone in Juneau was ridiculously friendly and appreciative toward us. In Juneau, everywhere we went, people were glad to see us and incredibly helpful. Marshall took us out on his boat for salmon fishing. Twice. I saw a humpback whale with a baby being closely pursued by a pod of hunting orcas.

John and Laura, a wonderful couple who work for the festival, drove us everywhere. When our performances ended, Greg, Eric, and I decided to take some leave and stay for a few extra days. John and Laura lent us one of their cars so we wouldn't have to rent one. Our new friends, Jan and Steve, opened their home to us for those extra nights, so we wouldn't have to pay for a hotel. The two of them also guided us on our hike to the glacier.

Ron is one of the benefactors of the festival. He asked us if we'd gotten to take a small plane tour of the area. We told him no.

"You can't come up to Juneau and not see the glacial cap," Ron said.

The plane tour of the glaciers was free, courtesy of Ron. So three days ago, through the windows of a small twin-engine plane, we all got to see the awe inspiring glacial cap that connects Mendenhall and some thirty other glaciers!

Now, as I turn my back on the cliff and head back to our car for one last evening in Juneau, I feel very grateful that the "President's Own" decided it was a good idea to send us here. Otherwise, I probably would have gone an entire lifetime without getting to see this glorious place. I think that a good part of the reason everyone here has been so appreciative is because they go eight months each year with no performing artists coming to town. What we and the other festival musicians did in Juneau isn't an everyday event for Alaskans, as opposed to Washingtonians, who on any given evening can probably find five or six different world-class performances to choose from. Not so up here. Until now, the "President's Own" has never sent performers to Alaska. I'm really lucky to be among the first.

MARINE CORPS ETHOS

We just finished our after-dinner entertainment program at the Marine commandant's home at Marine Barracks Washington, DC. Part of our Marine Band job is playing short programs for the commandant and his guests when the dinner is an official function. Kevin or Sara, our two fine Marine Band vocalists, usually sing three selections and a fourth pre-planned encore. Occasionally, they'll sing a classical aria, but most of the time it's pop tunes, show tunes, and a patriotic closer such as "God Bless the USA."

I've served under five Marine Corps commandants. The commandants are always gracious and appreciative, introducing us by name and playing up our role at the White House as members of the "President's Own" to the guests. I actually feel that I've become friends with both them and their ladies. Well, at least as friendly as you can get in the military when you're an enlisted marine and you're dealing with a four-star general.

General Michael Hagee , the thirty-third commandant would even go so far as to invite us to join the guests for a drink after introducing us, rather than having us quietly slip away after being offered congratulations. Kevin hesitated to join the party, but I happily accepted a cognac and convinced him he should at least have a beer. Funny how simple things like an after dinner drink can become a big issue when it comes to military etiquette.

Kevin's powerful voice could practically shift tectonic plates. After the applause dies down for our roof raising version of "Old Man River," General Conway, the thirty-fourth commandant of the Marine Corps, thanks us and talks about a great benefactor of our Corps, our guest of honor tonight. He's a man named Peter who runs a nonprofit to benefit the families of marines and law enforcement officers who've lost their lives in the line of duty. A pretty good cause, I'd say.

I know firsthand what a great, generous-spirited man Peter is. Three years ago, when General Hagee invited us to join the guests for a drink following one of our programs, I was speaking with one of them about my younger daughters, Nicole in college and Gabrielle preparing to apply. I've found through the years that when I'm put in a social situation with people I might not have a lot in common with, it's always safe to talk about family. Anyway, I like talking about them. Peter came by, introduced himself, and quietly handed me a business card and told me to give him a call. The card had an out-of-state address, and I immediately assumed that Peter was probably interested in having Kevin and me take a trip and do our show in civilian clothes for a private function. I didn't think about our short conversation until I remembered to call Peter three days later:

Peter: "I've been fortunate enough to see you play at the home of the commandant for years now. You're a great musician and a great marine."

Me: "Thanks very much. It's always a real pleasure to play at the Commandant's home."

Peter: "Well, I'd love to pay you back for your years of service. I couldn't help but overhear you talking about your situation with your daughters' education. It so happens that our foundation provides scholarships for the children of marines and law enforcement officers, and I'd like to include your daughter as one of our recipients. What I'm talking about is tuition for one entire year at whatever college she ends up going to."

Me: (After a long pause; I can't believe what I'm hearing) "Peter, I'm honored, but please, just take those funds and use them for the children of Iraq war vets or NYPD families. I haven't made anything like the sacrifices they have."

Peter: "That's what we do all the time, but with all you've done to represent our Corps all these years...well, I just really want you to have this token of our appreciation."

I accepted. I nearly argued with him to keep the scholarship. I know that, outside of playing under lots of pressure, I have one of the best jobs in the entire Marine Corps. I don't get shot at, IEDed, have to sleep in a tent when it's 115 degrees at night, and I don't have to leave my wife and kids for extended deployments in a war zone. But Peter values my service, and I can't deny that the scholarship will be a tremendous help. Once my youngest daughter Gabrielle leaves for college, Mary and I will be supporting three households simultaneously. It'll be tight, even with some money we've saved and Peter's unexpected gift. I guess he must really have loved our version of "Shenandoah."

As General Conway introduces Peter, I take the unusual step of making a public statement of my gratitude to the commandant and his guests. I tell everyone that Peter and I have a special relationship, and that he'll always have my gratitude and respect. General Conway continues speaking, commenting positively on Kevin's and my performance, both musical and verbal. When the general's done speaking, Peter comes over and shakes my hand warmly.

"One more great memory you've given me in the home of the commandant. Wonderful to see you again," he says.

I think I finally fully understand the sense of brotherhood that's the true ethos of the Corps. I've been hearing about it for years, but unlike most marines, I'll never know the bonds created by experiencing basic training at Camp Lejeune or by spending a solid year sharing a foxhole with my platoon in the remote mountains of northeastern Afghanistan. But Peter, this one elderly retired marine, has shown me firsthand the ethos of the Marine Corps—marines taking care of marines.

FAREWELL TO W

I'm upstairs in the White House playing on the Steinway B in the private quarters. I'm always a bit uncomfortable coming up here to play, probably because I feel like I'm intruding in someone's home. For the president and his family, I know that privacy is a rare and precious commodity. The social secretary, a couple of White House ushers, and five or six butlers are walking around briskly but without noticeable stress as they prepare for the Bushes' final lunch. Tomorrow, Barack Obama will be sworn in as the 44th President of the United States, and the Bushes will get on a helicopter bound for retirement in Crawford, Texas.

I generally start playing as soon as I'm escorted to the piano, even if the guests haven't started to arrive. I'm remembering my first private residence job for W. At that reception, I was standing by the piano with my arms behind my back in an at-ease posture when the president came in. He had extended his hand, saying, "Thanks for being here, marine."

"My pleasure," I replied.

The president paced around the room for a few minutes, then turned to me and said, "Why don't you sit down. You're making me nervous."

I complied and went into "If I Were a Bell" immediately, deciding that from now on when I played a private reception, the music would begin the moment I reached the keyboard, guests or no guests.

Since the election, the Bushes have hosted numerous private residence farewell dinners and receptions, with me being the only musical support. I've watched the president say goodbye to Supreme Court Justices Antonin Scalia, Clarence Thomas, and Samuel Alito. To Andrew Card and Karl Rove. And to current and former cabinet members Robert Gates, Donald Rumsfeld, and Alberto Gonzalez.

The president seems to have had a particularly close relationship with British Prime Minister Gordon Brown. A week ago, there was a dinner hosted for him and his wife, just the four of them. As they walked by the piano, Prime Minister Brown looked over his shoulder at me saying, "Lovely... simply lovely."

The president said, "Yup. This guy's one of the best piano players in America!"

And all these years, I didn't think he was really listening. Maybe I can use that quote on my promotional flyers when I retire.

It was a few nights later that I played for another of the farewell receptions, and Mrs. Bush came over and said, "I just want to thank you for all the lovely music you've brought into our home the last eight years. You've given us a lot of wonderful memories." She's always been very gracious toward me.

The nature of this type of work can make an artist feel like they're just providing "musical wallpaper," as the cynical freelance musician community is prone to call it, but validation by the president and first lady is certainly welcomed. Playing background or cocktail piano is sometimes viewed as second-class work by many in the Marine Band and musicians in general. But I know there's a real art to doing it well. I know the president likes country music and the first lady seems to like show tunes, so I may play a country music song followed by "If I Loved You." I play them quite softly but still with nuances of phrasing, and arrange them in a way that keeps them interesting to both the performer and the listener. I know that if I'm bored or disinterested while doing this work, people are going to know, if only subliminally.

At most of the events, the president and first lady meet and greet until all the guests have arrived. This takes place in the foyer where the piano's located, just outside of the Yellow Oval Room. Once everyone has gathered, the first couple usually offers to take the guests on a tour of the private quarters. There are a lot of Remington sculptures and Catlin paintings in the White House. I'm assuming the guests all get to see the Lincoln Bedroom. I can hear their voices in the distance but can't quite make out what they're talking about, though I do hear references to art works, as well as the names of some distinguished overnight guests from the past.

Today is different though. After everyone arrives, they all go directly into the family dining room, foregoing the tours and cocktails. All of these guests are either family or close personal friends. They've all seen it before, probably more than once. During the lunch, I can hear them talking and I'm sure they can hear me; however, they're in the next room where I can't see them. Amy, the social secretary, cues me to stop playing right after the butler staff finishes serving some sort of mouth-watering chocolate mound garnished with raspberries and mint leaves for dessert. There's a moment of silence, then I hear President Bush begin to speak. I can make out most of it, things like, "It's been a great ride. You've all been there for me...Laura and I want to thank you..." and so on. But what's most memorable to me about the speech is when he says, "No, this one's got alcohol in it. What the heck, we're out of here tomorrow anyway."

He gets some laughs and I join them, remembering how the president always had a benign non-alcoholic beer in his hand during all the cocktail receptions I've played. The entire speech, and the entire lunch for that matter, has the same feel as a last day of school before summer break. As I play them out, I'm thinking that President Bush is going to be real glad to get back to Texas once again to resume the role of the multi-millionaire gentleman rancher, leaving it to the next guy to be "The Decider."

PRESIDENT OBAMA'S INAUGURATION

I'm sure that tonight's in-place time is the latest I've ever been given for a Marine Band job. I got the call yesterday from operations, instructing me that I'll be playing for a White House reception that's scheduled to begin at 2300 hours. The Obamas are going to return to their new home for an after-party following a full day of official ceremonies, parades, and inaugural balls. Adding to the anticipation for me is that I'm to be the intermission pianist for Wynton Marsalis's Quintet. I'll be taking the subway to the White House, as I've been told our usual military transportation won't be able to get me anywhere near there with the millions of partiers and the cordoned-off streets that surround it. Either way, I had difficulty sleeping last night because I was concerned about making it into town.

I leave home at 1800 hours, knowing that I'll be making a first impression on behalf of the "President's Own" tonight. It turns out that the traffic and the subway volume aren't much of a problem, as I'm traveling in the opposite direction of the teeming masses. I run into a Marine Corps general and his wife on the train who say they remember me from pre-parade receptions at 8th and I (the oldest post in the Marine Corps and where I'm stationed). They're on their way to one of the inaugural balls. Everyone on the train looks emotionally charged and frozen. I wonder how the Obamas are going to have anything left in the tank for partying when they finally get home.

I walk a few blocks from the Metro stop to the White House and notice the streets aren't nearly as packed as I had expected. Word on CNN was that nearly six million people made it onto the National Mall earlier today for the festivities. My guess is that most of the locals have gone home by now and that most of the tourists are in local restaurants and hotels nursing hot chocolate, coffee, or maybe a shot of some warm cognac. It was pretty damn cold today and that's an understatement! I don't think it topped twenty-five degrees, and right now, it's probably closer to fifteen. I'm regretting that I didn't get any of the government-issue ear muffs.

I think about my band friends who had to march today. I know that most of them realize what an honor it is to be a part of something like this, but I also know the parade represents many, many hours of standing in the cold and waiting, as well as ridiculously early in-place times for both the parade itself and the rehearsals. I remember how, a few days ago, I was putting on my uniform in the locker room at 0745 hours to go play for one of President Bush's last receptions when the band came through the door in their "service B" uniforms. They had already completed a three-hour rehearsal. Just do the math. The human resources and logistics that go into something like this are absolutely mind-boggling, and I'm justifiably proud of how our band members handle it.

Security at the White House is no different than ever, although I enter from the Northeast Gate off of Pennsylvania Avenue instead of the usual Southeast one. When I enter the ushers' office, I immediately notice a group of new people coming and going. Of course, my usher friends are all still here, but President Obama's social staff has replaced Amy Zantzinger and the Bushes.

I ask Jim, one of the ushers, "You don't really think that the president is going to get back in time to come to this reception before he turns in, do you?"

Jim tells me, "The president said that he definitely wanted to make it back in time to catch a set of Wynton's." This tells me a lot about him. He loves music. He loves jazz. And he's OK with staying up late to party when it's called for.

Tonight's logistics are different than most White House events in that they've set up a stage in the East Room with the historic 1938 Steinway Grand and Wynton Marsalis's gear set up on it. The music's usually in the Grand Foyer, but tonight, I'm actually in the center of the reception. I start to play a few minutes after 2300 as guests begin to wander in. There seem to be a lot of prominent Democrats, including John Conyers and Harry Reid. Then I spot the "queen" out of the corner of my eye. It's Oprah. She's wearing the gown of gowns and seems to have a sizable entourage following her every move.

I stick to jazz. I've read that our new president likes Miles and Coltrane. I start with some Keith Jarrett, play a little Horace Silver and Bennie Golson, and then go into a few standards of Victor Young and Cole Porter. As I'm finishing "What Is This Thing Called Love?", I hear the sound of voices and a little soft laughter coming from the Green Room directly adjacent to the stage. At this point, I'm just starting Ellington's "Mood Indigo." Right as I finish the melody, a trumpet player jumps in with a solo break, leading us back to the top of the form. It's not just any trumpet player. It's Wynton Marsalis, and he's decided it's a good idea to sit in with me.

He looks at me briefly and says, "Just keep playin'."

Holy Crap! I'm trading licks with Wynton on this most beautiful and sultry of Duke's compositions at the White House on the eve of the inauguration of America's first black president. His sound is as round and beautiful as any trumpet player I've ever heard or played with. In the past year, I've been fortunate enough to play with two of the world's greatest, Phil Smith, principal trumpet in the New York Philharmonic, and Vince DiMartino, my old friend and mentor from the University of Kentucky, president of the International Trumpet Guild and artist on numerous performances and recordings with Doc Severinsen.

Wynton sounds as good as these "gods of trumpet," and the creativity of his solo lines are as brilliant as his sound is beautiful. After a minute or two, his bass player walks onto the stage and picks up his instrument and joins in. Then the drummer. Then the sax player. Now I'm playing with the entire Wynton Marsalis Quintet! They would sound great without me even playing a note. I haven't looked around the room because I'm so involved in the music, but toward the end of the tune, I become aware that there's almost no conversation. We get a significant round of applause at the end of the tune. I shake hands with the whole band, and Wynton asks me who I am and where I'm from.

The rest of the evening progresses the same way. I play the intermissions and each time during my last solo piano tune, Wynton and his band come and join me. When they play their own material, it's mostly funky New Orleans grooves with some interesting rhythmic twists and a few advanced jazz harmonies. I end up doing four songs with them. On the last number, "It Could Happen to You," Wynton walks around the room as he plays, checking out the acoustics in front of George Washington's portrait and the northerly windows that face Pennsylvania Avenue. I only experience one interruption throughout our alternating sets.

At around 0115 hours, our smiling new president taps me on the shoulder and says, "I didn't know you guys play this kind of music too." I tell him that we love to play jazz and that the Marine Band can do any kind of music he likes. We shake hands and I tell him, "Welcome to the White House. Congratulations!" He thanks me, then goes back to his guests, and I go back to work. At the end of the evening, I find myself talking with Wynton's piano player. He's a real nice guy, and I discover that we have a close mutual friend in Chicago.

I don't go and speak to Wynton because he's sitting at a table with the Head Usher, Admiral Rochon. The admiral's a good guy but well above me on the food chain, and I think he might not look kindly on my interrupting him. Before I know it, I hear a shrill whistle as I'm talking to the pianist, and Wynton calls on his guys to get going. Oh well, there's a missed opportunity for me, but I console myself with the thought that it looks like I'm going to have pretty good job security as long as President Obama's in office.

I say good night to the butlers and ushers and leave the building. I'm amazed that the secret service agents I pass on the way out don't look tired at all, even on a day as stressful for them as this one's been. I end up walking around outside for a good fifteen minutes at three in the morning, looking for a taxi. Some streets are still blocked off and the Metro stopped running at two. I can almost hear echoes of today's marching bands and see shadows of the throngs of people in what are now empty bleachers. What a day!

The taxi drops me off at 8th and I. I change out of my uniform, then take a blanket and pillow up to our staff NCO lounge to try and get a few hours of sleep. I hate not sleeping in my own bed, but I've got a rehearsal at nine in the morning of Olivier Messiaen's *Quartet for the End of Time*.

Bob performing with Wynton Marsalis and bassist Carlos Henriquez the night of President Obama's inauguration

THE PRESIDENT PREFERS JAZZ

This is my third trip to the White House since Barack Obama's inauguration. I caught on quickly that our new president is a big-time jazz fan, and that should make for a real nice four years for me. President Clinton was a jazz lover, too, but during his years in office, my section leader, Charlie, assigned himself to the majority of White House jobs, so I didn't get to benefit much from the president's musical preferences. My impression of Hillary Clinton was that her tastes in music leaned more towards 60s pop and folk.

Now, I'm being encouraged to play the music of John Coltrane, Miles Davis, Herbie Hancock, Wayne Shorter, and the rest of my favorite jazz artists, rather than just slipping in a few of their compositions between show tunes, pop, and standards as I would do for previous administrations. Over the years, I've tried to put my personal stamp on everything I play, but I don't think I've ever been in a situation where I've been encouraged to play many of my personal favorites on a daily basis like this. Besides, it makes things more interesting for me because I can experiment with some new harmonic, rhythmic, and melodic ideas on the job while hoping to continue to grow and improve. I even ran into President Obama following our second job at the White House and, after making some nice remarks about our five-piece jazz group, he said to us, "And thanks for throwing in the Miles and Coltrane. Don't think I didn't notice."

Today, I'm leaning more toward the older jazz, playing a lot of stride piano. This is where the left hand jumps between bass notes and chords while the right hand plays melodies and embellishments. I'm playing tunes by Fats Waller and Earl "Fatha" Hines. I also do some things in the style of Teddy Wilson and Oscar Peterson. I'm not in the same league as those geniuses of jazz, but I can approximate the style. I then decide to play a few selections from *The Gershwin Songbook*. This is a book that contains solo piano arrangements of some of the classic Gershwin hits written out by the composer himself. As with everything he wrote, these pieces have a distinct jazz influence. They're kind of like "Rhapsody in Blue" but on a much smaller scale. First, I play "The Man I Love," then as I'm halfway through "Oh, Lady Be Good," one of the president's aides leans over me and whispers in my ear, "Just stick with the jazz. The president likes the jazz." I'll have no problem catering to the tastes of this audience.

SMILEY

Smiley had always been one of my favorite people at the White House. There's a good reason that he received his nickname while serving as a White House butler long before I joined the Marine Band in '91. He had the friendliest and most easy-going attitude of just about anyone I've ever come across. I'm talking about Smiley in the past tense because sadly, I came to the White House today to play a memorial service for him. He died just a few days ago after suffering a massive stroke followed by a brief hospitalization. On a personal level, this is one of the saddest events I've ever played at the White House.

As I'm coming up the staircase toward the State Floor, I remember one of my favorite Smiley stories. When playing for dinners for President (W) and Mrs. Bush in the private quarters, Smiley would always bring me a glass of water. He didn't ask if I wanted it. He was just taking care of his friend. On this particular evening, I had nearly emptied my glass of water when the Bushes' cat, India, decided she was interested in the glass. She stuck her nose in the glass, took a few swipes at it with her paw, knocked it over, and casually walked away, leaving a watery mess where the hardwood floor meets the molding. I ordinarily wouldn't worry about a little spilled water, but this is the private quarters of the White House, and technically, we're never supposed to have any food or drink while working.

Smiley walked by and must have seen the small mess and the look of distress on my face. He made a gesture to me not to worry and after delivering a tray of salads to the president, first lady and guests in the adjacent Yellow

Oval Room, he showed up with a towel and made quick work of the mess. There are a lot of things for me to fret about when I go to the White House, but Smiley always, always helped me to chill.

As I come up the stairs, I see the tech workers setting up the East Room for the service, but the mood is definitely quieter than usual. I go to the ushers' office to check in and see what they want from me musically. It's always difficult with memorial services to decide what to play. I discuss the music with Admiral Rochon, the new head usher. He tells me they've put the upright piano in the East Room, and they'd like for me to play for about five minutes prior to the service as people are gathering.

I think about how nice it is that the Obamas offered to have the service here at the White House. I gather that even though the president has only been in office for a few months, his family has already become quite close to the butler staff. It's very unusual for me to be tasked to play in the same room where the speeches are given, but the admiral tells me that there is to be a short slideshow of photos of Smiley with his family and a number of presidents and staff members. I ask Admiral Rochon if I should play right up until the slide show ends and the service begins. After he says yes, I tell him that it's going to be awkward for me to get up and leave once the service begins, as the piano is positioned right by the stage and podium. I'm told that a seat will be provided for me, and I should remain in the room as a guest representing the Marine Band. The admiral adds that Smiley would want me to be there. For me, this is quite an honor.

I take my position at the piano, playing Debussy's "Reverie," Bach's "Sheep May Safely Graze," and Louis Armstrong's "What a Wonderful World" to accompany the slides. That's the best I can come up with in my attempt to comfort a family that lost its husband and father much too soon. I'd guess that Smiley was about my age (fifty-one), and his wife and daughters seem to be the same ages as mine. I'm reminded that death is somewhere in the background throughout our entire lives, but at my age, it's somehow starting to seem more imminent. I count my blessings as I watch both the slides and Smiley's grieving family. On cue, I find my seat, and a priest comes to the podium to say prayers and give an invocation. George, the chief butler (generally a man of few words), then gives a brief but heartfelt speech about how much he and his staff will miss Smiley. When Michelle Obama comes to the podium to speak, I realize that this will be the first time I've ever been in the audience for a speech given by the president or first lady. I've heard countless speeches from the Grand Foyer, but I discover that it's really different being in the room. I'm quite struck by what a pair of charismatic and articulate public speakers they both are as they eulogize Smiley. When Michelle Obama reads a heartfelt and exceptionally charming get-well card that Malia sent to Smiley during his brief time in the hospital, I feel without a doubt that a strong bond had been established between Smiley and the first family in a very short time. As I rush out at the end of the service to provide exit music on the White House grand piano, I know that coming to work here will never be quite the same.

DAVE BRUBECK

I'm in uniform and playing with a trio for the Kennedy Center Honors Dinner at the State Department. The Ben Franklin room where we play is probably the most beautiful space to perform in all of Washington. It's full of museum quality furnishings from the Federalist and Colonial periods. This is one of my favorite Marine Band jobs, as we get to see, and sometimes even speak with, prominent people from the arts and entertainment industries. This year, Dave Brubeck is receiving an award from the Kennedy Center.

Although I regularly play some of Brubeck's tunes, I contacted my old friend, the former Marine Band bassist, Dave Wundrow, a veritable encyclopedia of jazz and standards, for the purpose of coming up with more music for the job. Dave was nice enough to send me ten Brubeck charts for us to play during dinner.

After the cocktail hour, the room fills up quickly with men in tuxedos and women in evening gowns. We break out the Brubeck charts. As I'm looking around the room, it strikes me that an entire village in a third world country could probably be fed for a year with what was spent by these guests on their shoes. Then I find myself thinking that if it wasn't for affluent people like these with disposable income, I would have had a really difficult time trying to make any kind of a career out of playing the piano. I need to focus on these Brubeck tunes. Some of them are a bit tricky, so I force myself to stop thinking about shoe receipts.

People are starting to take their seats, and I'm feeling pretty good about how the trio sounds. The drummer and bass player are locking in well and generating a good swing feel. But then I notice an older man preparing to take his seat at the table in front of the trio. He's giving us agitated looks. I've become pretty good at picking up on subliminal messages from an audience after so many years of playing background music.

However, my attention's drawn away from him, when out of the corner of my eye, I become aware that someone is standing in the well of the piano and smiling at us. It's Dave Brubeck. He has a serene, nearly angelic smile as I'm soloing on his song, "Waltzing." As the solo is peaking, with dynamics and rhythmic activity picking up in both the drums and bass, the older gentleman at the adjacent table gets up and comes over toward us. Standing directly between Brubeck and me, in a louder-than-necessary voice, he asks, "Are you going to be doing this all through the dinner?"

"Doing what?" I ask in return.

"Playing this loud!" he says, now bordering on shouting at me.

I tell him that we'll bring it down as soon as this song is over. In disgust, he returns to his dinner, eating his appetizer in quiet anger. I've heard a lot of rude remarks and seen a lot of rude behavior toward musicians in my life, but I'm sure that this one wins first place. I look over at Dave Brubeck, and he's still standing there with the same beatific smile. Our trio launches into another one of his pieces (only slightly quieter this time), but he doesn't seem to want to go and sit for dinner, so he remains standing in the well of the piano, smiling. His son eventually comes over to take him to his seat, but first Brubeck pays us a few nice compliments and asks his son to take a photo of him with the Marine Band jazz group.

I'm reminded that years ago during the Clinton administration, I met Brubeck very briefly at the White House when he compared me to Miles Davis, saying: "You play the flat-5 at the end of that tune the same way Miles always did." I know I'm stretching things a bit to say he compared me to

Miles, but it sounds good in the telling.

There are a few things I can learn from this evening. Primarily, that I should never be surprised by the capacity for rudeness and ignorance in my audience. I'm convinced that our music critic this evening had no idea that it was Dave Brubeck that he had stood in front of while deriding the band. Secondly, I'm convinced that none of what happened with our surly guest mattered to Brubeck in the least. This senior citizen of jazz was just in another place entirely, enveloped by the simple joy of music, and needing to be reminded that it was time to eat at the age of eighty-nine.

MEL

This year's Kennedy Center Honors recipients just might be the best yet: Brubeck, DeNiro, Springsteen, and Brooks. That's right. Mel Brooks, who may be the funniest man on the planet. In fact, Mary gave me specific instructions that if I get to meet him to tell him that she thinks he's the funniest man on the planet. I'm really hoping that I get to give him her message.

Trying to come up with some music to play for Mel proved more difficult than I thought it would be. Of course, all of his songs are a little off color. The Marine Band generally obsesses with avoiding any music that could have even the tiniest hint of bad taste. However, when I asked my commanding officer about it, he just shrugged and said, "If they give a lifetime achievement award to Mel Brooks, I think they know what they'll be getting."

But the other issue is that I'm performing with a piano trio (piano, bass, and drums). Most of Mel's best songs are big Broadway-like production numbers. Then Mary suggested "High Anxiety." Not Brooks's most famous film but maybe his best. It's one of her favorite movies, and she loves the theme song, a satirical lounge lizard beguine. Mel sang it in the film and resorted to every piano bar one-liner and tacky vocal mannerism in the book. I think we own recordings of nearly everything Mel ever did, so I watched the video a few times to lift the song "High Anxiety" and write a lead sheet for us to play. I think the hardest part was trying to suppress my laughter long enough to write down the tune. I decided to couple the song with a soft, out-of-time introduction of "Springtime for Hitler." Very sentimental. I thought maybe Mel would find it amusing.

Mel is sitting by himself about three tables away from our group. The Ben Franklin room at the State Department is starting to become crowded, but there are still lots of guests filtering in from the cocktail hour. This is the perfect time for our Mel Brooks tribute medley. I'm not more than two measures into "Springtime for Hitler," when Mel gets up and starts walking toward us. By the time he reaches us, our trio is just beginning to segue into the intro for "High Anxiety." Mel looks a little puzzled at first, but as soon as he hears the melody in the piano, he joins us and begins to sing. I join him (I know most of the words), though both of us are singing softly. I don't expect him to hang around long enough to sing the entire song, but he does. I'm sitting at the piano with Mel Brooks, playing and singing one of his funniest songs! We conclude with the line, "High Anxiety...You Wiiiinnnnn!" He applauds and gives us that same goofy yet charming smile that I've seen in all his acting roles from *Blazing Saddles* to *Robin Hood, Men in Tights*.

Mel: "Who are you guys? What are those uniforms?"

Me: "We're the 'President's Own' Marine Band, the oldest professional musical organization in the United States."

Mel: "Wow! What a great job!"

Me: "It is, but not as good as your job. I heard you were in the military too—during WWII?"

Mel: (puffing out his chest) "You heard right! I was a corporal!"

Me: "Mel, while I've got you here, I've gotta tell you something. My wife said that if I got to talk to you, I needed to give you a message from her and tell you that you're the funniest man on the planet! And I agree with her!"

Mel: (with more than a hint of a Brooklyn Yiddish accent, pointing his index finger at me) "Tell your wife she has good taste!"

We all shake hands with Mel and congratulate him. As he walks away, we go into some Dave Brubeck tunes, the best-suited music associated with any of tonight's honorees for a piano trio. But it takes me a few minutes to get my mind off of Mel. You don't need to talk to him for very long to realize that in the flesh, he's just as funny as his film persona. He's the ultimate court jester for our times. He's the funniest man on the planet, and the funniest "Jew in Space."

THE CRUCIBLE

At the age of fifty-one, I thought I'd seen it all. But I was wrong. Tonight, I'm playing an AIDS benefit with Dixieland Direct at a club in southwest DC, ironically right next to a DC police station. I say "ironically" because The Crucible is an S&M club. Sadism and masochism.

Frasier, the club owner who hired us, seems like a regular guy. He's bearded, dark haired, balding, and about my age. He would frequently come out to hear our band at Colonel Brooks' Tavern by Catholic University, and after brief negotiations with our band leader Mike, he hired us, warning Mike that The Crucible is a "different kind of place." Mike, in turn, warned our group and recommended that we check out the club's website.

I was real busy preparing for a state dinner, so I didn't bother, figuring the place was probably a strip club or a gay bar, both of which I've played before. I should've taken Mike's advice though. Not that I'd have turned down the gig, but I would have been better prepared for the uniqueness of The Crucible.

When I walk in, I find a large, dark, cavernous space with an elevated stage on the opposite side of a large dance floor. There are long bars on either side and some high-top tables surrounded by bar stools. We'll be the second group playing.

Henning, our band's clarinetist, could probably fit in anywhere he goes. He's charismatic and knows how to have fun. He got here early and is playing blackjack with some of the regulars. It's Casino Night, a common theme for fundraisers. Probably the most striking thing about the room is the color scheme. Everything's black and silver. Kind of brings to mind a Doberman's spiked collar.

Nothing else seems out of the ordinary until I carry my keyboard backstage. This is where the club has stowed away the S&M gear, I'm guessing so the civilian population of potential donors won't be too uncomfortable. There are devices that look like medieval racks, chains hanging from boards, handcuffs, and lots of other gear that I choose not to look at too carefully. I'm starting to get visual images, and I'd prefer not to.

I go to the bar, find Mike, and grab a beer. The opening act takes the stage. It's two old friends strumming their guitars and singing the typical folk rock that I grew up listening to in the '70s, Eagles, Crosby, Stills and Nash, and Jimmy Buffet. Our friend, Frasier, is one of the singers. There's only one thing out of the ordinary. Frasier's wearing a skirt. Not a kilt, but a bona fide skirt. The creeping hemline is high enough that we can get a full view of knobby knees and hairy shins. When they're done playing, we take the stage. The audience is smaller than Frasier had hoped for, but they genuinely seem to enjoy our one-hour set. I learned a long time ago that music is pretty universal, regardless of ethnicity, culture, religion, or taste in sexual pleasure (or pain).

When we finish, I pack up quickly, and as I'm wheeling my keyboard across the dance floor to leave, I see an interesting looking couple walking arm in arm in front of me. She seems to be a pretty blond and they're both dressed formally. He's got a pencil thin mustache and is wearing tails. And a tail. Protruding from the back of his tux (seemingly attached to his sacrum) is what looks to be an oversized three-foot-long raccoon tail. It must have come off of a raccoon conceived of by Lewis Carroll. And as I get closer, I notice the blond has very broad shoulders and negligible hip definition. As I pull even with this interesting couple, she turns to me and strikes up a conversation. At this point, I'm certain that I'm talking to a man, as she (he) has an Adam's apple.

Interesting couple: "You're with the band that just finished, aren't you?"

Me: "Yes."

Interesting couple: "Oh! You guys sure sounded great! We love Dixieland! We loved you!"

Me: "Thanks so much." I can honestly say that I always appreciate positive feedback from an audience. Right now, though, I'm just ready to be in my car and on my way home.

Interesting couple: "Are you kinky?" (Talk about abruptly changing the subject!)

Me: "Afraid not...Just regular."

Interesting couple: "Oh, well. Too bad, but thanks for the music!"

At this point, I quicken my pace, load up my car as quickly as I can, and head for home on I-295 North. Throughout my career, I've generally taken pride in my ability to fit into whatever circumstances my gigs have called for. But somehow, I don't think I succeeded tonight.

The White House is only about two miles from The Crucible. Nationals Park, filled with families taking in an evening of baseball, is practically across the street. About a mile west of here is the Tidal Basin, where parents join their young children for paddle boat rides. And directly adjacent to the tidal basin are the Jefferson Memorial and the Washington Monument, filled with tourists year round. The Crucible is so very close to all this Americana, a warehouse-sized specialized club for those with more unusual tastes in entertainment.

OBAMA'S FIRST
STATE DINNER

Washington society junkies and the paparazzi have been waiting nearly a year for this night. Finally, there's to be an Obama state dinner. What kind of gown will she be wearing? What wines will be served with dinner? What will the after-dinner entertainment be? And, of course, the classic, "Who's on and who's off the guest list?" I can honestly say the only question I'm concerned with is the one about after-dinner entertainment.

Tonight is eventful for me because it's my first time playing in the private quarters since President Obama and his family moved into the White House. Until now, the president, the first lady, and I have had a few brief exchanges but no real conversations. They've both been gracious and appreciative and neither of them seem to be filled with the self-importance that tends to come with election to high office. Tonight, I'll be playing in their actual residence in the White House, not the museum floors.

Although the Bushes had me play in the private quarters quite a lot (especially during their second term), I understand the Obamas' hesitance to entertain in the residence part of the White House because of their children. Sasha's and Malia's lives are anything but normal for young American girls in the twenty-first century, and I'm sure it's important to their parents to at least attempt to maintain some semblance of normalcy in their new home. Having a uniformed marine pianist with exceptionally short hair regularly coming and going from your living room definitely wouldn't help the children feel like they're living the life of a typical American family.

The traditional state dinner protocol dictates that the president and first lady greet the foreign leader at the front door of the White House, walk them through the Grand Foyer, and up the Grand Staircase. At the top of the stairs, they'll find me playing the piano and see butlers holding trays of drinks and hors d'oeuvres.

Tonight when I arrive at the piano, I immediately sit down and start to play. As usual, I play a large dose of jazz, but for the Obamas, I've gotten into the habit of adding some 70s and 80s rhythm and blues (R&B) and pop. I saw up close how much the first couple loved this music at their first governors' dinner, where Earth, Wind, and Fire entertained for a solid hour of dancing. This great 70s R&B group was welcomed enthusiastically by the president and the governors, and we were able to position ourselves in the open doorway to the East Room, where I was not only able to watch and listen to the high energy show, but was also treated to the uniquely awkward sight of Arnold Schwarzenegger dancing funky.

After a few minutes of my playing tunes by Horace Silver and Stevie Wonder, the president sticks his head around a corner. As he's putting on his white bow tie, he smiles and says, "I thought that was you playing." I tell him to enjoy his first state dinner. He thanks me and disappears back around the corner. A few minutes later, I hear the sound of young girls talking quickly and giggling a bit. It's coming from behind me, and I can't make out what they're saying, but then I hear the president's voice rise above them and say, "Come on, girls, I'll introduce you to him." Seconds later, the president and his two daughters are standing over my right shoulder.

President: "Girls, let me introduce you to my favorite guy. This is Bob, and he can play anything on the piano."

Bob: "Nice to meet you. Mr. President, I know lots of songs, but I wouldn't go that far."

Malia asks me, "Can you play SpongeBob SquarePants?"

Bob: "My kids were too old to watch that. I don't think I've ever heard it."

President: "Come on, Bob, you can do that one. It's easy" (singing), "Who lives in a pineapple under the sea?" Sasha and Malia both shout, "SPONGE-BOB SQUAREPANTS!"

The president and his daughters continue their trio, and I realize this song is an incredibly simple British hornpipe (with non-traditional lyrics), so I join in. The song is very short, and when it's over, the girls cheer and the president says, "See, I told you it was an easy one." Thankfully, he was right about that. They say goodbye and thanks, and I go back to my routine. A few minutes later, the president and first lady come up the Grand Staircase escorting the turbaned Indian Prime Minister, Dr. Singh and his wife.

I've put aside any thoughts of repeating the SpongeBob song in ballad form and instead, play some very soft light classical. After the brief reception, the leaders of the world's two largest democracies head downstairs to begin a long receiving line. As I'm hurrying down a back staircase to join the Marine Chamber Orchestra to play through dinner, I'm struck by the irony that most people who are in attendance tonight are going to remember this evening for its elegance, for getting to meet a president and a prime minister, and for all the fabulous gowns and food. I'm going to remember it mostly for having had moderate success with faking a children's song while a famous vocal trio sat in with me.

NEW ORLEANS, PART 2

We've taken our places on the steps of the New Orleans' courthouse. It's Mike, Henning, and me—Dixieland Direct—getting ready to compete in the Battle of the Bands, our most significant gig at this year's French Quarter Festival. We're adding a local New Orleans bass player whom we just met. He seems to know what he's doing when we briefly do a "talk through." But our main concern is whether or not Harry's going to make it on time.

Harry's in the Army Band, and he's here in town playing with the Army's "Swamp Romp," a killer New Orleans group that's his brainchild. Harry used to live in New Orleans and he plays this kind of music as well as anyone. He also might be the best trombone player on the planet. No exaggeration. He's also a tremendous showman and a great friend. The issue is that Harry's Army group was playing earlier in the afternoon for some Habitat volunteers, and he wasn't sure whether he'd get back to town on time. He has ten minutes to downbeat, and as I wait on the courthouse steps, I have time to think back on the past few days.

Upon our band's arrival, we were immediately invited to a cocktail party in the backyard of Ralph and Helen who live in the Garden District. I'm not usually a day drinker, but in keeping with the spirit of the festival and our hosts, I joined in with a few glasses of wine. Ralph and Helen are big time fans of traditional jazz, so much so that upon retiring from their government jobs in DC, they immediately moved to New Orleans. They're fans of our group from years ago. When talking to them about New Orleans, I got the impression they hit the club scene almost nightly. They're a couple of older party animals, and they're also exceptionally nice people. They've made their home available to two of us, so Mike and Henning are staying with them for the duration. Their house is an early nineteenth-century home with fifteen-foot jalousie windows and an outdoor walkup entrance to the servants' quarters apartments. I'm staying in a hotel in the French Quarter, a room provided for us by the PRJC (Potomac River Jazz Club) from the Washington, DC region. A number of the club's members are also at the same hotel. Besides the financial support, the club members seem to be really excited to have DC represented musically here at the festival.

Close to thirty stages are set up throughout the Quarter for the festival, but they're reserved for local bands only. This festival is a celebration of New Orleans' unique musical culture, so I guess that's understandable. Funding for this festival is funneled through the local musicians' union, which means that we can play, but we don't get paid. Mike booked us in local clubs and bars for eleven gigs in four days. These gigs didn't pay either, but the New Orleans club scene has a wonderful tradition of passing around a tip bucket during the last set. When the room is full of traditional jazz lovers who've made a pilgrimage to the French Quarter Festival from every corner of the earth, the bucket take can become significant.

Basically, I'm breaking even for the weekend, but I'm really glad I've come. As satisfying as playing at the White House can be, this scene's a welcome change. The audience really listens. They're quiet during the subtle parts. They clap and yell after a burning solo. They wave their napkins over their heads when the tune climaxes. Sometimes, they even dance or parade in the aisles if the spirit moves them. All this is going on as I'm playing music I love with musicians I have a great bond with. Of course, you can't complain about the food either.

Somehow though, Mike managed to get our group included in the festival's Battle of the Bands. Henning was concerned that we only had one horn player in our group. I figured we would just do our thing, generate some excitement, and let the chips fall where they may. But now that I see the way this competition is set up, I understand his concern. The other bands are seven and eight pieces with three and four horn players. The winner is going to be determined by a decibel meter, measuring the volume level of our slightly intoxicated audience's response. So basically, whichever group raises the most hell wins.

At 1725, five minutes before downbeat, Harry arrives, walking quickly up the courthouse steps to join us. He reminds me a bit of the cartoon character Roger Rabbit, probably because he's skinny and approaches life with a seemingly limitless amount of energy and humor. As he takes his trombone out of the case, we talk through our program with him. Three songs: "Sweet Georgia Brown," "After You've Gone," and "Bourbon Street Parade."

The bands alternate, and I think we're holding our own after the first two numbers. The other bands are really good and fun to listen to, but I don't hear any soloists who can rival our horn players. "After You've Gone" goes over particularly well, thanks to the arranged riffs and drum breaks we lifted from a Benny Goodman recording, as well as the scorching solos played by Henning and Harry.

When we play "Bourbon Street Parade," we pull out all the stops. We use a New Orleans march groove on this one, and following the piano boogie-woogie break, Henning and Harry leave the bandstand and march into the crowd. Harry points his trombone slide at carefully selected women and a few unmistakably drunken men. Henning has the clarinet angled up toward the heavens and is wailing soulful melodies in the highest register of the instrument. Soon, the crowd forms up behind the two of them and we have an old fashioned, spontaneous New Orleans Mardi Gras second-line parade going on. After a few minutes, Henning and Harry make their way back up the courthouse steps to join the rhythm section for the last few choruses, changing keys to increase the energy one more time before the closing drum tag.

The audience goes crazy, reminding me for a moment of the crowds I played for twenty years ago when touring South America with El Puma. When the master of ceremonies announces each band while holding up the decibel meter, there's no doubt who won. We collect our first-place prize and go out for dinner at a fine restaurant (our only real gourmet splurge of the trip) with Ralph and Helen. I offer to treat Harry, but he's got to get back to his hotel to prepare for another Army Band job this evening. Boundless energy for the pinch hitter who helped seal the victory in New Orleans and then moved on to his next gig.

CODA

My daughter, Gabrielle, plays violin in a college rock band in Louisville, Kentucky, where she goes to school. Her group just won the university's Battle of the Bands. Following their victory, Gabi posted on her Facebook page: "Our band just won the University of Louisville's Battle of the Bands. Our prize was $300 worth of studio time. My dad's band just won the Battle of the Bands at the French Quarter Festival in New Orleans. They got a little plastic trophy."

THE SAINTS GO
MARCHING IN

I love New Orleans. I've performed down there with both Dixieland Direct and the "President's Own." The first time I ever visited New Orleans, I was touring with *Cats*, and we played at a beautiful old theater called the Saenger. I also volunteered to work on the Katrina cleanup twice. Once by myself with Habitat for Humanity, and the second time with my family, working for ACORN (Association of Community Organizations for Reform Now). I love the many different musical styles that originated and still thrive in New Orleans. I love the food and the carefree partying atmosphere. And I love the people. That's why I couldn't help but root for the Saints when they made the playoffs and eventually won the Super Bowl.

It's August of 2010, and today's White House job seems special to me, having personally witnessed the devastation of New Orleans. Today, the Saints are the guests of honor. In my nineteen years in the Marine Band, I've played for a lot of sports team receptions: Elway's Broncos, Jordan's Bulls, and even the Philadelphia Phillies, where I got to briefly thank shortstop Jimmy Rollins on behalf of my deceased dad (the world's most enthusiastic Phillies fan) for winning the World Series. But the boost the Saints' victory gave to the city that I've grown to love makes this extra special. I'm leading the Marine Dixieland Band, a musical style I've really come to feel at home with.

When I was first tasked to play this reception for the Saints a week ago, I strongly urged our operations office to recommend to the White House that we send the Dixieland Band rather than a generic jazz combo (usually a five piece group with only one horn instead of three, guitar instead of banjo, and bass rather than tuba). Our operations officer declined, probably thinking in terms of other commitments the band needed to fill, such as concerts, funerals, and summer parades. I was pretty disappointed and a bit frustrated. After all, we had a standing group that was stylistically perfect for this event. We even had tightly rehearsed material from an outdoor summer concert we had played recently. Well, it worked out anyway. Two days before the reception, I got a call from operations telling me that the White House had specifically requested our Dixieland Band for this event.

So now, our seven-piece Dixieland Band is raisin' a little Louisiana hellfire in the Grand Foyer of the White House, and the Saints football team is wandering the halls. We're a good deal louder than the usual Marine Band background music ensembles, and more people than usual are paying attention to the music. None of us are experts on New Orleans jazz (I've heard trumpet players who can literally play all of Louis Armstrong's solos note for note), but we've all listened and studied enough to achieve the right stylistic effect. We sound a lot like the French Quarter Festival parade bands that I heard and briefly marched with recently.

As the guests are finally all seated in the East Room waiting for the president's congratulatory speech and photo ops, Max, my contact from the White House military office, gives me the "cut" sign. When this happens at the White House, we don't finish the tune; we actually stop playing in the middle of whatever musical phrase we happen to be on. Presidential remarks always take precedence over musical architecture. We sit quietly for a few minutes, and then Max gives us the "go" sign. This is our cue to play "When the Saints Go Marching In." Our drummer kicks it off with a traditional snare drum march roll-off. Our trumpet player then plays the melody pickups, and we're rolling. The team starts to proceed from the State Dining Room, through the Cross Hall, and into the East Room. I warned the guys that we might have to play this song for a while, as football teams have huge rosters compared to most other sports, but the stream of players, management, and support staffers seems to be endless. A number of them give us thumbs up as they pass, but I can't help but feel a little sympathy for Dan, our wonderful trumpet player who's putting an awful lot of air into his horn in a pretty high register. Usually, he'd get a break as the other guys would play solos, but for this part of the gig, we need to provide constant melody. Finally, the last of the procession has passed by, and we can see from the Grand Foyer that the Cross Hall's empty. Max gives us the "cut" sign.

We all hear: "Ladies and gentlemen, the President of the United States, Barack Obama." There's no "Hail to the Chief" or presidential honors played today. That's usually reserved for more ceremonial events such as the awarding of the Purple Heart. I look around the corner and down the Cross Hall where I can see into the East Room. Thankfully, they've left the door open today. President Obama's standing on a podium with the entire Saints' football team positioned on risers behind him. The president's first words are: "Ladies and gentlemen, the 2010 Super Bowl champions...the New Orleans Saints!"

There's a huge amount of applause and a good deal of yelling in response. The president speaks a bit about the trials of Hurricane Katrina and the BP oil spill, and then about the resiliency of the people of Louisiana. He talks about what this football team has meant to their city. When he's finished, we play "Way Down Yonder in New Orleans" as the guests come into the Grand Foyer for a reception. At this point, we tone down the volume and intensity a bit, but there's still a genuinely festive atmosphere today, probably more so than any White House sports reception I've done. The city of New Orleans is well on its way back, and the Saints have certainly helped.

CODA

My next job at the White House is just a few days later. It's a routine bill signing with solo piano. Just playing the guests in and out. As I wait by the piano for them to arrive, one of the secret service agents walks up to me and we start talking.

Secret Service Agent: "How'd you like havin' the Saints here the other day?"

Me: "That was a cool one. I love New Orleans, and I was really pullin' for them to win the Super Bowl."

Secret Service Agent: "Well, the president loved your music."

Me: "Really? That's always nice to hear."

Secret Service Agent: "Yeah. You guys were playing, and the president was dancing around while he was waiting in the Red Room to be introduced. He told me, 'Man, those marines, they really can play some Dixieland!'"

SIR PAUL

It's December of 2010, and once again, I'm here in the Ben Franklin Room at the State Department for the Kennedy Center Honors Awards Dinner. This year, we get to play for one of my childhood idols, Sir Paul McCartney. I don't have to do any research to dig up music to play for Paul. I probably owned every album ever produced by the Beatles. In our young and romantic years, Mary and my special song was "Maybe I'm Amazed."

I did a few Beatles arrangements for tonight's gig, including "Come Together." I'm certain Sir Paul would like having John Lennon remembered as well. For background music, we also play "Here, There, and Everywhere," "Maybe I'm Amazed," "Got to Get You into My Life," and "Things We Said Today." This evening's guests include the usual collection of Hollywood standouts and musical performers, along with a number of politicians and wealthy arts patrons. We pretty much serve as attractive (optimistically), uniformed musical wallpaper. That's a good thing. I prefer not to have a repeat of a few years ago, when Kid Rock decided it'd be fun to heckle us throughout most of the dinner.

I get to play Harry Truman's beautiful nine-foot Steinway D piano whenever we're called to play for events at the State Department. This year, the State Department protocol staff has asked us to remain until the end of the awards presentation and play the guests out. In the past, we've always set up by a door in the southeast corner of the Ben Franklin Room, and after dinner, we quietly made our exit as the speeches began.

Following the dinner tonight, we all duck into the holding room behind us as soon as the speeches start, and find that it's been set up to take honorees' photos. So they'll all be walking by us wearing their Kennedy Center Lifetime Achievement Medals: Sir Paul, Oprah, Jerry Herman, Merle Haggard, and Bill T. Jones. As we wait, our drummer Steve strikes up a conversation with Sir Paul's bodyguard. The bodyguard tells us that McCartney and he run two miles together every morning and then do about an hour of weightlifting. He also tells us that he's never seen Sir Paul do a show consisting of less than thirty-five songs. Seems he's pretty hardworking for a guy in his seventies.

Through the door, I hear Smokey Robinson's name announced as the presenter for Paul McCartney. I immediately think back to when I played Smokey's show as a civilian at Meyerhoff Hall in Baltimore about a dozen years ago. Smokey was the real class of all the nostalgia acts I've played for. His conductor ran the rehearsal efficiently; the arrangements were faithful to the original tunes and clearly written, and Smokey's voice and energy level were still off the charts. Reflecting on that show brings a great song to mind for us to play, "You Really Got a Hold on Me," written by Smokey and sung by Lennon and McCartney on The Beatles' Second Album. I mention it to Glen, our bass player. If anyone in the Marine Band would know it, it'd be Glen. But he doesn't. I suppose my quasi senior-citizen status is in play, so I tell Glen to use his ear and follow me when we play it. He does have a great ear.

As we hear the final applause following the presentation of the last award, we open the door and quickly find our places behind our instruments, diving into a hard-driving shuffle version of "Can't Buy Me Love." Usually by this point in the evening, we're in our cars on the way home to our families. But I'm glad the State Department staff decided to have us play the guests out tonight.

Oprah, who has been sitting just a few tables away from us with Whitney

Houston and Julia Roberts, dances by us with a big smile on her face. The other honorees, including Sir Paul, choose to walk, giving us smiles and thumbs-up. Even with as much affirmation and audience adulation as the honorees have experienced in their lifetimes, the five of them still look pretty psyched to be wearing their new medals. They pass into the adjacent room to be photographed individually and as a group. A few minutes later, they come back out, and we go right into McCartney's "And I Love Her."

Sir Paul, Merle Haggard, and their entourages gather around the piano, and Paul begins to softly sing with us, "I give her all my love. That's all I do." I figure what the hell, this is probably the only chance I'll ever get to sing with Paul McCartney, so I join in. Paul seems to be fishing for the words a bit (he probably rarely does this one in his marathon shows), but he remembers them well enough to get through the song. He's definitely having some fun sitting in with the Marine Band.

At the end of that song, I tell him, "I've got one for you," and I go into "You Really Got a Hold on Me."

He smiles and says, "Too bad Smokey's already gone. He should be here for this one."

"Sure," I say, "but you recorded it too."

He smiles again: "Believe me, I remember." Paul again sings the song at half voice with us, and he remembers it well.

I begin to feel a little guilty because Merle Haggard is still standing next to Sir Paul, looking like he's enjoying himself, but also looking somewhat hopeful. Even though old-time country music's not at the top of my list, we go into "Mama Tried," one of Haggard's tunes that uses a freight train type of drum groove. I always kind of liked this one when I played it at Gill's Key Pub in 1981 (my only steady country music gig). We do a quick version and

Merle seems content.

Sir Paul and his entourage are gathering to leave. But first, we shake hands and I get to congratulate him. He thanks us, and he seems to be genuinely moved by the fact that we played his music. As they're all exiting the Ben Franklin Room, we go into "Let it Be," and I can hear Sir Paul singing along with us as he gets farther away, but now in full voice.

As the years have passed, I've gotten away from some of the music of my adolescence, but I still think that McCartney wrote some great tunes, and that his voice was (and still is) a divine gift. If someone had told me when I was twelve years old and the Beatles were in their prime that someday I'd get to meet Paul McCartney, play some of his songs for him, and have him sit in and sing a little with me, that alone would have made me consider my career a success. During the bad times, I need to remember that.

GORILLA BASKETBALL

We're on our way back to the barracks from Fort McNair. Kevin and I just performed a short after-dinner program for the Assistant Commandant of the Marine Corps, General Dunford. I'm quieter than usual on the short minivan ride back to 8th and I because I'm angry and frustrated following a brief conversation I had with a congressman at the general's home. It was, to say the least, disturbing.

I arrived at Fort McNair at around 1730 and set up my electric keyboard to play for the six o'clock cocktail hour. As always, the general, his wife, and their staff were very appreciative and cordial. When the guests went in for dinner, I stopped playing and got out the music for our program. Kevin, our vocalist, arrived.

We'd rehearsed at the barracks earlier and so we just talked through what we were going to play one last time. Our wait was long, but that was typical for these jobs. From the sounds of loud conversation and laughter coming from the dining room, I guessed the general and his guests were all comfortable with each other, a bit inebriated as a result of the cocktail hour, and probably on their second or third glass of wine.

There were only two guests and their wives. Both guests were congressmen who had won office only a few months earlier. I'm sure this dinner was the Corps' way of encouraging military-friendly voting on Capitol Hill. By the sound of things in the dining room, the congressmen and the general were quickly becoming very good friends.

Our after-dinner show went well. We didn't play any classical music because I try to avoid that when playing an electric keyboard, but we did a bit of Broadway, a Neapolitan song, and ended with "God Bless the USA." Everything appeared to be another satisfying yet unremarkable military duty job, until the congressmen came over to congratulate and thank us. The first one gave us a handshake and a "Semper Fi."

But congressman number two thought it'd be nice to chat with us for a bit. We got on the subject of basketball because I mentioned that I had studied at the University of Kentucky.

The honorable congressman told us, "When I was in college, we used to play gorilla basketball!"

"What's that?" I asked. "It's just basketball with tackle football rules. Y'all go over and play for the president a lot, don't you? Well, you know the president; he plays a lot of hoops. Why don't you ask him? I'm sure he could explain gorilla ball to you better than anyone!" The congressman gave us a meaningful smirk and then chuckled at his own attempt at humor. Then he added, "Maybe I shouldn't have said that now that I'm working here in Washington."

But I don't think he really felt that way because he was still laughing. Kevin didn't join him in laughing but just stood there with his unwavering West Virginia smile. I couldn't help myself. My jaw dropped, and I just stared in disbelief. It seems to me that if you're a racist and you have to work with congressmen and women from all over the US with all kinds of backgrounds, it might be better not to let anyone know your true feelings. Not only did our congressman let us know, but he seemed to find it amusing. When he realized that Kevin and I weren't joining in his fun, he said his goodbyes and went to look for friendlier conversation.

In my early years of playing gigs in Miami, I found myself on a number of jobs where people would make racist, anti-Semitic, or anti-Hispanic remarks. I wanted to fit in, go with the flow, so I wouldn't speak out against any of them. But later on, while I was living in Kentucky, I decided I'd heard enough and that I'd stop passively accepting this kind of crap anymore. I once confronted a man at a bar when he made anti-Semitic remarks. Another time, I cut short a lesson I was teaching when my piano student showed herself to be a bona fide racist. Neither of them apologized. Actually, they both just tried awkwardly to change the subject. Ironically, neither of them was from the South. One was from Chicago and one from Cincinnati. I know that I didn't change either of their minds, but it certainly felt better not to be complicit by my silence.

Tonight, I was in uniform and definitely in no position to argue with the "honorable" guest. So as we're returning to the barracks, all I can think about is what this means for our country. I had hoped that as a nation we'd moved beyond the substantial overt racism that existed in Congress when I was a kid. I guess that I was just being naïve. I get very frustrated thinking about how I have to keep my mouth shut because I'm representing the Marine Corps and wearing the uniform. The only thing I can think of to make amends is to put it in my memoir once I retire.

STEVIE WONDER

It's February of 2011 and we're playing at another reception for In Performance at the White House. As usual, we play background music as the audience gathers in the East Room. I don't call many straight-ahead jazz tunes, but we do play a fair amount of funk, Motown, and Stevie Wonder classics. We've already played "Don't You Worry 'Bout a Thing," "My Cherie Amour," "Stand By Me," "Just the Two of Us," and "Cold Duck Time." "Cold Duck Time" is a 60s Eddie Harris funk tune that once prompted President Obama to announce to family and friends at a Thanksgiving party, "I just want to point out that the marines are really cookin' today."

I like Motown a lot. I remember most of the tunes from my childhood and adolescence in the 60s and 70s. I've found that I like it even more as I've aged and left behind some of the pompous hard rock that used to appeal to me in my teens. Disclaimer: I still love Jethro Tull and make it to their concerts whenever they're within a hundred miles of DC. But this is African American History month and tonight's White House performance features this wonderful genre of music.

We get the cue to stop once everyone's seated in the East Room. The president, vice president, Mrs. Obama, and Mrs. Biden are all introduced, and the show begins. Unfortunately for us, the ushers close the doors because all these In Performance events are filmed live. The room is packed tight, so we only get to listen through the door. The ushers do thoughtfully offer to let us and the White House social aides go down to the Map Room and watch the show on an HD large screen TV. A couple of our guys take them up on it, but

I decide to just listen through the keyhole.

As is always the case, all races, age groups, and sexes are represented in the performance. I hear a great duet of "You Really Got a Hold on Me" by Smokey Robinson and Cheryl Crowe and a credible version of "The Way You Do the Things You Do" by one of the Jonas Brothers. But my favorites have to be Seal's "Can't Get Next to You" and John Legend doing "Ain't Too Proud to Beg." Stevie Wonder comes out toward the end of the program and sings "You Are the Sunshine of My Life," followed by a full cast version of "Dancin' in the Streets." All the performers, including the song's original performer, Martha Reeves, the president, first lady, and Berry Gordy, the founder of Motown, end up on stage singing and dancing. Through the door, it sounds just a few decibels short of a musical earthquake.

The concert ends, the doors open, and we go into "Mercy, Mercy, Mercy," one of the soul/jazz standards we play a lot. Most of the performers give us a nod or a wave as they walk by, and Randy Jackson, the bassist and band leader, stops by and speaks with a couple of our guys for a minute or two. All the guests, performers, staff, and even the building itself, seem to be on a musical high. It's the most positive vibe I've felt in the White House since the night of President Obama's inauguration. We keep playing for a solid hour and a half. I may be imagining it, but it seems to me that our five-piece combo sounds better than usual, cranking out jazz standards and some instrumental Motown. By now, most of the guests are gone, but I still hear a few voices coming from the State Dining Room. The group has been playing continuously, so I tell them to take a break and I'll play some solo piano.

At that moment, I see Stevie Wonder himself walking into the Grand Foyer with an escort (I guess it's his manager). I was just wondering what I'd play and this decides it. I go into "All in Love Is Fair," one of Stevie's most beautiful ballads from the early 70s. When I get to the third measure, Stevie starts singing the beginning of the tune at full voice. I jump back a couple measures to join him. It's pretty seamless, as now my first two solo measures come off as an introduction. His voice sounds remarkable in this room. Actually, it sounds remarkable anywhere. I'm amazed that I'm playing this song with him under these circumstances. I'm just plain awestruck, but I manage to stay with him, play pretty well, and make some music. Stevie gets to the final phrase, slows down a little, and sings, "All in love is fair..." Then he shouts, "You guys play great!" before he turns and takes his ear-to-ear smile with him as he quickly walks out of the Grand Foyer and down the stairs. There's a look of awe on the faces of my Marine Band colleagues and appreciative smiles on the faces of the ushers and butlers who stopped to listen. This is without a doubt one of my best nights at the White House.

CODA

I told Mary about it and she was really excited. Stevie's been one of her favorites since long before I met her in 1976. I was wound up enough that it took me quite a while to fall asleep that night. I woke a few times to find that I could still hear in my "mind's ear" the echoes of Stevie's voice. His glorious, joyful voice was still bouncing around inside my head, and I'm sure, still floating around the Grand Foyer of the White House.

JERUSALEM OF GOLD

Tonight, Kevin and I have been tasked to perform an after-dinner program at the Marine Commandant, General James Amos's home for the Israeli military attaché and his wife. Attachés are foreign embassy staff, and they generally function as important points of contact for the US military on issues of mutual defense interests. About a week before the gig, Kevin presented me with the program he wanted to sing. I generally don't ask him or Sara to make program changes, but this time I had an idea. I suggested that maybe he could sing "Jerusalem of Gold."

From what I remember of my childhood, this song is nearly as important to the Israeli people as their national anthem. It has a strong association with Israel's improbable victory over the entire Arab world during the Six Day War of 1967. Kevin was a little hesitant at first, but I told him that it isn't difficult, and he agreed to sing it, even with the last verse in Hebrew.

Thinking about the prospect of Kevin singing in Hebrew takes me back eight years ago to when General Jones decided to make Gomer Pyle (Jim Nabors) an honorary marine. The night after the ceremony, Kevin and I performed at the commandant's home for the general, Ms. Jones, and Gomer.

When introduced to Gomer, Kevin proceeded to gush with praise, "You know, Mr. Nabors, when I was a little boy growing up in West Virginia, my family and I were all watching an episode of Gomer Pyle together on our TV. It happened to be an episode where you sang. I turned immediately to my mama and said, 'Someday, I'm gonna sing like that. I want to sing just like Gomer Pyle!'"

Gomer looked pretty pleased. After the job, as Kevin and I walked back to the band's locker room to change and go home, I said, "Damn, Kevin! You sure were piling it on high and deep with the Gomer Pyle hero worship routine!" Kevin looked me right in the eye and told me in his rural West Virginia accent that every word he had said was true. Kevin's probably one of the most honest and sincere people I know. Gomer really was his role model. Now Kevin's getting ready to sing in Hebrew?

I went over the Hebrew pronunciations a bit with Kevin when we rehearsed, but he already seemed to have it pretty well learned, though I detected a bit of inescapable southern vowel combinations. Mentioning it would have only made him feel self-conscious and likely wouldn't have changed anything. Anyway, I know that when performing for people from a foreign country, it's making the effort to play music of their culture that really means something to them, and that definitely holds true this evening.

We end our usual program with "Old Man River," and General Amos gets up, thanks us, and asks if we might possibly be prepared to give them one more selection. Of course, he knows we are. Kevin gives a nice short speech about the relationship between our two countries and the significance of "Jerusalem of Gold." It's obvious that the guests are pleased with our selection. As Kevin begins singing, I can clearly see tears welling up in the eyes of the Israeli attaché's wife. When he segués into the Hebrew language on the last verse, she asks if she can join him. Kevin gestures for her to come up, and suddenly the two of them are standing side by side in the well of the piano, singing Hebrew in full voice, the Israeli officer's wife and the simple marine country boy from West Virginia.

I don't cry, but I could if I let myself. I think of my Jewish ancestors who fled to the US to escape pogroms in the Ukraine and my Israeli cousins who've lost a child serving in the Israeli army. Music can surely be powerful medicine, and tonight everyone in the commandant's home leaves knowing it firsthand. Kevin and I did our job.

3 November 2011

Dear Master Gunnery Sergeant Boguslaw,

Bonnie and I want to personally thank you for researching and performing "Jerusalem of Gold" for our honored dinner guests, Major General and Mrs. Shamni. This song holds great significance for the Major General and his wife, as it does for all of the people of Israel. It was wonderful to hear Mrs. Shamni join in on the rendition.

Your performance made an outstanding impression and added a very special touch to the evening. I know it meant a lot to our friends and close allies. Thank you for the time and effort you put into the preparation and performance. You did an exceptional job. Keep up the great work!

Semper Fidelis,

JAMES F. AMOS
General, U.S. Marine Corps
Commandant of the Marine Corps

MGySgt Robert Boguslaw, USMC
United States Marine Band
Marine Barracks Washington
8th and I Streets SE
Washington, DC 20390

Masterbums... what to treat you provided to Gen Shamni and Hadas... Thank you!

TRINIDAD

We're on stage at National Academy for the Performing Arts, Port of Spain's recently built beautiful performing arts facility. The hall seats twelve hundred, and there are probably close to a thousand in the audience tonight. Earlier in the evening, during a pause in the concert, I made a speech that probably was the closest I'll ever get to acting as a diplomat. I talked about cross-cultural communication, close ties between our countries, and Jazz Appreciation Month. Even though I've spoken during educational presentations and a few times during concerts, this is by far the largest audience to ever be victimized by my rambling communication style. My speech turned out better than I expected. Mary, who at one point taught public speaking classes, told me to keep it brief, to the point, and to speak slowly and clearly. I took her advice, managed to avoid a disastrous international incident, and then gladly returned to the relative safety of the piano bench.

The piano is a top-of-the-line Bösendorfer that responds beautifully, and the musicians on stage with me are Eric (the only other marine bandsman beside myself), Jeff (a brilliant saxophonist from Nashville), Brian (the drummer who was the impetus behind this trip and serves on the faculty of the University of Trinidad and Tobago), and Tamba (a brilliant local hand drummer/percussionist who specializes in Afro-Cuban music). The concert was already burning before Tamba joined us. We played some originals by Jeff and me and a few jazz standards.

I didn't know what to expect when I agreed to make this trip with Eric. The way Eric presented the idea was something like, "You wanna go to Trinidad and do a jazz concert and teach some classes with me and a few old friends of mine?"

I asked Eric if his friends were good players.

"Well, it's been a while, but I remember them being good."

On this trip, everything's been better than I could possibly hope for. On our first rehearsal, Brian and Jeff nailed one of my more difficult original tunes, "The Way." They'd done their homework, and not only did they play the notes and navigate the difficult rhythms perfectly, but they made music out of it on the first try. Eric "remembering them being good" was an understatement.

We started the concert as a great quartet; then the energy level ratcheted up substantially when Tamba joined us for John Coltrane's "Afro Blue." By the end of the first half of the concert, we could feel the audience's excitement growing. I almost wanted to skip the intermission so we wouldn't lose our momentum. And Boogsie, reputed to be the world's greatest jazz steel drum player, hasn't yet joined us. Boogsie is a living legend in his native country. Steel drums were invented in Trinidad, and the Trinis also stake a credible claim to being the birthplace of Calypso.

When Boogsie first showed up at the university to rehearse with us, he seemed a little agitated. I can't be sure, but my first impression was that he was skeptical of US Marines who are also musicians. He's of medium height, a little overweight, and probably in his mid-sixties. As we'd been warned by Brian, Boogsie's English was borderline unintelligible and he doesn't read music, as is the case with many Trini musicians. If he wants anything musically different on his featured tunes, he has to explain himself verbally. Everyone in Trinidad speaks with at least some Caribbean accent, understandable to varying degrees. But when Boogsie talks to us, it comes out as a barrage of unintelligible consonants and vowels concluded with an

"OK." At least when he said "OK," I knew when to nod my head.

So we ended up communicating musically. When I asked him what he wanted for an introduction or an ending, he muttered something and then demonstrated on his steel pan. We picked it up. When we were working on "Who Can I Turn To?" which he selected, he said something to me, and I thought I could discern the word "chord." I gestured to the piano, and he sat down and showed us his harmonies for the tune on the keyboard. We then traded riffs a bit, and his extremely well-developed aural skills were quickly obvious. What an ear. Anything I played he could pretty much play back to me immediately on his pan.

Playing steel drums is very physical, and it was amazing to watch him get around the drums when we rehearsed. The act of making music seemed to transport him back to his youth. By the end of rehearsal, it was clear to us that we passed the test, and that Boogsie was looking forward to the concert.

Boogsie's been introduced, and he's walking across the stage to join us to thunderous applause. He approaches his pans, and as the applause dies out, he goes into a wonderful solo introduction to "Who Can I Turn To?" I wouldn't have thought the subtleties of phrasing, articulation, and dynamics were even possible on this instrument. Boogsie makes it look and sound so easy. He sustains tone for long melodic notes with a controlled and nuanced tremolo. By the time he cues us in, he's captured the audience. After Boogsie completes the melody, we take our turns soloing. All the solos go well and then it's Boogsie's turn. By now, I realize that I'm performing with a truly great artist who is a musical force of nature, and his solo doesn't disappoint. As his solo seems to be ending, he looks expectantly at me and plays a riff over the first phrase of the tune. I answer him, not by repeating his lick, but by reshaping it and turning his musical question into an answer. He poses a new, slightly modified riff based on what I just played, and so our musical conversation begins. We're not trading 8s, 4s, or 2s as is the usual convention among jazz musicians. We're just talking, and where one musician's response ends, the other's begins. The audience realizes that something special is happening, and they applaud loudly in the middle of our dialogue. I'm even aware of some laughter when our musical conversation becomes humorous. We end the tune, and as we all stand for the applause, I think that the language of jazz has allowed something unique and truly cross-cultural to happen tonight.

Tamba comes back on stage, and we end with a rhythmic local calypso number, "Santimanite," followed by an encore of "Green Dolphin Street" that Boogsie chooses to play at breakneck speed. At the end of the concert, Boogsie seems to have a bit of difficulty coming back out to the stage for bows. He's out of breath. Word is that his health isn't the greatest, but when he was behind that steel pan, you'd never know it.

Alex is one of the US embassy staff who helped put this mini-tour together. The embassy worked along with University of Trinidad faculty, Brian, and his wife, Deborah, to produce this tour. I mention to Alex what a great job they've done in setting this up and getting such a large turnout. Alex congratulates me and says, "You've got to consider that there's lots of oil in this part of the world. Venezuela, who's not on the best terms with the US, is only twenty-five miles from here, and the Chinese built the facility you played in tonight. Any cultural exchanges that improve our country's standing in Trinidad are really, really important. And tonight, you guys certainly helped with that!"

A lot of Trinis went home happy tonight, including the president of the university and the prime minister. I like to think that music can help a little bit to change things for the better.

CODA

In April of 2013, we are invited to return to Trinidad to hopefully recreate the magic of 2012's trip. It is a great time once again, but musically it doesn't quite live up to the standard we set earlier. The main hall at the university is taken, so our big concert is outdoors in a public park. I play an electric keyboard instead of the grand Bösendorfer, and we play without Tamba, who couldn't get out of a previous commitment. Boogsie joins us and plays great, but the vibe just isn't quite the same. Unfortunately, when something magical happens in this lifetime, we can't just will it to happen again and expect it to be so.

But in another way, this second trip to Trinidad is even more amazing than the first because Mary came with me. During the first Trinidad trip, I had the distraction and anxiety of knowing she was at home in bed following serious cancer surgery. The surgery followed four months of chemotherapy, and as with all cancers, her recovery was not guaranteed. When I suggested that I take a pass on the first Trinidad trip, Mary's response was "Don't be crazy. You're not passing up an opportunity like this!" I argued a bit, but she was adamant. Our grown daughter, Nicole, was living at home while working on her master's degree in cello performance at Catholic University, so I knew Mary would be well cared for.

Throughout her illness, all the doctors and nurses told Mary that she should take a nice trip when her treatments were over. Joining me in Trinidad for this second trip was what she chose, even though I brought up the possibility of traveling to Italy. Given what she had been going through last year, it was so uplifting to see her swimming laps at our hotel pool, playing with Brian and Deb's girls on the beach in Tobago, or having her sit in and sing with us during our Tobago show. Our group still sounded great (particularly a mind-blowing jazz arrangement Jeff did of Copland's "Fanfare for the Common Man"). But what I'll remember most about my second trip is my sweet wife coming back to life.

EMBASSY OF THE
UNITED STATES OF AMERICA

THE AMBASSADOR

May 4, 2012

Colonel Michael J. Colburn
"The President's Own"
United States Marine Band
Marine Barracks Washington
8th and I Streets, SE
Washington, D.C. 20390

Dear Col. Colburn:

    I want to thank you for allowing Master Gunnery Sergeant Boguslaw and Gunnery Sergeant Sabo to participate in Port of Spain's Jazz Month celebration. Their concert on the evening of April 26th, 2012 was nothing short of spectacular; together with other American and Trinidadian musicians they electrified the audience. Your ensemble of very talented musicians was truly amazing and I was extremely touched by their beautiful rendering of 'Who Can I turn to'. During their brief stay I know they touched many young musicians here by conducting a series of master classes throughout the country.

    Following the concert, many of my friends expressed to me how impressed they were at such an awe-inspiring performance. My hope is that the people of Trinidad and Tobago appreciate your band's invaluable contribution and unique talent.

    I look forward to future collaborations with the United States Marine Band.

Sincerely,

Beatrice W. Welters
Ambassador

cc: GySgt. Eric Sabo
       MGySgt. Robert Boguslaw

PORT OF SPAIN, TRINIDAD AND TOBAGO

344

SWEET HOME ALABAMA

Most of the time, nothing terribly dramatic happens at a typical Marine Band White House job. We (or I) show up, go through security screening procedures, and get a rundown of the event from Max, our contact in the White House military office. We play on cue and cut the music when given the signal at the precise moment that the president or first lady are about to make their entrance. Today's event is for the University of Alabama football team, who just recently won the National Championship. This should be routine. We know the usual drill for these sports team receptions. Except this time, I screwed up.

The team is ten minutes away from making their entrance, and I forgot to bring the music for the university fight song. I've never done this in my twenty years with the Marine Band, but in this job, all it takes is one complaint from the White House to dig a serious pothole in the middle of one's career path. Our exceptionally efficient library staff normally coordinates with our operations office to announce at our weekly muster the specific music that needs to be picked up and carried for certain jobs. Unlike most of the sports team receptions we've done, the announcement wasn't made this time. But I know that ultimately, as the group leader, it's my responsibility to see that we're prepared. This one's definitely on me.

About an hour ago, we arrived at the White House and went down to the men's mezzanine to get our gear. We then set up on the South Lawn, where we could easily see the president's podium and the bleachers for the team to assemble behind him. As usual, about two hundred folding chairs were put in place for the guests, and the butler staff set up a couple of bars serving iced tea and cold water. No beer and wine on a weekday morning. We played our usual mix of jazz standards with a few Latin and pop tunes thrown in. Not surprisingly, one of the 'Bama players walked by and asked us if we could play "Sweet Home Alabama." I try to avoid heavy rock tunes when our group is set up to play background jazz, but we all knew this one so we played some Skynyrd. We generated lots more interest from the audience for that one than the Pat Metheny tune we just finished, although I'm sure they aren't used to hearing Skynyrd with a valve trombone playing the melody. Ryan does a great job on trombone. We also threw in "Stars Fell on Alabama," a standard well known and loved by the older Alabamians.

Then, about fifteen minutes before the team is scheduled to make their entrance, Max comes up to me and says: "Now, you've got that fight song ready for the announcement of the team, right?"

Oops.

Ryan suggests we listen to the song on his iPhone and see if we can find sheet music for it on our handheld devices. But the group has only two iPhones between us, and five of us need to read the music. We listen quickly to the fight song, but it's too long to memorize on the spot. Ryan finds the sheet music online, but it's too small for any of us to be able to read it. At this point, I ask Max (who's looking both slightly amused and disturbed at the same time) if I can have our Marine Band Library fax it to his office.

"Sure." He gives me the number, and sends one of his aides up to the military office to receive the fax and make five copies.

When I call the librarian, she drops whatever she was doing (as is always the case for the White House) and faxes it right away. But now nearly ten minutes have gone by, and we're trying to hold on until the cavalry shows up with the sheet music. I can see the Alabama team and coaches lined up over my right shoulder, ready to march in to a fight song we don't have yet when given the signal. Finally, Max's assistant comes out of the south portico carrying a bunch of loose papers. I can't tell if he's walking really fast or running really slow.

We cut our last tune off, and as soon as he hands me the music, Max says, "Now!"

We're all competent sight readers and this music's not difficult, but it would have been nice to have had thirty seconds or so to look it over. Fortunately, it goes well. After all, a fight song's a fight song (though it helps if you know the melody). After the reception (handshakes, photos, and gift giving), Max and the Marine Band guys are getting a chuckle out of the crisis we just averted. I chuckle with them, but I sure wasn't laughing when we were in the middle of it.

It crosses my mind that marines who are living and fighting in foxholes in Afghanistan would find my panic over this more than a bit silly. But this is what my job is, and I do always try to get it right. Today, I've come to the conclusion that I definitely prefer the White House gigs where nothing out of the ordinary happens.

DYSTONIA

I've just left the colonel's office after being informed that my career with the "President's Own" will soon be over. Following one of our infrequent yet frustrating section commanders' meetings (picture lots of talking with rarely anything significant being accomplished), the colonel asked to speak with me in his office.

"As you know, we've discussed the fact that you may be asked to retire before your rank and position in the organization would dictate if your condition should worsen. Well, that time is here."

I'm sure the colonel had given this a lot of consideration, but his delivery of the news was astonishingly casual. The colonel acknowledged the fact that I was being given a year's notice (instead of the customary two, due to my condition), but I was upset enough that most of it didn't really register. I could feel this coming, and I've always had the attitude that I'd be fine when it did. I made a modest living by playing and teaching before joining the Marine Band, and I can certainly do so after my retirement. I'm still reasonably young, fifty-five. Plus I'll have an adequate pension. I also know that it's been a great career. So why am I so angry and frustrated?

I realize it's because for the last seven years, I've been struggling to overcome focal dystonia, and my command (at least for the past five years) has made me feel that my career has constantly been in jeopardy. From my perspective, they've paid lip service in terms of encouraging me to receive treatments and supporting my attempts to recover, while at the same time showing no signs of confidence that I ever would. It's a hell of a thing to have hanging over me when I'm trying to make music, and I already have the significant pressure of frequent performances at the White House.

In 2005, I managed to set up a lesson with the brilliant jazz pianist and teacher, Kenny Werner. We ended up spending the entire hour trying, unsuccessfully, to get me to be able to gently lift the fourth finger of my right hand. The only thing I got out of the lesson was Kenny's advice that I'd better see a doctor. I returned home and prepared for a performance of Mozart's Concerto no. 21 with the "President's Own" Chamber Orchestra.

On the first day of rehearsal, I was confronted with serious DC traffic gridlock, even worse than usual. But when I arrived, I still had an hour to warm up. Unfortunately, another keyboard player was struggling to find sounds on a synthesizer for a separate rehearsal. As section leader, it's my job to try and help, so I plowed through a computerized bank of electronic sounds looking for synthesized celeste and harp patches. As I stood over the synthesizer looking at the LEDs, my stomach started doing flips in anticipation of sitting in front of an orchestra full of friends and colleagues and feeling unprepared. I needed to be warming up with scales, trill exercises, and etudes.

Our directors frequently give us speeches about how marines always need to be ready to perform at a high level under adverse circumstances. But I played what was probably the poorest first rehearsal of my career. The colonel knew I was having unspecified hand problems and canceled my concerto performance.

I had experienced some of my most satisfying classical performances while soloing with the "President's Own": Beethoven's Concertos no. 1 and no. 4, Schumann's Concerto in A minor, Mozart's Concerto no. 24, and Carl Maria von Weber's "Konzertstücke." That was over now. The embarrassment in front of my colleagues and the blow to my self-esteem was devastating. Over the next few weeks, I slid into a serious state of depression and began to realize I did have a serious problem and that I needed to seek help. That was the beginning of my journey in search of recovery.

The first neurologist to work with me through the military medical system misdiagnosed my condition as "essential tremor," basically meaning there was nothing that could be done except to prescribe drugs to reduce the shaking in my right hand. Eventually, I got a referral through a friend to see the chief of neurology at Columbia in New York. The doctor examined me for about fifteen minutes, then stated unequivocally that I had focal dystonia.

I realized I'd wasted two years with treatments for the wrong condition. During those two years, however, I'd done a pretty credible performance of the tremendously difficult Mendelssohn C-Minor Piano Trio, in uniform with Marine Band colleagues, as well as a few civilian pops concerts with Marin Alsop (a wonderful conductor) and the Baltimore Symphony Orchestra, which featured a lot of solo piano. Leon Fleisher (one of the giants of classical piano and another dystonia sufferer) gave me ten minutes of advice by phone. That conversation inspired me to go for a number of deep-tissue massage treatments called Rolfing. I was hopeful my condition would improve. But my command warned me that my career was in jeopardy.

The colonel told me that people do not recover from dystonia. "Once a 'dystonic,' always a 'dystonic,'" he said. But I'd done enough research to know that his assertion was incorrect. I redoubled my efforts to get well. I went for physical therapy, acupuncture, massage therapy, body-mapping instruction, and attentional focus training (a rigorous regimen aimed at re-wiring neural pathways). I received training from Jan Kagarice, an intense and brilliant instructor of attentional focus, who basically cured herself of multiple sclerosis using this method. I even saw a psychic healer who I'm convinced was genuine. It was all expensive and time consuming, though I'm certain those treatments enabled me to keep playing.

I was very, very fortunate to have found a group of compassionate and caring healers. I began lessons in Alexander Technique with Cynthia Mauney, a gifted teacher. Alexander Technique is based on the notion that we human beings lose touch with our sixth sense, kinesthesia. As we go through our daily activities (including playing musical instruments), we tighten and lock our muscles, and eventually nerves, without being aware of it. Alexander Technique helps to release and regain control of muscles, nerves, and joints. It's been effective enough for me that I've become a firm believer in the "sixth sense."

During my dystonia years as a marine, I did have a number of fine performances that led me to believe I was well on my way to recovery, as well as some poor ones that made me want to walk away from the piano and never return. The idea of playing the piano as an artistic pursuit has become an all-consuming source of physical struggle and emotional frustration. Sleep deprivation and nearly constant anxiety have become a way of life. As I walk down the hallway and exit the command suite, I feel this seven-year battle I've fought has been lost, but I'll continue to wear the uniform and represent the Marine Band at the White House and the home of the commandant to the best of my ability for another year. I was a gig warrior before the Marine Band and will still be one when I hang up the uniform for the last time.

CODA

It's May of 2013 and I'm walking to my car. In the distance, I can hear the Marine Band closing with Morton Gould's arrangement of "Dixie." The piece is clever, but not terribly sophisticated, pretty typical of the music we play for our outdoor Summer Pops concerts. I'm not in any danger of getting caught in the end-of-the-show traffic rush. All two thousand members of the audience will probably stay for the fireworks when the "Armed Forces

Medley" ends. Wolf Trap is a large outdoor theatre, and every year their season kicks off with a Marine Band concert followed by an awe-inducing fireworks display. Most audience members bring picnic baskets and lawn chairs. You can't get much more Americana than this.

I left as soon as my part in the concert was done. I quickly changed my clothes and collected my garment bag and briefcase at the end of "Medley from Ragtime." Although I played well and I like the music from that show a lot, I experienced absolutely none of the emotional, spiritual, or personal satisfaction that one gets from sharing music with a large and enthusiastic audience. Zero on the musical-fulfillment meter.

A few years ago, I took some "body mapping" lessons with my old college friend from the University of Kentucky, Jerald Harscher. Jerry's method has met with substantial success in treating dystonia patients. Toward the end of our sessions, Jerry told me that there was also something called "the mental map." He then asked me if I thought of myself as an artist. I thought long and hard and then responded, "No, I'm a craftsman. I'm someone who cranks out parts for concerts and songs for background music." A bit perplexed, Jerry looked at me and said, "That's interesting because when we were in graduate school together, literally everyone at UK, faculty and students, all thought of you as a great artist." Something must have changed.

ANNIE LENNOX

It's the summer of 2012, and it's the United States' turn to host an international AIDS conference. It's amazing how much things have changed with respect to this horrible disease since I first heard about it in the early '80s. For years, we all knew that an HIV diagnosis was a death sentence. Nowadays, nearly everyone can receive treatments that slow down or even stop the progression of the virus. I do know, however, that there are still places in the world where the disease is a scourge, and it's not to be taken lightly here at home either.

President Obama has decided to invite the organizers of this conference to the White House for a large reception tomorrow afternoon, and I'm coming up empty-handed in my efforts to think of musical material specifically suited for this one. AIDS and HIV isn't a subject that readily lends itself to music. I do remember, however, that Annie Lennox has been very active with this cause in the past, and I recall reading that she's a spokesperson for this organization. I'm guessing she'll be there. Unfortunately, the only song of hers that I know is "Sweet Dreams" from the Eurythmics days, almost thirty years ago now.

I'm getting ready to give up and resign myself to playing the usual variety of jazz that our quintets do, when I remember a brilliant Herbie Hancock album called *Possibilities*. This recording is one of my favorite collaborative albums of all time between jazz and pop/rock artists. Herbie recorded with different singers and songwriters on every cut: Sting, Carlos Santana, Johnnie Lang and Joss Stone, Jon Mayer, Annie Lennox, and others. I also remember the lyrics of the song Annie sang, called "Hush, Hush, Hush." It's one of the saddest songs I've ever heard. It tells the story of a parent who watches his child wasting away with AIDS in a hospital bed. Some of the lyrics suggest what might have been, and some allude to hopes of reincarnation. Not your standard Porter and Gershwin fare. Although, come to think of it, I've always suspected that it's no coincidence that Gershwin wrote "They Can't Take That Away from Me" and "Our Love Is Here to Stay" (his last song) just a few months before a brain tumor killed him.

Anyway, I take a seat at the computer with a YouTube clip of "Hush, Hush, Hush" and write out the music by ear in a little less than an hour. There are a few tricky harmonic changes, but it's well worth the effort. After all, it certainly is a brilliant song, and the power of its emotional content is visceral.

The Grand Foyer is full of people and the noise level is intense as we go from jazz standards such as Clare Fisher's "Morning" to John Coltrane's "Moment's Notice." During most of these jobs, I still find myself at least a bit amazed that we can make any music at all with the acoustic challenges we face at the White House. All the drummer has to do is gently tap his ride cymbal if he wants to compete with the guests. When the crowd's large enough, I sometimes have difficulty hearing some of the band members who are standing no farther than five or six feet away. But somehow, we manage to start and stop together and make some music in the middle.

As the social staff lets the first guests up and we begin to play, I see Annie Lennox walk by us. She gives us a smile of recognition that most musicians will generally give each other when unexpectedly coming across a performance of some kind. After arriving, she quickly leaves the foyer, probably to greet President Obama in the receiving line. But now she returns, and we're in-between selections. I quickly pull out the sheet I wrote for "Hush," which I've kept handy, and I let the other guys know that I'll take this one. (The arrangement on the recording of this song is well suited to a solo piano version.)

Annie Lennox immediately comes over to the piano and looks over my shoulder at the scribbled chart, sees the title, and begins mouthing the words. Surprisingly, she seems a bit unsure of them. Since I listened to it at least six or seven times yesterday, the lyrics are still fresh in my mind, so I prompt her a bit and even hum along lightly. She remembers as she goes, singing more assertively as the song progresses from a sad lullaby to a joyful dream-fantasy of lives still to come. As the arc of the song melts back into the sad lullaby section, I look at Annie and detect a few tears in the corner of her eye. I realize that we're both crying. I can't say if it's because of the song itself or remembrances of loved ones lost to AIDS or, in my case, the joy of playing this song with the wonderful original artist in this setting. When we end, I stand up and she gives me an emotional hug.

"How'd you learn that song? I haven't sung it since the day we recorded it!" she says.

I tell her I'm a big fan of the *Possibilities* album and that "Hush" is one of my favorites. I also tell her the lyrics seem pretty meaningful for today, so I lifted it from the CD yesterday. She thanks me and then moves on to rejoin her friends. Some of the guests stopped and listened while she sang, though many remained absorbed in their drinks, food, and conversations, not noticing that something special had just happened. But that really doesn't matter. Not to me or to Annie.

DAVID

It's October of 2012, and I'm sitting in the pit of the Hippodrome Theatre in Baltimore playing the Keyboard 2 book for the national tour of *Wicked*. I'm not the world's biggest modern musical theater fan, but I'm finding that I like most of the music in this particular show. I was hired to be the "sub" keyboardist, just playing one or two shows a week. As I play, my attention focuses on one of my favorite *Wicked* songs, "For Good." My part in this song is pretty important and exposed, and at one point, I realize there are only two instrumentalists accompanying the powerful Broadway diva on the stage. One is me. The other's my brother, Dave.

David and his wife Debby travel with this show. He's been playing *Wicked* for almost three years now, and for nearly thirty years, he's made a good living by playing a constant stream of Broadway hits. *Cats, Les Miserables, Sunset Boulevard, Ragtime, Some Like It Hot* (with Tony Curtis), *Mama Mia*, and probably some others I'm forgetting. He's really good at it, and I'm under the impression that he's got a national reputation within his field. When I spent three months playing *Cats* with Dave, right before joining the Marine Band, I don't think I ever heard him miss a note. He claims that he did, but I couldn't tell. But now it's been over twenty years since we played *Cats* together or any other professional gig, for that matter. Once again, Dave and I are in an orchestra pit together, playing a brief trio—two Boguslaws and a diva. The lyric of "For Good" is a beautifully crafted reflection on friendship and the positive influence human beings can have on one another. When I think about those who've been a positive influence on me, my teachers, Fred and Lucien, usually come to mind, or my parents, or Pat, my childhood nanny, or my wife, Mary. But playing this song with Dave has gotten me thinking all the way back to my childhood.

Right in the middle of the show, I'm transported back to the basement of our childhood home, Dave and me strumming on a guitar and mandolin, singing Beatles, Grateful Dead, and Doc Watson tunes. And even farther back in time, Dave, my sister Nancy (on flute and vocals), and me reading arrangements from the first published songbooks of Elton John, James Taylor, and Cat Stevens. Dave and I shared a lot of music back in those days. And now, some forty years later, we're sharing the accompaniment for Steven Schwartz's climactic power ballad. I force myself to come back to the present. The end of "For Good" is not hard to play, but it does require that I give the conductor my full attention.

As far back as I can remember, I've wanted to be like my big brother. That may be understating things a bit. I think what I actually really wanted was to be my big brother. He played the piano, and consequently, by the time I was five years old, I was hounding my parents incessantly to let me take lessons, too. Our teacher told me I could start when I turned six, and I punctually reminded him of that during the week of my sixth birthday.

David was also an excellent French horn player. Not coincidentally, I took up the horn in the fifth grade. He got involved in a Renaissance period recorder ensemble as a senior in high school, so I learned the soprano recorder, enabling me to join the group when they needed a fifth part for some of the madrigals they liked to play. In high school, Dave also started getting seriously into the guitar, and I got him to show me some chords on the instrument. But he eventually encouraged me to learn the mandolin instead so we could do some bluegrass music together. And there were non-musical things as well.

I tried but failed to live up to the standards he set as an excellent student.

I tried unsuccessfully to whip myself into shape, so I could be on our high school football team like Dave had been. And I certainly aspired to have a pretty girlfriend like he did in his last two years of high school. He also got me listening to some of the newest and best hard rock of the day, The Who, Jimi Hendrix, Cream, and Jethro Tull. We played horn duets together (far preferable to practicing), golfed together, and went to lots of concerts together. I recall always feeling that he was so much superior to me at everything, and the gap between us was insurmountable—typical little brother psycho-dramas.

In the summer of '76, we spent a wonderful five weeks together visiting my grandparents in London. Although the castles, cathedrals, museums, and pubs of the city were exciting, the best part of the trip was the eight days Dave and I spent hiking in Scotland. Nothing but rugged mountains, quiet pine forests, beautiful lakes, and rolling heather for miles and miles. We stayed in youth hostels. Dave and I were fanatical enough about our music that we carted my mandolin (which fit in my pack) and his guitar (which Dave carried by hand) on hikes up and down mountains, sometimes for distances as much as twenty-five miles in a day. This allowed us to play some bluegrass or Celtic folk music every time we stopped for a break. At one hostel where we stayed, we were joined by a Canadian lumberjack who played spoons. I was skeptical, but he played well and we jammed for quite a while. Another hostel's owner and manager recorded the two of us playing a few of our original tunes, telling us he liked to record any of his guests who were musical. I sometimes wonder if he still listens to that recording from the summer of '76. We also spent the latter part of that crazy summer putting our acoustic trio, Final Frontier, together with Bob, my talented college musician friend.

After that summer, though, I rarely saw Dave. As siblings do, we went our own ways and got on with our lives. I spent most of my time in Miami. I aspired to be a classical concert artist, studied some jazz, wrote for and played in a few original rock bands, and found some new role models. Back in Philadelphia, Dave became a fine jazz player and an excellent wedding band musician. But he also became quite in demand as a musical theater performer, and that eventually became his career. Dave has the ability to read a part and follow a conductor simultaneously, the ability to change styles instantly, and the ability to play the same show nightly for a period of years while still maintaining his concentration, focus, and energy. He still does all those things really well. It's been twenty years since we worked together, and here, sitting in the *Wicked* pit, I can tell that he still "brings it" every night.

So here we are, working together once again to get an audience excited, two aging musicians who first played together and developed a bond through music nearly fifty years ago. Brother Dave and me.

HOUSE OF CARDS

Much of my professional life has been spent on the periphery of fame. Presidents Bush I and II, Clinton, and Obama have all received foreign dignitaries while I provided background music nearby. Stevie Wonder, Paul McCartney, Jeff Beck, and Paul Simon all performed in the adjacent East Room while I listened by the door, prepared to run back to the piano at any moment when given the cue that the show was done and it was time to start the reception music. Probably the closest I came to fame was playing for El Puma's shows, but the thousands of fans were screaming for Jose Luis Rodriguez, and the frenzied females in the audience who rushed the stage were throwing themselves at him, not the second keyboard player.

I'm fine with being on the outside looking in on the world of stardom, whether it's the life of a politician, a pop idol, or a film star. But the gig I'm doing tonight is going to take me to the next level. It's my Hollywood debut (actually, filming in Baltimore). Tonight, I'm going to be playing air piano on a film shoot for a scene from *House of Cards*, the Netflix miniseries.

Last week, I got a call from my friend Ed, who works at the Baltimore Musician's Union. Ed was providing the musicians and music for a number of different scenes in *House of Cards*. The shoot was to be a twelve-hour call from 1600 to 0400 to mime a tune that we would prerecord. We were asked to play a "cool lounge background jazz number in the style of Brubeck's 'Take Five.'" But it had to be a preexisting tune written prior to 1923. Obviously, the producers didn't want to pay residuals to a composer. They wanted a 1950s cool-jazz style using a pre-swing era tune. I offered to write something to fit the style. They didn't want to have to pay me residuals either. No surprise there.

So I went through a list of songs from the early twenties and teens and finally settled on two ideas: a tune called "Indian Summer" by Victor Herbert that has some nice harmonic movement, and a version of W.C. Handy's "St. Louis Blues" that I arranged using the same rhythmic feel as Brubeck's "Take Five." We recorded them both on Sunday for the director to choose from. That was the fun part of this gig.

Right now, it's nearly 0330, and Mike, Chris, and I are all standing in a hospitality tent with about seventy extras. Talking to some of the extras, I'm shocked to discover just how little they're paid. And the director's assistants talk to them as if they're wayward school children in need of some serious guidance. I guess the allure of seeing one's self on television is worth it to them. Maybe some of them hope to be "discovered" when the camera pans across the room for a few seconds.

The gig started out with a quick visit to a make-up artist. We were then escorted to an alcove just outside a hotel special-event room where the faux cocktail party was to be filmed. There we waited until around 0730. Chris, Mike, and I exhausted our conversations regarding families, careers, and music. I tried a few of my old jokes, with limited success. At one point, the sound man fit us with a tiny earbud, so we could hear the recording we'd made the other day and hopefully, mime accordingly with the music. We were asked to make a jazz recording, and no self-respecting jazz musician would ever play the same tune the same way twice. Basically, I had no idea what patterns my hands and arms were moving in when we recorded "Indian Summer" three days ago. Oh well. I figured I'd just wing it and hope they didn't get a shot of me doing an ascending arpeggio while the sound was descending. At 0730, we were suddenly expected to move fast and get in place for our mimed performance. When the director yelled "Action!", we moved our hands over the instruments as if we were playing. The extras milled about, mouthing silent conversations. One or two of them thought I was a good stage prop, so they faked conversations with me. Good thing it was faked because by the time we did the fourteenth take, whatever I would have said would require serious editing.

Between each take, the director played back what was recorded, and we were all firmly encouraged by his assistants to remain silent. This went on for three hours, and by the time we got a break, I was thoroughly convinced that making movies is not my thing. We were given another two-hour break, followed by another three-hour session of miming the same tune, and now they're finally telling us we can go home. They got what they needed.

While driving home, I struggle a bit to stay awake behind the wheel. It occurs to me how fortunate I am to spend my life working at something where there's almost never literal repetition. Even playing classical music in large ensembles can leave significant room for individual interpretations. That just wasn't happening for me in *House of Cards*.

CODA

I'm getting rave reviews for my performance in *House of Cards*. Lots of family and friends calling and emailing to tell me how much they loved seeing me in Season 1, Episode 10, for all of .78 seconds. I've probably gotten more feedback for my performance in this show than for both of my CDs combined. But I get the biggest kick out of hearing our trio's version of "Indian Summer" as the soundtrack for the entire scene when slut girl comes on to and picks up the unsuspecting politician. My only problem with the show now? I just can't understand why the producers decided to put Kevin Spacey on all the promotional billboards instead of me. What were they thinking?

MY LAST WHITE HOUSE JOB

It's a hot July day, and our Marine Band Jazz Quartet just finished lining up our instrument cases and music along the wall by the entrance to the White House off East Executive Drive. I've been doing this for years and am used to the secret service and the canine sweeps of our gear. The EOD (Explosive Ordnance Device) agents who come to inspect us today are particularly thorough, thumbing through what seems to be every page of every fake book. They tend to be the most thorough when there's been a recent threat of some sort. Weapons would be picked up by the metal detectors that we all have to pass through, but I've been told that the hands-on inspections are for potential chemical agents that may be missed by the electronic eyes.

One of the secret service agents says, "Hey Bogie!" to me. I tell him that today is my last White House job, then we shake hands and say goodbye.

I'm actually surprised at how unemotional I feel as I enter the White House, the place that's been the highlight of my recent years with the "President's Own." I think I'm probably emotionally exhausted after all the anger I've experienced in the last ten months. After being told that I would be forced to retire with one year's notice, I found myself waking up at night and lying in bed for hours, unable to fall back to sleep.

My sleeplessness gave me plenty of time to figure out what was bothering me. At first, I thought it might be the sadness of not getting to work with the world-class Marine Band musicians anymore. But I realized after a while that although this does make me feel a bit sad, I fully expect to continue working with some brilliant musicians (including some of my Marine Band colleagues) in the DC area. Then I thought my sleeplessness might be caused by worry about my financial situation. But I concluded that that's not the reason because I'm pretty confident of my ability to play and teach enough to make ends meet. I'm sure I'm not losing sleep because I'll miss my friends. I certainly can keep in touch. I finally came to realize that I was losing sleep for one plain and simple reason: I'm simply mad as hell at my commanding officers for disrespecting me and my service to the Marine Band for the last twenty-two years. The anger is intense enough to keep me awake. Admittedly, my ego and self-image are fragile.

I can recall performances of extremely difficult music that I've done on behalf of the Marine Band at the Library of Congress, as well as chamber music performances at Marine Barracks Washington, DC, that received positive reviews in the *Washington Times*. I recall the time when Pope Benedict XVI visited the Bush W. White House, and I called a Catholic musician friend to ask him what was appropriate to play for him. I found out that Pope Benedict was a serious classical pianist, so I selected classical piano works including, of course, the music of Chopin. I told the colonel afterward that the pope complimented my performance of a Haydn sonata when celebrating his birthday at the White House with the Bushes. The colonel's response was, "You're looking for approval in the wrong places."

*Bob and Mrs. Bush with Pope Benedict XVI on the occasion of the
Pope's birthday, 2008*

I realized my commanding officer didn't care about the pope's opinion. It was useless to speak up for myself. The directors believed only they themselves were qualified to judge me.

I've had an excellent relationship with President Obama, Jeremy Bernard, the social secretary, the ushers' office, and the butlers, as well as the marine commandant. I don't kid myself into believing that the Marine Band is going to fall apart without me and that no one can take my place when I retire, but after today's job, after twenty-two years, it's over. I need to focus on all the great experiences I've had wearing this uniform that I never would have had otherwise. I know I need to redirect my energy and possibly take Mary's advice to seek out some anger management counseling. It's my last time at the White House, and only three days from now, I'll be on terminal leave. For now, though, it's time to direct my emotional energy to today's job, my last at the White House.

The University of Louisville men's NCAA basketball champions are the guests of honor. Coincidentally, my two youngest daughters both completed their bachelor's degrees at this university. Both Gabrielle and Nicole would love for me to come home with some autographs by the players. As we enter the building, I see the Louisville team ambling down the hallway in front of us, pausing to look at a series of beautiful presidential photos. Their youth, height, and athletic build give them away.

There's a thirty-something blonde woman looking at a photo of President Obama, Mrs. Obama, and Stevie Wonder. She smiles as I walk by and comments, "It's going to be good hearing you all play again." I say something about how cool it is that she's come to the White House with the Louisville Cardinals. She then tells me that she used to work here during the Clinton Administration, and that it's great to get to come back.

I think, what the hell, and I ask her if she can help me get a few autographs for my daughters who are alumni. She looks at me with feigned skepticism and tells me that she'll only help me if I have something from U of L for them to sign on.

"It just so happens that I have the University of Louisville Alumni magazine right here," I say. What a coincidence.

"Oh, my gosh," she says, "I'm the editor of that magazine. I'll see what I can do for you."

As I thank her and hand it to her, I think that today might be one of my good karma days after all. Ten minutes later, we're setting up in the Grand Foyer, and she comes back with the magazine signed by the coach with the added message: "Go Cards!" I thank her again and tell her how excited my daughters are going to be. She asks me what their names are and I tell her, "Nicole and Gabrielle." She writes the names down, asking for the correct spelling. I'm hoping that the two of them might make it into the next edition of Louisville Alumni magazine.

A few minutes later, two of the Louisville guards come over and start looking over the historic White House piano. I figure they're guards because they're not much taller than me but young and athletic looking.

Guard number one says to number two: "Go on, dawg, play me some Beethoven."

Guard number two says: "Play Beethoven? I'll bet you can't even spell Beethoven."

I interrupt their fun and ask them if I can get two more autographs for my daughters. They both seem real happy to sign, and just like the coach, they write "Go Cards."

We finish playing a forty-five minute set as the Louisville visitors assemble in the Grand Foyer and then proceed to the East Room for the president's speech and a photo-op. We then play the Louisville fight song while the team is introduced, and now the president is speaking, recognizing the accomplishments of these young men who excel at his favorite sport. One of the assistants to the social secretary comes up to me and tells me the president would like to meet me in the Red Room following his speech, so we can get a photo together. He's heard that I'm retiring and that this is my last White House job for the marines.

I get up and go wait in the Red Room. Five minutes later, when President Obama enters, the first thing he says is, "Bob, you're not leaving us, are you?" I mutter something about it being time for me to move on. He then asks me about my plans, and I tell him that I'm going to play more civilian gigs and probably teach more.

The president tells me, "Well, don't be a stranger. Let us know where you're playing around DC. We'd love to come and see you."

I seriously doubt that that'll ever happen, but it's a real nice thing for him to say. The president and I pose for one last photo. As he leaves to do a receiving line with his Louisville guests and I turn to go back to my quartet, I tell him what an honor it's been to play for his administration for the last four and a half years. And I mean it.

Back on the bandstand, I'm thinking about what an excellent way this was to end my White House career, when Daniel, my good friend from the ushers' office, walks by and tells me that there's a gift for me in the cabinet next to the piano. He tells me that he has to go to a meeting before this event is over, so he says a quick but heartfelt goodbye and wishes me well. He quickly adds that the gift is a pen from Camp David. He tells me that it's the very pen that was used by Germany's Prime Minister Angela Merkel to sign the G-8 "Camp David Declaration" last May. I am speechless. It's an amazing gift, an incredible gift from Daniel.

As I finish packing up and helping the drummer with his cases for the last time, I think how this is just what I need for my last White House job. I need to be reminded about the great music, the great friends, and the many historic events I've gotten to be a part of, however small that part was. Yes, karma is with me today. When the East Gate of the White House closes behind me, I don't even look back. I know it's time to move on.

Bob with President Obama at Bob's final White House performance,
2013

PIANOS

As instrumentalists, pianists are in the unique position of being forced to constantly adjust to different instruments. Gigs might be played on any instrument ranging from "mint condition" Hamburg and New York Steinway concert grands to poorly maintained inexpensive uprights. The difference between the touch and sound of these various pianos is enormous, and that's not even including modern sampled electronic keyboards. If I play a repeated note with the same finger, starting very softly and eventually increasing the dynamic level to its maximum, I can assess the instrument's capability. Generally, I can get close to twenty different volume levels on the best grand pianos. On a good upright, maybe ten. And on an electric "touch-sensitive" instrument, probably five at most.

I'm sure that kind of touch sensitivity was the reason the great classical concert artist, Vladimir Horowitz, would transport his own Steinway Grand from city to city by train, bringing his personal piano technician with him to all of his recitals. Jazz artists such as Keith Jarrett and Oscar Peterson also had very specific clauses written into their contracts regarding instruments to be provided and technicians to be on hand for concerts.

As a gig warrior who occasionally moonlights as a concert artist, I've seen the entire spectrum of instruments. Hotels and restaurants are notorious for keeping their instruments beautifully shined and polished while failing to tune, regulate, or voice them, sometimes even for a period of years. I guess they figure that most people listen with their eyes. Of course, there are exceptions. Last night, I played a three-hour background jazz duo gig with one of DC's (and one of the nation's) finest bass players, Tommy Cecil. It was a corporate reception, and we were mostly just providing "musical wallpaper," but I had a great time because the Ritz Carlton provided me with a well-maintained Steinway Grand, and we played lots of jazz standards. People were talking and milling about as we played, although a few stopped and listened. Overall, I went home feeling that this wasn't such a bad way to make a living. What a difference twenty-four hours makes.

Tonight as I'm driving home, I'm thinking there's a good chance I'll wind up retraining for a new career at the age of fifty-six. Tonight's gig may have been four of the longest hours of my professional life. I'm sure if I racked my memory, I'd eventually come up with something worse, but right now it seems that way. Aha, now I remember! The time I uncontrollably shivered my way through a five-hour wedding while wretchedly sick with pneumonia, sitting under a ventilation duct with cold air blowing on my back throughout the entire gig. Maybe tonight can't beat that, but it definitely deserves second place. I've never played publicly on an instrument so horribly out of tune.

"I don't think anything you just sang is a note." That's one of my favorite sardonic quips from my cellist daughter, Nicole. It comes to mind after I spent thirty seconds trying out tonight's piano.

The event planner saw my pained expression and asked, "Is the piano OK?"

I played a few of the "I-don't-think-these-are-notes" notes for her and simply said, "It's pretty out of tune." She asked me if it'd help to lower the piano lid. I wanted to tell her that the only way that that would help would be if closing the lid would make the piano inaudible, but I behaved myself instead and just responded with, "Um, nope." "Well, the guests will be arriving in half an hour, so we'll just have to make do," she told me.

While playing the gig, I couldn't bring myself to look up at any of the cocktail consuming corporate types. It's unimaginable to me that anyone would think what I was doing sounded good, and probably for the first time in my life, an instrument made me feel embarrassed. I was aware that most of my audience probably wouldn't make the distinction between the player and the piano. But I know that even Art Tatum or Glenn Gould would have sounded like aural defecation if they played on that instrument.

Tonight's gig makes me think back on Restaurant St. Michele in Coral Gables. I worked there a couple of nights weekly in '83 and '84. Despite the restaurant's dreadful, never-tuned piano covered with a poorly applied coat of white paint, it was a good job for me. The owner let me play whatever I wanted to play, so I regularly used the job to try out Mozart, Haydn, and Beethoven sonatas along with pieces by Chopin, Bach, and Schubert in preparation for upcoming piano competitions. I didn't hard sell the idea of the value of an investment in a tuning to the owner, but I did mention it more than once.

One time while playing the gig, I saw Whit Sidener (the head of the University of Miami's jazz program) come in with the great jazz pianist/keyboardist, Bob James. The two of them whispered something to the hostess and she escorted them to a table at the farthest point in the restaurant from the piano (and me). Not a coincidence.

But what turned the tide and finally convinced the owner that a tuning was a good idea was when a friend of his remarked, "That piano's so out of tune, it could turn the wine to vinegar!" Amazingly enough, when I sat down to play the next evening, the piano had been tuned. But while driving home tonight, I'm thinking that if the St. Michele piano could turn the wine into vinegar, then the "Presidential Suite" instrument I just played probably turned the baked salmon into salmonella.

Of course, there are two sides to every story. On the 1993 Marine Band tour of the northeastern US, I got to perform as a soloist in Carnegie Hall, Boston's Symphony Hall, and Philadelphia's Academy of Music. No problems performing on their instruments. In 1992, some exceptionally wealthy friends of my sister in law hired me to visit the Manhattan Steinway showroom on their behalf to pick out a seven-foot B-model instrument for their new home on Jupiter Island. I spent about three or four hours happily moving from one beautiful instrument to the next. A short time after that trip, my satisfied customers actually called me and hired me to play a private solo recital at their magnificent new home on the piano I had selected as the New York showroom's best "B." That was definitely a gig I couldn't complain about.

But probably my greatest experience with playing the world's finest instruments came about because the Marine Band director decided to purchase a new nine-foot Hamburg Steinway D. The band hadn't bought a new piano since the 1960s. Unfortunately, pianos don't appreciate in value as they age in the same way that stringed instruments do. It was time for a new one, and I was ecstatic when I heard that Colonel Colburn had authorized and funded a brief trip to Hamburg for me and a small group of colleagues to select a new grand piano. You wouldn't dream of buying a top-of-the-line new car without taking it for a test drive. The same goes for a piano.

The Hamburg trip was incredible. We were wonderfully wined and dined by the president of Steinway International, but the highlight of the trip was a four-hour guided tour of the Steinway factory. We saw the entire by-hand manufacturing process, from lumberyard to chemical wood treatments to framing to harp and sound board installation to stringing, and finally, to the showroom. And what a showroom!

We selected the new Marine Band piano out of fifteen glorious Hamburg Steinway D's. They were all magnificent. A colleague and I both kept grading sheets as we went from one to the other. Any of them would have been wonderful, but amazingly enough, the two of us ended up with the same two instruments topping our lists. We bartered a little and came to an agreement on a final selection. The instrument had a huge and resonant bass sound. The high notes were brilliant without being brittle or percussive. The piano felt as if you were resting your fingers on a lovely soft cushion when the keys were depressed. And a single struck note seemed to sustain for at least thirty seconds. It was possibly the best piano I'd ever gotten to play on.

That's the standard I use to judge tonight's travesty of an instrument. Maybe if I'd never gotten to play that beautiful Hamburg Steinway, or one of Carnegie Hall's concert instruments, or spent twenty-two years getting to play on the White House's magnificent custom-built Steinway, tonight's situation wouldn't have bothered me as much. But I don't think so. I've taken pride over the years in my ability to make at least some music under all kinds of adverse circumstances, whether playing on poor instruments, with poor musicians, or in front of hostile audiences. But tonight, there just wasn't going to be any music made with that instrument. I think what's bothering me the most is that tonight I lost some of my remaining self-respect. If Vladimir Horowitz, Glenn Gould, Oscar Peterson, or Keith Jarrett had sat down and played one scale on that "piano," they would have immediately turned around and walked out of the room. But I'm not them. I'm a gig warrior, and gig warriors don't do that.

HERBIE HANCOCK

I'm watching the 2013 Kennedy Center Honors performance on TV. It's the first time in the four months since I retired from the Marine Band that I've regretted missing a military gig. Herbie Hancock finally received this well-deserved, high-profile lifetime achievement award. It's especially bittersweet for me because I've met Herbie a number of times. You could say that we're friendly acquaintances.

I'm watching as the awards show pays tribute to his modal jazz roots, his role in the development of funk and fusion, and his eventual influence on rap and hip-hop. Herbie's a genius. He's one of the primary influences on nearly every jazz pianist (myself included) in the last fifty years. In a way, I've modeled myself after him by trying to keep my hand in lots of different musical idioms. I would really have loved to be at the White House to personally congratulate him. I frequently remind myself about how fortunate I am to have had the career I did in the Marine Band and all the experiences that came with it.

The first time I met Herbie was in 1991 at the Kennedy Center Honors dinner held in the Benjamin Franklin room at the State Department. I had been in the Marine Band for nearly a year, but I was still starstruck by all the celebrities and politicians surrounding us. Our jazz trio was in-between tunes when our drummer Dave blurted out, "Oh my God, there's Herbie Hancock!"

I tried to act calm, even though my heart was pounding. I called Herbie's tune, "Dolphin Dance." My solo was going reasonably well when I looked up to see Herbie standing at the other end of the piano. He leaned over the piano toward me, smiling and laughing and said "————" I couldn't hear a word because the noise level of everyone conversing at once was so great. I just nodded and smiled. We played out the rest of the gig with me distracted by the thought of possibly approaching him while he ate to ask him what he had said. Of course, we had explicit instructions from our command to never do that (rule number one for these types of jobs). So I stayed put, and spent the entire bus ride back to the barracks regretting I'd never know what he'd said to me.

For years, I harbored the hope that I'd run into Herbie again, so I could ask him what he had said.

It finally happened at the 2002 Kennedy Center Honors Dinner. Herbie was the first one in the room when the State Department protocol assistants opened the doors. He walked right over to where we were set up and found his name card on the table directly in front of us.

He turned to us, laughed, and said, "Your worst nightmare, I'm sitting right in front of you." It's kind of like being asked to take a turn-around jump shot with Michael Jordan standing next to you. But my mind was on something else.

I said, "Herbie, I've been waiting over ten years to ask you what you said to me in 1991 when you were here for the Kennedy Center Honors dinner and I played 'Dolphin Dance.' You were smiling and laughing, but the room noise was loud and I couldn't hear a thing you said to me."

He told me, "I probably said you sounded great, or maybe I just told you to keep your day job." He laughed, and I could tell right away he wasn't serious. Apparently, he couldn't remember the exchange at all. I really didn't expect he would, but asking him about it did take a load off my mind.

We stood together and discussed his recent CD, *The New Standard*. I complimented the great group he put together to record jazz arrangements of songs such as "Scarborough Fair" and "Norwegian Wood." He told me he was no longer interested in making recordings of unrelated songs, but instead, wanted to do only CDs that had a theme or concept. To my slight embarrassment, he then asked me if I'd heard his new recording titled *Gershwin's World*. He seemed really proud of it, and rightfully so, as I later discovered.

I was awkwardly apologizing for not staying current on his releases when one of the State Department protocol assistants came up and said, "I know Mr. Hancock is irresistible, but the guests are coming in, and we need you to start playing."

Herbie shrugged as he walked away.

"Thanks for answering my question," I said. "It's been bugging me for years."

We played Herbie's "Cantaloupe Island." When it ended, he turned from his conversation and gave us a thumbs-up.

About five years later, I was tasked to play solo piano at the White House for a Valentine's Day celebration. When I checked in with the ushers' office, they told me Herbie was to be the after-dinner entertainment. Just Herbie and the famous custom built White House Steinway Concert Grand. Solo. I played for cocktails and dinner. After dessert was served in the East Room, Herbie was introduced and played a beautiful and introspective twenty-minute set. Fortunately for me, they left the doors open, so I was able to see and hear everything he was doing. I found myself assimilating some of his chords on "Someone to Watch over Me," which I'm sure he was playing for the sake of Valentine's Day. Then I was carried away by an exceptional version of his tune "Maiden Voyage." Eventually, I found myself trying to figure out a syncopated rhythmic vamp he inserted in the middle of the form.

Then it struck me that with all the years that had passed since I first heard him, Herbie had become one of the senior statesmen of jazz, and he possessed a kind of wisdom in his playing that only comes with the passing of time. Great musicians, at this point in their lives, no longer have anything to prove. Consequently, their art manifests itself in its purest form because no other motivation exists for them other than the desire to express the inexpressible mysteries of existence and perceived universal truths. That's precisely what Herbie was doing.

After he was done, I started up again in the Grand Foyer, playing the guests out on a small Steinway upright. Gigi, Herbie's wife of nearly forty years, came over and told me that she was really loving my playing.

I was in between tunes so I took a moment to tell her, "I'm so glad you came over. It struck me while your husband was performing that there's great wisdom in his playing. Please tell him that as the years have passed, he's truly become a master."

She smiled, pointed at me and said, "You're a master, too."

I think that the only time anyone ever said anything that made me feel that good was when Mary agreed to marry me, after I'd spent seven years periodically popping the question. This gracious woman who'd spent the last thirty-eight years listening to Herbie play had called me a master. Herbie said hello to me before leaving, and this time he asked for my name. "Well, Bob," he said, "I'm sure I'll be seeing you again."

I did see him a few more times at the White House, most notably when Paul McCartney received the Library of Congress Gershwin Prize. Herbie performed "Blackbird" with Corinne Bailey Rae, a fine young jazz singer. It was beautiful playing. Herbie has an uncanny ability to make any song in any style sound like he owns it. On his way out, he walked by our five-piece Marine Band jazz group, raised his eyebrows, and smiled as I played a few adventurous chords during my solo on Bud Powell's "Bouncin' with Bud." He shouted something across the band as he left the Grand Foyer. I couldn't hear what he said, but this time it didn't matter. That was the last time I saw him until President Obama's second inauguration.

We'd been instructed to take a break as another group was about to start playing in the East Room. They were the featured act, and as usual, we were just providing reception music. I walked to the cross hall to try and get a glimpse of who the civilian entertainment was, and I saw Herbie and Gigi standing with their backs to me. They were far enough from me that I couldn't approach them without being conspicuous in my red polyester/wool blend coat with gold polished globe and anchor buttons. I just wanted to say goodbye, and tell him what an honor it was to have gotten to know him.

Not many people get to meet their heroes. I not only got to meet one of mine, but I was also very, very fortunate to have gotten to know him just a little bit. I've heard he's a Buddhist, and he certainly has that air of serenity and gentleness about him that I associate with meditation practitioners. In addition to the music, he also seems to be an exceptional person. I'm really happy for him as he receives his lifetime achievement award from the Kennedy Center. In my mind, there's no one more deserving.

THE PRESIDENT'S
NOT HOME

I'm walking into the White House to play for a holiday reception on December twenty-second. Tonight, my family is with me: my mom, Mary, Nicole, and Gabrielle, as well as my niece, Mary, who's come down from New York with her fascinated and fascinating, beautiful daughter, Eleanor. We entered through the Northwest Gate on Pennsylvania Avenue, escorted by Jim, one of my friends from the ushers' office. I'm wearing a coat and tie, and all the ladies are dressed beautifully. Nicole and Gabrielle are carrying their instruments (cello and violin) with them, so they can join me in providing musical entertainment for this particular holiday reception. This isn't an official holiday party. The guests are all part-time workers who augment the full-time staff for nearly four solid weeks of Christmas parties. They work constantly, starting at the end of the Thanksgiving weekend. A couple of years ago, the ushers' office decided these workers should enjoy a White House holiday reception just like the full-time staff. They bring their immediate families and enjoy the Christmas decorations, a light buffet, and some eggnog.

Daniel is probably my best friend in the ushers' office. He asked me if I'd provide some holiday music as a paid civilian. At the end of the first of these receptions, he handed me a check. I saw it was from his personal account. That was when I realized this whole party was paid for by the ushers.

"Daniel, I don't feel right about accepting this," I said. "I didn't know that you and the other ushers were bankrolling this reception."

"No. I insist you accept it. That was our understanding."

"Well, you know that we work together all year, and you guys always treat me well and really help me out."

This is true. They always see I get fed when food's available, and they help with cues to play or not play when needed. Dennis even got me into the back of the East Room for the Paul McCartney Gershwin Prize tribute show!

"OK, but if you guys have me back next year, I don't want to be paid. It'll be my contribution to the cause."

"Of course we'll have you back next year. And next time maybe you'll bring along your family!"

That was three years ago, and this reception has now become an annual event to look forward to for both the White House workers and the Boguslaw family.

So here we are, standing just outside the ushers' office by the closely guarded elevator that goes up to the private quarters. But the president and first lady aren't home today. They got out of town yesterday for a family vacation in Hawaii. I don't blame them for skipping this one. The entire month of December, the two of them spend around two hours at each reception greeting and posing with guests on almost a daily basis. Sometimes twice in a day. It makes me glad I never followed my childhood inclination to go into politics.

The president may be out of town, but the secret service agent standing by the elevator still looks pretty uncomfortable because my mom's standing so close to it (and to him). Mom seems happy, even though she's struggling a bit with arthritis, and she's telling us about her childhood visit to the White House when she met Franklin Roosevelt and got to sit in on one of his "fireside chats." Her uncle (my great uncle) was president of the National

Press Club at the time, and she reminisces about how easily the two of them entered the White House, made a quick left turn, and walked up the grand staircase to the private residence.

I let her finish her story and then suggest to her that the secret service agent might feel a bit happier if she were to move a few feet to her right instead of standing directly in front of the elevator. We're waiting in this smallish alcove because a tour is just now finishing up. Throughout the Christmas season, there's a nearly constant flow of people passing through to check out the decorations.

After about a five minute wait, Daniel comes out, welcomes us, and tells us that this particular tour is winding down, and it'll be a half hour before the reception guests begin to arrive, so why don't we go and have a look around.

"Anything off limits?" I ask.

"Just not the private residence. Anything else is fine. You all are family." A tremendously nice thing for him to say and do for us. Our family now has private viewing privileges of the entire museum part of the White House for a half hour!

After getting my fill of the beauty of the Christmas decorations, I sit down at the one-of-a-kind concert grand that I play most of the time when I work here. This instrument dates back to 1938, when Steinway and Sons gave it to the White House as a gift. The piano sits on legs carved in the shape of eagles, and it has wonderfully painted scenes of American musical life on the body of the instrument. I'm not sure what the wood is, but the finish has a lustrous glow to it. It's positioned in the Grand Foyer in between a couple of eighteen-foot Christmas trees. I take out some music, but I only need it for later when Nicole and Gabi join me. For right now, I dive into a few jazz arrangements of Christmas carols I've played for years, "Silent Night" as a jazz waltz (a la Miles Davis's "All Blues") and "God Rest Ye Merry Gentlemen" with a bright swing feel and some added chords.

After a few numbers, Gabrielle comes in with her violin case and takes out her instrument. The girls are going to take turns and then play some Christmas trio arrangements with all of us together. Gabrielle plays a movement of the Bruch violin concerto as I accompany her with the orchestral reduction. Then, she does a couple of movements of one of Bach's solo violin partitas. Nicole and I then play the first two movements of Dvořák's masterful cello concerto. Both girls play great, and I feel justifiably proud. We then follow the classical pieces with a number of Christmas tunes, played as a trio. When the girls finish and start packing up, I invite Mary to sit in and sing one with me.

I've asked her before when we've come for these receptions, and she's refused, but this time she agrees to do "Christmas Time Is Here," Vince Guaraldi's beautiful waltz from *A Charlie Brown Christmas*. As wonderful as it is to get to bring my family to this reception and give the kids a chance to play, Mary's singing has got to top the list of best things about this gig. She doesn't sing at her strongest, but she still sounds beautiful. She's still a bit weak because for the past year she's been fighting cancer through chemotherapy, radiation, and surgery. It's been a long haul, but now she's slowly returning to normal. A little something extra to be grateful for this Christmas.

The reception's over, and now we're all putting our coats on before venturing out into the below-freezing DC night. The family seems to have had a really nice time. I can tell because everyone looks so content. I think that even pretty little Eleanor realizes she's been part of something special tonight. Throughout the reception, I greeted nearly everyone who came through the Grand Foyer. I've gotten pretty good over the years at being able to play with divided attention. We recognized each other as respected coworkers who had once again completed another Christmas season of long hours and hard work.

But now, as the family and I are leaving, we run into George. George is the head butler, and he's been at the White House since the 1960s. I've already introduced the family to Daniel and my other friends in the usher's office, and now they get to meet George. He says hello to everyone, but before we leave, he turns to Nicole and Gabi and says, "Now girls, your father is a great man. Don't ever forget that. Your father's a great man."

I don't think he could have said anything nicer, this older gentleman who's spent his entire adult life around truly great people. But he's wrong. I'm not a great man. Gandhi, Mandela, Abe Lincoln, and Martin Luther King were great men. My teacher and mentor, Fred Coulter, was a great man. I'm just a musician who, with a little bit of talent, some hard work, and lots of good fortune, has managed to make a life for himself and his family doing something he loves.

Bob with daughters, Nicole and Gabrielle, at the White House,
1994

ACKNOWLEDGEMENTS

There are too many people who have given me their support and encouragement with regard to this book for me to possibly mention them all. There are also quite a few great musicians who didn't make it into the book because all that they did (without much in the way of quirky gig stories) was share with me tremendous amounts of guidance and faith in my abilities and musical instincts. I could have written chapters for each of these individuals. A few that come to mind who weren't mentioned: Aaron Clay (Bass), Ron Diehl (Saxophone), Dennis Diblasio (Saxophone), Dave Stambler (Saxophone), James King (Bass), Tom Baldwin (Bass), Regino Madrid (Violin), Claudia Chudacoff (Violin), Alan Wonneberger (Drums and sound engineer), Pete Minger (Trumpet), Stewart Miller (Bass), Al Hood (Trumpet), Max Murray (Bass), Frank Russo (Drums), Gavin Davies (Drums), Alan Dale (Drums), Ronnie Shaw (Drums), John Legg (Pianist), Kim Miller (Violin), Dave Kane (Pianist and editing!), Dick Carter (Bass), Victor Dvoskin (Bass), Charlie Powers (Cello), Mike Montgomery (Bass), Dave Einhorn (Bass), Ronnie Miller (Jazz Piano and Jazz Comp Teacher), Mike Gerber (Jazz Piano Teacher), and Lance Brunner (Musicology Professor). I've learned an incalculable amount from all of you. I plan to pay it forward to some of today's wonderful up-and-coming young musicians who are following in our footsteps. Thanks also for additional editing help from Debby Liebman, Dave Boguslaw, Kent Ashcraft, and Mary Boguslaw.

Many thanks to my Mom and Dad for supporting me to the fullest, even when they understandably had their doubts about my chosen career path. Many thanks to my brother, David, who's been an inspiration to me ever since I was old enough to understand what it meant to be inspired.

Thanks to my sister, Nancy, for being my closest childhood friend. I know if she had lived beyond the age of eighteen, she would have been a great supporter of mine and we would've remained lifelong friends.

Many, many, thanks to my brilliant former teachers, Fred Coulter and Lucien Stark. There's no way I ever would have gotten to where I am today without their selfless giving of time, energy, and considerable knowledge. Lots of gratitude to Colonels Bourgeois and Foley of the "President's Own." My first dozen years in the Marine Band were a joy due to their belief in me and the opportunities that they afforded me.

Thanks to my daughters, Hosanna, Nicole, and Gabrielle, from whom I've learned patience, humility, and renewed joy in the wonder of life's growth and discoveries.

The biggest thank you goes to my wife, Mary. I can't overstate what it's meant to me for the last thirty-seven years to have gone through life with someone who loves me so deeply, and believes in me as both a human being and a musician. Her feedback, enthusiasm, and encouragement in relation to the development of this book has been completely invaluable.

And finally, to Scott Giambusso, a great friend and a wonderful bass player. Thanks a million for the cool idea for the title!

IF YOU'RE A FAN OF THIS BOOK, WILL YOU HELP ME SPREAD THE WORD?

There are several ways you can help me get the word out about the message of this book...

- Post a 5-Star review on Amazon.

- Write about the book on your Facebook, Twitter, Instagram – any social media you regularly use!

- If you blog, consider referencing the book, or publishing an excerpt from the book with a link back to my website. You have my permission to do this as long as you provide proper credit and backlinks.

- Recommend the book to friends – word-of-mouth is still the most effective form of advertising.

- Purchase additional copies to give away as gifts.

Available in Paperback and eReader at these and other great retailers.

amazon   **BARNES&NOBLE**

www.bobboguslaw.com